AF269954

GREAT

AMERICAN

INVESTMENTS

GREAT AMERICAN INVESTMENTS

A HISTORY OF

THE BOLD INITIATIVES

THAT SHAPED A NATION

Charles D. ELLIS

BESTSELLING AUTHOR OF *WINNING THE LOSER'S GAME*

WILEY

Published by John Wiley & Sons, Inc., Hoboken, New Jersey.

Library of Congress Cataloging-in-Publication Data

Names: Ellis, Charles D., author.
Title: Great American investments : a history of the bold initiatives that
  shaped a nation / Charles D. Ellis.
Description: Hoboken, NJ : Wiley, [2026] | Includes bibliographical
  references and index.
Identifiers: LCCN 2026008429 (print) | LCCN 2026008430 (ebook) | ISBN
  9781394436750 (hardback) | ISBN 9781394436774 (adobe pdf) | ISBN
  9781394436767 (epub)
Subjects: LCSH: Public investments—United States. | United
  States—Economic conditions.
Classification: LCC HC110.P83 E45 2026 (print) | LCC HC110.P83 (ebook)
LC record available at https://lccn.loc.gov/2026008429
LC ebook record available at https://lccn.loc.gov/2026008430

COVER DESIGN: PAUL MCCARTHY
COVER ART: © GETTY IMAGES | SIMON2579
SKY10154963_042326

CONTENTS

CONTENTS

PREFACE

In the dark first year of COVID when it didn't appear that our country could get "its act together," there was high anxiety in our family. But I have always been an optimist and kept thinking about how our nation had risen to do remarkable things—often as unlikely as tackling a pandemic. In that year when we were all basically housebound, I started a list of the audacious investments in our country—the Louisiana Purchase, the race to the moon, and a dozen others—and started reading more about them. I became a student of these "America's Great Investments." What captured my imagination were the stories: Although they differ in time and place, most were the result of the vision and determined work of one individual or a small group, who despite formidable resistance, worked through the political process to gather sufficient support to turn their vision into reality. I had neither the interest in nor the appropriate resources to do the rigorous research and careful citations that would be expected for a publishable book. This project was intended just to be for fun, with copies for family and friends who might enjoy an informal tour of the stories behind these Great American Investments. I am honored that John Wiley & Sons, my long-term publisher, thought it might deserve a wider audience.

My hope is that this compilation underscores how this country has relied on individuals who have risen with imagination and perspicacity to make our nation better. In this moment when there are so many concerns about the national scene, I hope it reminds us that we need to find and support leaders who are focused on uniting and propelling our commonwealth.

I am indebted to scores of authors who educated me during my self-study of these topics. I apologize for not offering them the attribution that they are due, but I am genuinely grateful for the education—and inspiration—they offered.

Charley Ellis

February 2026

INTRODUCTION

These 14 Great American Investments, while often very different from each other, are bound together in many ways. They all make America a better nation. Each required a government commitment, and this usually meant successfully navigating through the political process, which took time and required strong, sustained, and skillful leadership. Typically, the leadership came from a few dedicated, tenacious people with the vision and requisite skills to recognize and seize opportunity.

Alexander Hamilton, in leading the federal government to assume the debts of all the states—and the states to accept the financial obligations and burdens—understood the collective potential power of our nation and the importance of cooperating together to accomplish what could never be done so well, if at all, by the separate states. When we Americans have come together to make bold investments in a better America, the results have almost always been remarkably favorable.

Of course, these Great American Investments were not easily made. In fact, one of the overall messages of the fascinating stories in this happy collection is that most might not have happened at all.

The Great American Investments share another compelling characteristic. Each contributes significantly to America being the country its citizens so deeply love. Who would be willing to have any of them disappear? Imagine for a moment an America without our national parks, Social

Security, the Louisiana Purchase, our many "land grant" universities, or our interstate highway system.

Each investment has a unique history, but they have a pattern. While they all may seem obvious in retrospect or easily taken for granted today, most once faced determined opposition. They began with an individual with strong enough enthusiasm to work through the political process to get a collective national commitment. It was seldom easy and usually took a long time and energetic determination. How individuals with a mission overcame obstacles makes for a series of adventure stories that are both interesting and inspiring.

One of these stories, the Marshall Plan, was an enormous investment by Americans, not in the country they would want to live in but in a world they would want for America. Somewhat similarly, the National Institutes of Health, by far the world's largest funder of research about disease, makes all the resulting discoveries available to everyone worldwide—immediately and without charge—America's great gift to the people of the world.

Of course, we Americans do not have everything: We do not, for example, have as strong a healthcare safety net as other advanced nations. So, the question is fairly asked: While we enjoy and take pride in the achievements of our predecessors, what might we do in our time to help create the America of the future?

What we do know is that if we ever lost the benefits of the Great American Investments, we would have lost something special about America.

1

SOCIAL SECURITY

By far America's largest investment in preventing late-in-life poverty among the American people, Social Security is one of the most popular and successful programs of the American government. It was guided past the Scylla and Charybdis of Constitutional law and the Depression by the political skills and determination of an astute, no-nonsense woman: Frances Perkins, the first woman to serve in a Presidential Cabinet.

Through Social Security,[1] Frances Perkins has had more direct and indirect impact on the lives of more Americans and on our nation's economy and society over more years than all but a dozen other major public servants. Yet, for most of us, she is unknown. Chances are she wouldn't care.

Frances Perkins's unrelenting focus was on getting justice for working Americans through effective government programs. Still, she may have been quietly pleased that the name most frequently given to girls born in 1936—the year after Social Security was made the law of the land—was Frances.

---

[1] The common term for the Federal Old Age, Survivors, and Disability program. It covers 94% of individuals employed in the United States, but not six million state and local government workers covered by other plans.

Perkins was exceptionally private, and, while a gifted public speaker, she shunned public recognition. She was the first woman to serve in a President's Cabinet and one of the longest to serve—just over 12 years. Her most consequential achievement was the creation in 1935 of the revolutionary set of programs we now call Social Security.

Social Security currently pays out over $1 trillion in annual benefits, assuring retirees and their families of a basic income for life. So well-loved by millions of Americans, Social Security is considered the untouchable political "third rail" among government programs. It has been the most important and enduring domestic accomplishment of Franklin Delano Roosevelt's remarkable administration.

FORMATIVE EXPERIENCE

Frances Perkins made several personal decisions while a student at Mount Holyoke. Throughout her life, she embraced the college's founder Mary Lyon's charge to "Go where no one else will go and do what no one else would do." She majored in physics—with chemistry and biology as minors—to develop her capabilities in working with data and objective analysis. She became deeply interested in social issues in an economics course that included observing working conditions in nearby grimy factories and reading Jacob Riis's *How the Other Half Lives*. Riis's descriptions and photographs seared Perkins' imagination and the impact of that book remained with her for life.

Before she was 30, she had changed her name from Fannie to Frances, her church membership from Congregational to Episcopal, and her political party from Republican to Democrat. (She also changed her age by two years.) Religion would always be a central part of Perkins's life. While working in Washington, she regularly went to a cloister for a day or two of silence, prayer, and meditation. On her mother's blunt recommendation—"There, my dear, that is your hat. You should always wear something like this. You have a broad face. Never get a hat that is narrower than your cheekbones because it makes you look ridiculous"— she adopted tricorn hats that she would usually wear all day.

Perkins presented herself as she wanted to be seen so she and her policy proposals would be taken seriously in a men's world. She kept a large red envelope labeled "Notes on the male mind." Comfortable with formality, she would be startled by Senator Wagner—even after 20 years of working together—calling her by her first name. She liked the "high church" liturgy of the Episcopal Church. Perkins was "old school" formal, using *one* to avoid using *I* and dressing as though a full generation older. She chose dresses in plain black or dark blue with white collars, believing that this made her look more like men's mothers and so increased the chances of their accepting her views as serious and wise. She did not like airplanes, so she would travel using trains and buses, often changing several times to get to her destination. She kept a copy of her will in her purse so, if she died, she wouldn't cause anyone any trouble.

EARLY CAREER

After college, she taught school in Lake Forest, Illinois, and worked part time at Hull House, a leading settlement house. (In 1891 there were six settlement houses in America. In 1905 there were 200, and in 1910, over 400, showing the increasing need. Fully half the people over 65 were in 1,300 old age homes in 1930.) Perkins later moved to Philadelphia and then New York City to join the Consumers League. As a young social worker, she dealt directly with poor Black people for the first time when she secured a job with the Philadelphia Research and Protective Association.

Both immigrant and Black girls who traveled to Philadelphia searching for employment in the booming city were met at the boat piers or railroad terminals by unsavory agents who offered them lodging and employment—as prostitutes. The Philadelphia Protective Association assigned Perkins and two Black assistants to meet the new arrivals and direct them to reputable boardinghouses and employment agencies. Perkins was instrumental in closing down several of the disreputable "agencies." City officials, drawing on recommendations from the Protective Association, eventually required licensing for lodging houses.

As Secretary of Labor years later, Perkins adhered to the principles of equality for all. As a former social worker, Perkins conceived the Department of Labor to be the listening post for the government, "the place where the poor people of the Nation could come with their complaints and obtain assistance."[2]

TRIANGLE FIRE'S IMPACT

At 4:40 p.m. on March 25, 1911, Perkins had been enjoying tea with a group of friends at a handsome house overlooking Washington Square in New York City when the butler announced a serious fire at the nearby Triangle Shirtwaist factory. The cloth the young women there were working with was unusually light and quickly burst into flames. The factory was on the 8th, 9th, and 10th floors of an even taller building. The layout of each floor made a funnel toward the small elevator—so the women could be checked for possible theft when leaving.

Fire escapes were narrow and rickety. City fire hoses had too little pressure to reach the high floors where the fire burned, so they could not help.

---

[2] Of President Franklin D. Roosevelt's circle of advisors, Perkins was not the only member considered a champion of Black causes. Black leaders also turned to Works Project Administrator Harry Hopkins and Secretary of Interior Harold Ickes. Together, this troika would often pool their efforts to advance the social programs of Black people, often calling on Eleanor Roosevelt for additional help.

Many jumped. Perkins would never forget the image of young women leaping from the 8th floor windows. The tragic event confirmed her career commitment to improving working conditions for labor. In Perkins's mind, that was when the New Deal was born.

A citizen's committee on improving working conditions was established and Perkins, on the recommendation of Theodore Roosevelt, was hired as group executive. Perkins[3] became an expert on workers' health and safety; she led legislators on inspection tours of factories to see for themselves the dangers of unfettered industrialization. Thanks to her work, New York State soon had the nation's most advanced workplace safety regulations.

The 1918 election was the first time women could vote in New York State. Perkins worked hard in Al Smith's successful campaign to be governor. Smith convinced her of the importance of party membership to organize efforts for change, so she became a Democrat in 1920. He appointed her to the New York Industrial Commission, making her the first woman appointed to a senior administration position. Her job was to clear out corruption in the state labor department. In Smith's fourth term as governor, he appointed her chair of the Commission. Paying \$8,000, that role made her the state's highest paid public official. Perkins became a skillful lobbyist for social reforms and worked with Smith to limit the working week for women and children to "only" 54 hours.

As Smith's most trusted advisor on labor matters, she got to know Franklin Roosevelt. When Roosevelt became governor (and Smith lost to Hoover in the presidential race), Smith urged FDR to keep Perkins. "You better not let her get away from you. She is able and conscientious." Despite Smith's caution that men might not react well to reporting to a woman, FDR made her Industrial Commissioner for New York State in charge of

---

[3] On September 26, 1913, she married Paul Wilson in Grace Church at 10th and Broadway. No family or friends were present. He was 37, she was 33. Financially, they were comfortable with their combined salaries. Paul also had inherited some wealth.

the entire State Labor Department. She reorganized the state's employment agencies and increasingly focused on unemployment insurance.

When President Herbert Hoover falsely claimed that unemployment was ending, Perkins made national news when she repeatedly called him out with figures proving the opposite and said his "misleading statements" were "cruel and irresponsible." She began to work with leaders from other states to figure out how to protect workers and promote employment by working together.

Perkins developed remarkable skills at thinking through the sequence of steps by which she could achieve extraordinary results. She was described by a female friend as a "half a loaf girl: take what you can get now and try for more later." That incrementalism worked well in politics and in government, particularly for those who were, like Perkins, persistent, selfless, and well-respected. Perkins also understood power, planning, anticipation, and timing. Not only was she unusually able to visualize a multistep sequence of clever moves but she was also remarkably adept at understanding how best to work with Smith—and then with Roosevelt. She developed a reputation for unusual effectiveness, a reputation that would increase steadily over her career.[4]

THE CRUCIAL MEETING

As President-elect, Roosevelt signaled to others that he wanted to appoint a woman to the Cabinet *and* he wanted that woman to be Frances

---

[4] She convinced Governor Roosevelt to be the first public official in the nation to commit to unemployment insurance. Roosevelt sent her to England to study the British system with a stern admonition that he was "opposed to the dole" with benefits paid out of general revenues with no contributions required of the workers. (Such contributions by future beneficiaries would later be central to the design of Social Security.)

Perkins led in a series of New York State anti-Depression programs, demonstrating her political pragmatism and senior management capabilities. While labor union leaders might object to having a woman who was not a union member running "their" department, FDR knew how important the votes of women had been to his election and was looking for ways to signal the dynamic change he was already calling the New Deal.

Perkins. Various women's groups took up the challenge of building support. Of particular importance to Perkins was the view expressed by Episcopal Bishop Charles Gilbert of the Diocese of New York who wrote, "I really believe that it is God's own call. If it is, you cannot refuse. If it is a job to which God has assigned you, what man thinks is of no consequence."

When a person gives a poor man shoes, Perkins wondered, is it for the poor man or for God? She decided it should be for God. As Perkins would say years later, "I came to Washington to work for God, FDR, and the millions of forgotten, plain, common working men." Working for God came first and would show clearly in her strong, unwavering determination. She knew who she was, why she was in government, and what she intended to get accomplished. Perkins's deep belief that she was doing the work of the Lord would also put the daily difficulties of the process of political persuasion into the context of her major mission to serve the millions of ordinary workers she knew needed help.

On February 22, 1933, Roosevelt asked Perkins to meet with him at his Manhattan home on East 65th Street at 8:00 that evening. Thinking ahead as usual, Perkins came prepared. She had made a list of her priorities: a 40-hour work week, a minimum wage, workers' compensation, abolishing child labor—to keep children in school and save jobs for adults—federal aid to the states for unemployment relief, universal health insurance, a more effective federal employment service, and what we now know as Social Security.

Perkins and Roosevelt both knew that the major reforms on her list would face great challenges—both political and legal. Armed with a strategic approach to problem-solving centered on a remarkable ability to understand both individuals and groups, Frances Perkins chose her long-term goals carefully and then adapted to prevailing circumstances *and* selected the best people to work with her.

Believing God was on her side, she played to win.

CONSTITUTIONAL QUESTIONS

Roosevelt appreciated that sophisticated observers believed that some of the reforms on her list—particularly by changing the federal laws rather than working state-by-state—might face a Supreme Court challenge where they would likely be ruled unconstitutional. Perkins was, as usual, prepared and direct. Perhaps, she offered, Roosevelt would not want her as Secretary of Labor because if she were appointed, she would work hard to get her list of changes made.

The program received Roosevelt's hearty endorsement, and he told Frances he wanted her to carry it out.

"But," I said, "have you considered that to launch such a program we must think out, frame, and develop labor and social legislation, which then might be considered unconstitutional?"

"Well, that's a problem," Mr. Roosevelt admitted, "but we can work out something when the time comes."

"And so I agreed to become Secretary of Labor after a conversation that lasted but an hour."

Roosevelt, being Roosevelt, did not give his explicit commitment to the items on her list, but she did get his authorization to go ahead and see what she could accomplish. With Perkins being Perkins, that was all she would need.

Her initial focus would be on her top priority: Social Security to prevent old-age poverty. Roosevelt looked at her and nodded thoughtfully. Then, as would soon prove to be typical of his approach to major decisions, said, "All right. I will *authorize* you to try, and if you succeed, that's fine." (And by implication, if you fail, don't expect much help from me.)

"Well, that's all I want. I don't want you to put any roadblocks in my way. We'll see what we can do. There are plenty of people who want change badly and will work for it." They both understood FDR would be committing to massive unemployment relief, a giant public works program, minimum wage laws, abolition of child labor, and the old age insurance program we now call Social Security.

When he said, "I suppose you are going to nag me about this forever," she confirmed that she certainly would. Both knew that the constitutionality of the program was a central question. Perkins's next step would be to get an effective group to study the subject and develop specific proposals for legislation.

TAKING CHARGE AT LABOR

When Perkins got to Washington for the swearing in of the Cabinet, she had several awkward moments, including being unable to find a taxi and her inauguration ticket directing her to the wrong door at the White House. But she managed to make her way to the ceremony in time, and soon had her balance.

When reporters asked what they should call her, she replied, "My name is Perkins."

"Yes, but what do we *call* you? How should we address you?"

"Miss Perkins," she suggested. But that would not do.

"But we say 'Mr. Secretary' to the Secretary of State or 'Mr. Secretary' to the Secretary of the Interior. What do we say to *you*?"

Adumbrating her deft political skills, she turned to the Speaker of the House who was standing nearby and said that as an expert on parliamentary procedure, he would know best. Speaker Rainey declared that they should use the same formality for her as for men serving at the same rank. "You call men Mister Secretary. You will call her Madam Secretary." And so it was for her 13 years *and* for all her successors.

Secretary Perkins moved quickly to establish herself at the Labor Department. After the swearing in, she went first to the Willard Hotel to check with her secretary for any messages from Hoover's Labor Secretary Doak. There were none.

Looking up the number in the phone book, she called outgoing Secretary Doak's office and, after a long wait, finally got through to him. "You know I've been sworn in."

"I read in the newspapers that the whole Cabinet was sworn in. I didn't know whether you were going to stay in Washington or not."

"We were all asked to stay, and take up our duties at once."

"Oh."

"I'm here and thought I'd come over while you're still here." Then she surprised him by saying she would come over in half an hour. When she arrived, Doak's office surprised *her*, not so much by its being rather shabby, which it was, but because it gave no sign that Doak would ever be leaving.

Perkins moved quickly. She asked Doak to introduce her to his senior staff before lunchtime, and then she asked that he arrange to have his personal items packed while at lunch. She assured Doak that they would immediately be taken to his residence, and that after lunch he would be taken to his home by the limousine he always used. After leaving Doak, the driver was to return to the Labor Department for reassignment. Meanwhile, Perkins would stay at the Department as she had some letters to dictate.

Perkins's first strategic decision was to take control of the Bureau of Immigration. For Perkins, immigration was not nearly as important as the issues on her list when she met with Roosevelt: unemployment, public works, minimum wages, abolition of child labor, federal aid to the states for direct relief, and old age or retirement insurance. Even though the number of immigrants, due to the new quota law, had been declining, immigration dominated the Labor Department with 3,659 employees out of a departmental total of 5,113 and $10 million out of a total budget of $13.5 million.

Doak had focused narrowly on one aspect of the Department's work: deportation of aliens of the "radical element" and "alien agitators" through Section 24—which many in the Department believed a disgrace. (In 1932, a group of Section 24 investigators and local Detroit police had surrounded a block of buildings late at night and, without any warrants, had forced their way into rooms and apartments and arrested 606 people and thrown them in jail. This operation proved to be a serious overreaction. All but two were citizens or legal aliens.)

In just the past week, Doak—whose brother and nephew were both Section 24 men—had cleverly converted all men in the unit to civil service status. This meant they could not be dismissed or transferred unless proven to be derelict in their work, a notoriously cumbersome and slow process. If all the Section 24 men were "protected," how could Perkins assert control?

Perkins soon had a solution, provided by senior staff member Robe Carl White, a Republican who had agreed to stay for a while to help in transition. White strongly opposed the Section 24 crowd and their practices and advised Perkins to simply not ask Congress for more money than already appropriated. Since past appropriations were almost entirely spent, with no new money, Section 24 would soon evaporate.

Perkins saw Roosevelt privately in his office and explained the situation. "Go ahead and clean them out," he said, chuckling, "You are lucky to have that way of doing it. Just let them go." Perkins promptly terminated 86 of the Section 24 people, including Doak's brother and nephew—for lack of funds.

The reaction to the break-up of Section 24 within the Department was immediate—and enthusiastic. People wanted to know their Department was doing its work properly. Perkins never mentioned corruption: only that funds would not be available.[5]

---

[5] Good advisors on policy were not always good administrators. In reorganizing the Labor Department, which had long been a dumping ground for political patronage purposes, Perkins aimed at both greater efficiency and greater effectiveness. The senior team Perkins steadily assembled would be recognized as one of the best in Washington.

That same night, the Department's annual reception and ball were to be held. Despite being told at the last minute, Perkins immediately committed to go. She asked White to join her in a receiving line, but neither he nor anyone else would know the names of all the guests. Perkins's solution was typically pragmatic. She would give her name and a smile, confident that each person would give his or hers in return. Later, when she saw no one dancing, she turned to White and asked him to join her in getting the dancing started. It had been quite a day and had sent good news and good feelings flashing throughout the Labor Department.[6]

Returning to her office after dinner the next night, Perkins discovered a group of men rifling the files. They were led by Special Assistant Secretary for Labor Garsson, who had just been asked to submit his resignation. As usual, Perkins was direct.

"What are you doing, Mr. Garsson?"

"You know we're all out, but the notice was so sudden we had no time to get our personal belongings and correspondence."

"These files cannot be *personal*. They look like official files of investigations. Surely, anything personal must be in your desks and not in these files."

"We just wanted to get a few little belongings."

"Take nothing from these files, sir. Return tomorrow for personal items when the office is open, and now leave this building at once!" She demanded the keys to the files and had the locks changed the next day.

Once in office, Perkins was a driving force behind the Roosevelt administration's massive investment in public works projects to get people back to work. She successfully urged the government to spend $3.3 billion on schools, roads, housing, and post offices. Those projects employed more than 1.5 million people in 1934.

---

[6] *Time* magazine would put Perkins on its cover for August 14, 1933.

DESIGNING SOCIAL SECURITY

Perkins got Roosevelt to agree to have the working group responsible for organizing what would become the Social Security program kept small and report directly to him. They also decided to have the small group be entirely Cabinet members. Perkins's committee had Henry Morgenthau from Treasury, Henry Wallace from Agriculture, and Attorney General Homer Cummings. Its small size made the Economic Security Committee easy to organize and lead. (Adjunct working groups were, of course, professionally staffed.)[7]

Perkins charged the committee with developing pragmatic legislation that would fit with "a practical knowledge of the needs of our country, the prejudices of our people, and our legislative habits." Roosevelt felt strongly that "We've got to leave all that we can to the states. All the power should not be in the hands of the Federal government. Just think what might happen if all the power were concentrated here and Huey Long became president!"

Roosevelt wanted to be sure Social Security participants had a *property* right not just a civic right to their benefits. Roosevelt's view was that it was politics all the way. "We put those payroll contributions there to give the contributors a legal, moral, and political right to collect their pensions and their unemployment benefits. With these taxes in there, no damned politician can ever scrap my program."[8]

---

[7] The technical board working with the Economic Security Committee was led by Arthur J. Altmeyer. Before he came to Washington to be Perkins's second Assistant Secretary of Labor, he had served as secretary of the Wisconsin Industrial Commission. Edwin Witte, who had been chairman of the economics department at the University of Wisconsin and knew how best to work with academics and enlisted them for their expertise. Roosevelt agreed with his acting budget director to shift the Committee's employment assurance proposal over to Harry Hopkins's public works program. Otherwise, all of the Committee's recommendations went intact to Capitol Hill. (Edwin Witte reported in his book that $87,550 was initially set aside from the Federal Emergency Relief Administration. Total expenses rose to $145,000.) Actuaries were provided by the Lions Club of America.

[8] Perkins, *The Roosevelt I Knew* (New York: Viking Press, 1946).

Roosevelt didn't want to use the word *social*, which still meant the dole to him, so it was called the Committee on Economic Security. The Economic Security Bill was renamed the Social Security Bill in the House Ways and Means Committee in early 1935. That was fine with Perkins, who would observe, "Semantics meant nothing to me!"

Congress authorized the Committee before adjourning, but did not provide an appropriation to cover expenses. So Perkins went to Roosevelt for advice, and he said "Well, look, Harry Hopkins has got all that money for relief, so go get some of Harry's money."

"I don't think that's legal, is it? It belongs to Harry."

"Oh well, you can get it. Borrow people; just borrow what you need for staff. Agriculture has them. Labor has them. The Army and Navy have them." Perkins took $125,000 from Harry Hopkins on a promise that the money would all be used to hire experts who were unemployed, particularly university faculty.[9]

Nothing in legislation is ever simple. Perkins, as chair of the Committee on Economic Security, knew she was short on time and long on complexities when the Committee began its work on June 29, 1934. Their goal: a fully developed program by the following New Year's Day—just six months away!

The small size of the Economic Security Committee and the fact that it reported directly to the President had major advantages in getting agreement on specific recommendations. But time was soon running out and decisions had to be made. (Committee meetings were usually held in Perkins's office with sandwiches served.) Health insurance was eliminated due to opposition from the medical profession. The only one of the Act's 10 programs that was a pure federal program was Social Security. That was because actuaries had

---

[9] Civil War pensions, which kept getting increased, were widely seen as corrupt. (Their costs were covered by general revenues provided by high taxes.) In some northern states, 40% of males 65 and older received Civil War pensions while virtually no one received them in formerly Confederate states. Senator Hugo Black, noting that Confederate states paid pensions to their veterans out of state funds, wanted to know if the states would get credit for their payment. Perkins assured the Senator, "The numbers must be small, so it could easily be worked into the system."

made it clear that given worker mobility, reasonable accuracy of actuarial estimates would only be feasible with a national program.

Democrats supported Perkins's program because it won votes and was humanitarian. For Perkins, Social Security was also for Jesus's sake because it brought the City of God closer to the cities of toil and industry.

CONSTITUTIONAL CHALLENGES

In spring 1935, the Supreme Court had declared key pieces of New Deal legislation unconstitutional. To many, this meant that Social Security—if passed by Congress as expected—might well be declared unconstitutional too. Perkins's work appeared to be in jeopardy, but she was prepared with two bills she had kept in her desk drawer in case the law was struck down by the Supreme Court. One would authorize the federal government to set wage and hour standards in an industry; the other covered government contracts. It was based on Felix Frankfurter's suggestion that it might be done by linking state-by-state cooperation to the purchasing power of the federal government. The federal government, he believed, had the power to determine the working conditions under which goods it purchased were manufactured.

In a conversation with Roosevelt about the likely fate of the legislation, Perkins had assured him, "Never mind, I have something up my sleeve. If NSA doesn't put a floor under wages and a ceiling over hours, we have to be prepared with something else."

"What have you got?"

"Two bills that do everything you and I think important. I have them locked in the lower left-hand drawer of my desk against an emergency." Throwing his head back, Roosevelt laughed, "There's New England caution for you!"

Then Perkins got a lucky break. Once again deciding to do the proper thing, as befit her personal preference for formality, she went to tea. Mrs.

Harlan F. Stone, wife of the Supreme Court justice, would be "at home for tea" on Wednesday afternoon. Perkins arrived at 5:45.

"In Washington, you don't go to parties just because you want to go, you know: you go because you have to go. I went up to Mrs. Stone's house and presented myself. There were a lot of people already there. I went to the dining room to get a cup of tea and met Mr. Justice Stone who had just come from the Court and was getting his cup of tea. We greeted each other and sat together to have a chat."

"How are you getting on?"

"All right."

After a pause, she continued, "Well, you know, we are having big troubles, Mr. Justice, because we don't know—in the current draft of the Economic Security Act which we are working on—what would be a wise method of establishing this law. It is a very difficult Constitutional problem, you know. Different ones of us are guided by this, that, or the other case. We don't know which way to go."

Looking around to be sure nobody could hear him—because it would be improper for a member of the Court to advise either the executive or legislative branches of the government on any matter that might come before the Court—Justice Stone put his hand up by his mouth to ensure confidentiality and said very quietly, "The taxing power, my dear, the taxing power. You can do anything under the taxing power."[10]

As Perkins would later recall, she asked no further questions. "I went back to my committee and never told them where I got my information. As

---

[10] In 1866, the Congress passed an act levying a 10% tax on bank notes issued by state banks. The real purpose of this measure was not to raise revenue, but to eliminate state bank notes from circulation. So effectively was its real purpose accomplished that little, if any, revenue was ever collected under this act. The validity of the statute was challenged on the ground, among others, that it was not a true revenue measure. Its constitutionality was, however, upheld in *Venzie Bank v. Fenno* (8 Wallace 553). Another striking case involved the oleomargarine tax. The obvious purpose was driving yellow oleomargarine out of the market in view of the fact that it was frequently served to the public as butter. The validity of the measure was questioned, and its character as a tax measure was assailed, without success in *McCray v. United States* (195 U. S. 27, 59).

far as they were concerned, I went out into the wilderness and had a vision—and said firmly, 'The taxing power of the United States! You can do anything under it.' And so it proved."

Reflecting on later legal developments, Perkins spoke of watching with anxiety as the first case went to the Supreme Court. "The favorable opinion was written in elaborate, fine social language by Mr. Justice Benjamin Cardozo. Mr. Justice Stone voted with him. So, we were safe on Constitutionality, but not yet on legislation." While the federal government had had almost no engagement with social programs in the past—leaving social programs to the various states—it took a leading role with the New Deal. And Frances Perkins was the lead player.

DEVELOPING THE LEGISLATION

Perkins developed great skill in knowing when and how to bring specific matters to Roosevelt's attention. Perkins made a regular point of having a private hour with FDR every week or 10 days to go over and reinforce agreements and decisions already made. She had learned that a telling story or personalization was key to his grasping any abstract concept and that she usually had to reaffirm her point several times in a meeting to keep it clear to him. Perkins knew Roosevelt was prone to changing his mind. So, before meeting with him, she would prepare a one-page memo of the options—so he could select one. "Are you quite sure?" She would ask to fix his choice in his own memory. Then, she would return to the decision a third time—after being reminded of the opposition he would face—to be sure he confirmed his decision, asking, "Is that still okay? Is it all right?"

She knew that Roosevelt abhorred a one-way dole and favored insurance in both concept and specific terms *and* embraced a strong link between payments and benefits. He wanted workers to have a moral, political, and legal right to collect their benefits, so he would categorically reject relying on general revenue financing.

On November 13, 1934, Roosevelt addressed a group of national leaders at the White House, saying, "Old age is one of the most certain, and for many people, the most tragic of all hazards. There is no tragedy in growing old, but there is tragedy in growing old without means of support."

Pragmatic politics were exercised at every stage and everybody involved joined in making the case for passage. Perkins herself gave over 100 speeches. (Perkins was named one of the five best speakers by a poll Washington's radio stations, and in another poll, she was named the most prominent woman in the world.) Specific groups that might provoke resistance such as lawyers, domestic workers, or agricultural workers were each taken out. The main drive was to get the basic bill passed. (Unemployment had peaked at 24.9% in 1933. In 1935, unemployment was still high at 20.1% *and* the unemployed had been out of work even longer.)

Perkins had arranged for the appointment of three prominent citizens to the first Social Security Board, which was chaired by John Winant (later, a New Hampshire governor, ambassador to the Court of St. James's, and, until an untimely early death, a serious candidate for president). She left administering Social Security to them and went to work on other items on her to-do list.

During Spring 1935, politics and competing "easy solutions" were daunting. With 87% of American families having incomes under $2,500 in 1935, the Townsend Plan—which was naive, but promised benefits that were obviously attractive (with a monthly payment of $200 per person over 65 and $400 for couples)—had strong appeal and gathered over 500,000 members in some 3,000 clubs. Its adherents were an "army of the aged." While Dr. Townsend's plan was quickly seen by experts as unrealistic, his commitment to a federal program was broadly appealing to many people. (An even more naive alternative—the Ham and Eggs movement—was based on widely distributing $30 every Thursday.)

The Social Security Act got held up by Louisiana Senator Huey Long's filibuster and a dispute over whether private pensions might enable corporations to opt out of old age insurance. In September, Republican candidate Alfred Landon attacked Social Security as "unjust, unworkable, stupidly drafted, and wastefully financed." This attack caused John Winant to resign as chairman of the Social Security Board so he could offer his services to the Roosevelt campaign as defender of the Social Security program.

The President's Economic Security Committee could not resolve on the vital question of an entirely federal system versus a blended state-federal system. Perkins and other members of the committee each changed their minds numerous times, often within a few hours. A final resolution was needed and time was slipping by.

As Christmas 1934 approached, Perkins brought Hopkins, Wallace, Morgenthau, and a few senior staffers together at her home after dinner. She locked the door, and ushered the group into her dining room where she provided one bottle of whiskey. Perkins insisted, "We have to settle this tonight!" Having taken what Perkins called a solemn oath that there would be no further review or vote changing after that meeting, the committee members stayed in session for six hours—until two in the morning.

Then, on Christmas Eve afternoon, Perkins and Hopkins met with the President for several hours and won his approval and a commitment to deliver it with a special message to Congress. The initial payroll tax of only 1% would increase gradually to 3% by 1948 and benefits would not begin until 1940. The program would be self-supporting until 1965.

At the last minute, Roosevelt discovered a provision that might result in the government paying some future benefits out of general revenues. He would have none of it! That would be dole. Roosevelt wanted Social Security to be entirely self-financing so it could never be made a political football. To accommodate the President, changes were quickly made. On Morgenthau's recommendation, the rate of tax would begin at 2%, not 1% and would rise gradually to 6% over 12 years, not 5% over 20 years and exclude from old age coverage farm workers, domestic servants,[11] and workers at establishments with less than 10 workers. The increases raised the trust fund's expected size by over 300%.

The committee report was presented on January 17, 1935. Happily, the process had moved too quickly for opposition to get well organized. During debate on the House floor in April, the name of the program was changed from Economic Security to Social Security. Otherwise, the proceedings were uneventful. (A little noticed "detail" was added: to collect benefits, the worker had to stop working. In later years, this "detail" would become a major provision.)

PERKINS'S BROADER IMPACT

Perkins's legislative agenda would be part of the 1936 election campaign and provided for a 40-hour work week, prohibition of child labor, safety and health standards, and a minimum wage to be set by the Secretary of Labor in accordance with the "prevailing minimum wage in the industry operating in the area."[12] Perkins was also a major force behind such New Deal initiatives as the Civilian Conservation Corps and the Public Works Administration.[13]

While old age insurance was quite popular, there was opposition in Congress to unemployment insurance, where the anticipated floor debate threatened to produce amendments that would create an inferior bill that

---

[11] The first two groups included many Black workers.

[12] While both Roosevelt and Perkins had not favored the Wagner Act that created the National Labor Relations Board, when it was sure to pass both houses of Congress, the President came around.

[13] Perkins was the first Secretary of Labor to show any interest in the state labor departments. When she did so, year after year, she was well received. She added to the favorable feelings with appealing touches such as awards for state leaders: red ribbons for minimum wage success, blue for maximum hours success, and green for success in restricting child labor. She also arranged to give a signed greeting from the President to the delegate who had come the farthest.

would not pass. So, Perkins and Roosevelt combined the two into one bill with the states administering the unemployment part. Compulsory health insurance was nearly included until the American Medical Association weighed in about "socialized medicine" and got it removed.

People were living longer, thanks to improving healthcare. Work was shifting from farm to factory, from countryside to city, and to smaller dwelling units with less ability to accept more family members who were too old to work. Workers were increasingly on their own rather than part of an extended family. Craft skills were less important than physical dexterity, so older workers who could not keep pace with a production line were simply let go. As a result of these pressures, labor reform movements had become the norm in industrialized economies.

In 1935, the average American worker's life span was only 66 years, so benefit years after retirement at 65[14] was not a concern since half of the population did not live to claim any benefits. (Today, the average is not 66, but 86—an increase of 20 years. Central to any thinking about pensions, all those extra years have been added to one part of the balance: retirement. This means that each of us needs to understand that during our working years, we need to save enough—combined with Social Security benefits—to cover all our expenses for 20 more years than our great grandparents. And end-of-life health care keeps getting more and more expensive, thanks to advances in diagnostic technology and sophisticated medical care.)

Finally, in August 1935, the Social Security Act was passed by overwhelming votes of 372–33 in the House and 77–6 in the Senate. When FDR signed the Social Security bill into law on August 14, 1935, he said, "If the Senate and House of Representatives, in this long and arduous session, had done nothing more than pass this Bill, the session would have been regarded as historic for all time."

---

[14] Retiring at age 65 in the United States related back to its introduction in Bismarck's Germany in 1883.

The first Social Security payroll deductions began in 1937, and the first benefits were paid on January 17, 1940: 65-year-old Ida Mae Fuller of Vermont received the first Social Security check for $22.54.

SUMMING UP

Looking back, Perkins said,

One could hardly have believed that it would be possible when we first began. I've always said, and I still think we have to admit, that no matter how much fine reasoning there was about the old-age insurance system and the unemployment insurance prospects—no matter how many people were studying it or how many committees had ideas on the subject or how many college professors had written theses on the subject—and there were an awful lot of them—the real roots of the Social Security Act were in the great Depression of 1929. Nothing else would have bumped the American people into a social security system except something so shocking, so terrifying, as that depression.

Another reason was that most European countries had enacted similar programs 20 years before.

Years after Perkins retired, she said, "One thing I know: Social Security is so firmly imbedded in the American psychology today that no politician, no political party or political group could possibly destroy this act. It is safe. It is safe forever *and* for the everlasting benefit of the people of the United States."

At the time of Roosevelt's death in April 1945, Frances Perkins was the longest-serving Secretary of Labor in history and one of only two cabinet secretaries to serve the entire length of the Roosevelt presidency. In 1944, a piece portraying Frances Perkins in *Collier's* magazine described her accomplishments over the previous 12 years as "not so much the Roosevelt New Deal, as the Perkins New Deal." When Perkins left the cabinet, only one item on her long list—health insurance—had not been established.

That is why many observers considered Perkins the principal architect of the New Deal.[15]

As biographer George Martin wrote, "She was more than good as an administrator, and as a judge or legislator, she was quite extraordinary. She had a judicial temperament and a strong sense in all situations of what was fair. She was always open to new ideas and yet the moral purpose of the law, the welfare of mankind, was never overlooked." As David Brooks wrote with admiration years later, "She had more than a career; she had a calling."

Time and again, "conservative" politicians have sought to "privatize" (or even eliminate) Social Security. This may appeal to those who have not understood the essential need for a fund to ensure support for Americans in their retirement. Great advances in healthcare have extended the lives of Americans, but 65 continues to be the accepted norm for retirement. So, our Social Security system is challenged by the burden of paying out benefits for much longer per person than it was originally designed. This cannot continue. We need to shift the fulcrum by increasing our working years and have 70 or 72 be the new retirement age. As riots in France have signaled, this change will likely meet resistance, but it is the most realistic way to respond to the increasing lengths of lives.

* * *

---

[15] Before leaving the Department of Labor in June 1945, Frances Perkins stood in the department's auditorium, and, while a full orchestra played, shook the hands with every member of her department. The following year, President Truman appointed her to the United States Civil Service Commission, a position she held until 1953. Still, Perkins needed to earn money, first to cover her husband's costly care and then to do the same for her surviving daughter. So she began a new career of teaching, writing, and giving public lectures, ultimately serving as a lecturer at Cornell University's new School of Industrial Relations until her death in 1965. Charles Wyzanski, serving as a young solicitor to the Department of Labor before going on serve as a much-admired federal judge, began as a skeptic, but became a great admirer of Perkins. (When, as a young member of her staff, he thought he was not up to the job, she went to Felix Frankfurter, who enlisted Supreme Court Justice Louis Brandeis to persuade Wyzanski to stay.) His mature appraisal was that she stood out as "one of the noblest, strongest characters I have ever encountered. On Social Security, she had a vision that was as practical as it was far-sighted. In social vision, she was superior to all of the great persons I have known. In courage, none exceeded her. In loyalty to principle and to persons, none were more commendable." Wyzanski identified Perkins's doctrine as having two parts: First, economic conditions are subject to human improvement by intelligent action, and, second, authority for undertaking the improvement must come from the national government.

The following were particularly helpful sources for this chapter:

- George Martin, *Madam Secretary Frances Perkins* (Boston: Houghton Mifflin, 1983).
- Francis Perkins's oral history for Columbia University.
- Francis Perkins, *The Roosevelt I Knew* (New York: Viking Press, 1946).

2

ERIE CANAL

The Erie Canal was the longest and the most successful canal in the world when it was built in the early 19th century. Innovations were crucial to the success of what was then the largest engineering project on the planet. The history of the commitment to build the canal was almost as complex as its construction. The canal was critical to both the economic and political development of the nation.

The importance of connecting regions, particularly those separated by the Appalachian Mountains, goes back to George Washington and his 1796 farewell address. Washington worried that settlers west of the Appalachian Mountains might bond with either the English or French Canadians or the Spaniards to the south. He warned that this might prove divisive unless we could forge one community of interest as a nation. As Washington explained, "Any other tenure—whether derived from its own separate strength, or from an apostate and unnatural connexion with any foreign power, must be intrinsically precarious."

President Jefferson's Treasury Secretary, Albert Gallatin, agreed and advocated an efficient nationwide transportation network that would stimulate a community of interests and unite people in every part of the nation.

Nothing else within the power of government could do more to reinforce "[the] union, which secures external independence, domestic peace, and internal liberty." In 1808, with the national debt likely to be paid off soon, Treasury Secretary Gallatin proposed spending $2 million annually over 10 years on internal improvements with up to $3 million for a canal between the Hudson River and Lake Erie.

Canals had a long history of connecting people. In 220 BCE, the Babylonians built a canal from the Tigris to the Euphrates. During the 5th century, the Chinese began the Grand Canal (over 1,000 miles long), and in the 11th century, the Dutch built many canals with locks. In the 15th century, Leonardo da Vinci designed 18 locks to climb 80 feet. In the mid-18th century, the Bridgewater Canal in England was built to carry coal 10 miles from mines in Worsley to Manchester with an aqueduct over the River Irwell. This history inspired the small group who, with determination, promoted the Erie Canal.

When New York was seeking federal funding, the nation had only three canals as long as two miles and none was profitable. The world's longest canal was only one-tenth the length of the proposed Erie Canal.[1]

MANY FATHERS

Gouverneur Morris was one of the early "fathers" of the Erie Canal, and may have been the first to envision a canal from the Hudson River to Lake Erie. In 1800, on his return from diplomatic service in France, Morris speculated in land and traveled to the wild back country of New York State. He celebrated the land as excelling "in soil, in climate—in everything."

---

[1] These three canals were the South Hadley Canal, the Turners Falls Canal, and the Dismal Swamp Canal.

Another early supporter of a canal was Jesse Hawley—a flour forwarder. In 1805, while he was incarcerated in debtor's prison, Hawley published a series of 14 essays in *The Genesee Messenger* that argued for a system of canals. Hawley never explored the route himself, but the Erie Canal would be remarkably close to the one he proposed. His essays covered all aspects of construction, including a total cost estimate of $6 million—or $120 million in today's dollars—only $1 million shy of the final cost. Hawley's essays laid out not only the value of a major canal but also explained how to bring the concept to fruition. He proposed that the financing should come from the federal government.

Another among the Erie Canal's many fathers was Elkanah Watson, a businessman and agriculturalist who persuaded a group of influential New Yorkers of the canal's likely merits. The group included his friend Jeremiah Van Rensselaer, a large landowner and lieutenant governor of New York State. Watson and his group were impressed by the abundant produce of the interior farmlands and by the natural salt deposits near Onondaga Lake. Both would benefit from low-cost water transportation to New York City—and beyond. Watson wrote a positive report and shared it with his friend, state Senator Philip Schuyler, who had just visited the Bridgewater Canal in England.

Schuyler—wealthy, a war hero, and father-in-law of Alexander Hamilton—was ready to make a strong effort to win the legislature's support. With Schuyler's help, a long proposal was submitted to the state legislature in 1791 that advocated converting the Mohawk River into a suitable waterway. The plan, entitled The Mohawk Improvement Bill, was to build a series of locks to get past the worst parts of the Mohawk River. Five locks built of wood would bypass Little Falls over a one-mile stretch—each lock lifting or lowering boats by nine feet. Then, two additional locks over two miles would enable boatmen to shift to larger, Durham boats that could carry 20 times as much weight. This cut the travel time substantially—from one day to one hour—and gave the argument for a canal a major boost by opening the water route to Oneida Lake and Lake Ontario.[2] Unfortunately, that plan proved hopeless because the Mohawk River's rapids were far too formidable.

In the 11 years following their 1792 charter, the Western Company converted a long section of the Mohawk River into a deep-water passage. While converting the whole river would prove impossible, this was conceptually an important step toward building the Erie Canal. Experience also showed that private financing would not be enough: public financing would be required. By this time, the idea of a canal was being seriously discussed, and would soon reach James Geddes, an engineer and New York State legislator. Geddes discussed it with Jesse Hawley, who quickly became a strong supporter.

Joshua Forman, a state legislator from Utica, enthusiastically advocated connecting different parts of New York State via canals and arranged to have a feasibility survey conducted at state expense. When the appropriation was cut back, James Geddes, an engineer, paid an additional $73 out of his own pocket (which was later reimbursed) to have the Irondequoit Valley, east of Rochester, included in the survey. The review, which estimated building costs of the canal at $10 million, brought good news. The Genesee River could provide the required water for an embankment high enough to carry a canal between the hills on either side of the valley. So, Forman audaciously proposed that the canal should go across the Irondequoit Valley on an artificial embankment 68 feet high and over 500 feet wide, "a surface not surpassed in the world for singularity." The concept would become a major feature of the Erie Canal.

---

[2] In a 1798 report, the cost of going 200 miles from Albany to Geneva had been cut from $100 to $32.

WAITING FOR A LEADER

President Jefferson scoffed at the idea presented to him by Forman as being at least 100 years too soon. "Why, sir, here is a canal of a few miles, projected by George Washington, which, if completed, would render this a fine commercial city, which has languished for many years because the small sum of $200,000 necessary to complete it cannot be obtained from the general government, the state government, or from individuals—and you talk of making a canal 350 *miles* through the *wilderness*. It is little short of madness to think of it this day!"

Before construction of the canal, odds had favored separation of the western states from those east of the Appalachian mountains—as Washington had feared. However, Forman did not retreat, and his parting words to Jefferson were prophetic, "The State of New York will never rest until [the canal] is accomplished!"[3]

The Holland Company (a consortium of six Dutch banks that had lent money to Gouverneur Morris before he got into serious financial difficulties in 1779) held title to most of western New York State. That organization's manager, Joseph Elliott, saw the great value a canal would add—at least $1 million—to his company's land value. So, he arranged to offer the state over 100,000 acres—in alternating lots of 160 acres each—to encourage building a canal that would, drain swamps, increase land value, and direct it in a way that would bring the most value to the company's land holdings.[4]

---

[3] Another political fight surged forward as two villages fought to be chosen as the canal's terminus on Lake Erie. The combined populations of Buffalo and Black Rock, rivals for the terminus on Lake Erie, *totaled* only 700. Finally, Buffalo won. Its subsequent growth proved how great were the stakes of the fight.

[4] This offer came with a stipulation that the state would pay the tax on the land, and that if the canal was not built within 15 years, the land would have to be returned.

Petitions to begin canal construction usually cited America's rivalry with Canada in transatlantic trade. The compelling reason for an interior route to Lake Erie was clear: Going to Lake Ontario would surely result in losing most of the lucrative trans-oceanic freight to nearby Montreal.

In 1810, Thomas Eddy, a director and treasurer of the Western Inland Lock Navigation Company, was convinced that a carefully conducted study by appointed commissioners would lead the legislature to endorse the canal. He convinced State Senator Jonas Platt, who had doubted such a major project could be undertaken by private investors but was certain it could be accomplished by the state. Eddy and Platt recognized that they needed strong political support and went to DeWitt Clinton, who had shown no interest in the past, but now—needing to champion a great cause—seized on the canal as "an object of the highest public utility and worthy of the noblest ambition."

The New York legislature appropriated $15,000 in support of a commission to arrange financing, acquire the interests of the Western Inland Lock Company, seek grants of land from owners along the proposed route, and approach Congress for financial support. The total cost was estimated at $20,000 a mile or $6 million total and the expected time to completion was 10–15 years.

For realists at the time, the capital costs were enormous. More daunting, the skills required for success in such an adventure in engineering were not available, *and* the politics were demanding. The federal government refused to help. With 93% of Americans still living on farms, the benefits and challenge of building a 353-mile artificial waterway through the mountains and forests were far from understood. What was clearly understood was that the 1792 attempt to make the Mohawk River navigable from Albany for nearly 100 miles into the interior had been a failure.

DEWITT CLINTON

The canal faced daunting financial and engineering challenges, but these were modest compared to the greater political roadblocks put in place by skilled and ambitious practitioners like Martin Van Buren and Tammany Hall.

Canal supporters found their leader in DeWitt Clinton[5] who was brilliant, arrogant, politically connected, and ambitious to gain more power and higher office. A serious intellectual, he strengthened the American Academy of Arts and Sciences, established the Historical Society, and wrote numerous articles on academic matters with a keen interest in science and nature (particularly ornithology). He was a compelling speaker, a former United States Senator, three-time mayor of New York City, as well as lieutenant governor (and would later be governor of New York State).

To realize his political ambitions, Clinton believed he required major success with a highly visible project. So, he made the canal his great cause.

In March 1811, a state commission—nominally chaired by Gouverneur Morris, but effectively led by DeWitt Clinton—reported that an overland canal was feasible and should be undertaken by New York State. (That commission still anticipated federal help.) As Chairman Morris declared, "The wisdom, as well as the justice of the national legislature, will no doubt lead to the exercise on their part of prudent munificence." The commission concluded that the whole venture should be dug, forever scotching any thought of using rivers for part of the project.

---

[5] Clinton's many activities stretched his time and money thin. Hostile political forces gained control of the legislature and removed him from office as mayor in February 1807, but not before he had seen the benefits of playing patronage. Only 38 years old, he was determined to fight again.

Given the War of 1812, the federal budget had gone from steady surpluses to a record deficit in 1814. So, financing the canal would be left to New York State, where the political opposition seemed to be gathering momentum. Moreover, farmers distant from the canal worried about having to pay higher taxes while receiving little direct benefit. Then, Clinton's opponents forced him out of office as mayor. By 1815, friends of the canal were seriously discouraged and close to giving up hope. Clinton bemoaned, "The commissioners were frittered down into a board of consideration—without power and without money!"

His uncle, George Clinton, having served as Jefferson's Vice President, had hoped to become president. DeWitt Clinton had even stronger ambitions for the presidency from 1808 onward. In 1811, Clinton regained control of the Council of Appointment—the same group that had tossed him out as mayor—and had himself returned to office. (Through a fluke, he also became lieutenant governor of New York State.) The group that had great influence on nominations for national office in those days was unusually small, and the Clintons were in the middle of it. DeWitt Clinton began building his base for election as president. As unlikely as it would seem today, he hoped to attract some Federalists over to his Republican base.

During "Mr. Madison's War," Clinton focused on the military threat posed by the British. At his request, he was granted a military commission as a major general but was denied an active command. Worse, in March 1815, the Council of Appointment removed Clinton from office as mayor. For the first time in 18 years, he was out of political office. His only public position was as a member of the state's Erie Canal Commission, a role that Clinton seized on as his road back to power.[6]

---

[6] In 1810, Clinton had kept a wide-ranging record of his trip along the intended pathway of the canal that covered local politics, flora and fauna, possible future industry, and complaints about local accommodations.

By 1815, the tide was changing and beneath the surface, the canal venture was gaining strength. A new commission was organized by DeWitt Clinton and the wealthy business leader and politician Stephen Van Rensselaer—and other "go-ahead" leaders. They agreed to divide what they called "The Great Western Canal" into three major sections. A modest tax would facilitate the substantial borrowing needed to finance building the canal.[7]

DeWitt Clinton recognized that a fully operational canal achieved on time and on budget by 1824—the end of Madison's second term—would be a superb basis on which to run for president. Clinton was free of administrative duties and able to channel his considerable energy, talents, and political connections on building the canal.

Recent military experience gave credence to the importance of the canal for shipping heavy cannons and other arms. Equally important was the evidence that a robust home market should be a major focus, since overseas markets, as shown during the recent war, could not always be relied on. As Clinton led the public campaign for support of the canal, the importance of internal transportation became clearer and clearer. Between 1815 and 1816, major meetings were organized in two dozen cities and towns around the state to develop public interest and demand attention from the legislature.

Still, tough battles lay ahead for the canal *and* for Clinton—whose arrogance and acerbic personality continued to cause him trouble. While the power to achieve major objectives such as free schools and freeing slaves were his focus, he had little tolerance for the everyday "retail" politics needed to get popular support for his major projects. He was brilliant and far-sighted, but he showed too clearly his sense of cultural and intellectual superiority. He would not compromise and was dismissive of those

---

[7] Cost control was helped by completing the construction in 7 years, not the anticipated 12 years.

who disagreed with him. Also, he had insulted too many people. His strongest political enemies were gathered together in one power center: Tammany Hall. Clinton exhorted, "It remains for a free state to create a new era in history, and to erect a work more stupendous, more magnificent, and more beneficial than has heretofore been achieved by the human race." While built by a single state, the motivating concept of the canal was nationalism, not state identity.

GETTING STARTED

While politicians squabbled, engineers working on the canal made steady progress. In late 1820, work began on the section running from Utica to the terminus at Albany, where a wharf three-quarters of a mile in length had just been built on the Hudson River. The Erie Canal would need 83 locks to raise and lower the barges 675 feet over the 363 miles from Albany to Buffalo. Each lock would be 90 feet long and 15 feet wide and lift or lower each boat 8 feet, 4 inches.

In making a strong case for constructing the canal, Clinton declared, "The inhabitants of the same country should be bound together by a community of interests, and a reciprocation of benefits: that agriculture should find a sale of its commodities; manufacturers a vent for their fabrics; and commerce a market for its commodities: it is our incumbent duty to open, facilitate, and improve internal navigation." Later in the same grandiloquent document, Clinton pointed out how the canal could reduce sectionalism. Details were worked out and specified in a tightly reasoned and well-documented 12-page advocacy report. In the report, Clinton argued that "our merchants should not be robbed of their legitimate profits" and public revenues should not be "seriously impeded by dishonest smuggling" nor the commerce of cities supplanted by "the mercantile establishments of foreign countries!"

Then, swinging over to the positives, Clinton explained that the canal would help pay off the public debts, pay for "great public improvements, encourage the arts and sciences, and foster the inventions of genius—and carry more riches on its waters than any other canal in the world." Clinton concluded with this stirring admonition: "Delays are the refuge of weak minds!"

This splendid memorial made the project be called *Clinton's canal*. On April 15, 1817, the Canal Bill was passed.[8]

CONSTRUCTION

The commissioners had hoped to bring William Weston, an experienced engineer, from England, but he declined due to age and poor health. So they turned to amateurs Benjamin Wright and James Geddes for the western and middle sections—and hired Charles Broadhead for the eastern section. (Fortunately, the canal would connect with many rivers, providing ample water.)

Construction began near Rome at dawn on July 4, 1817. In October 1819, the section from Rome to Utica was completed and filled with water. By 1820, the canal would extend 90 miles to Montezuma, and in 1824, the last lock was built near Albany. Construction would have none of the major advantages of Europe's great canals. The length was 25 *times* longer, population far sparser, and, with the exception of Dewitt Clinton, no powerful luminaries were advocates. Only 7% of the state's population lived within

---

[8] While opponents could not stop the canal movement, they did delay construction by 18 long months, thanks to clever political moves by Martin Van Buren and a call for "more research." US Senators Clay and Calhoun proposed a Bill in Congress sponsoring internal improvements that included $90,000 a year for 20 years to build a canal across New York State; but after passing by just two votes, it was vetoed by President Madison. Clinton struck back with "Whatever gloss may be thrown over this reprehensible conduct of Mr. Madison, it connects with jealousy of the growing prosperity of New York!"

easy reach of the canal. In today's dollars, the cost of the canal would be over $100 million![9]

So, how do you dig a ditch 4 feet deep and 40 feet wide for hundreds of miles through dense, primeval forest? Nobody had ever done such a thing! The answer came down to hard labor. Stakes were driven 60 feet apart—40 feet for the canal plus room for the towpath for horses or mules on one side and a berm on the other side. The engineering challenges were daunting: with shovels, axes, explosive powder, and mules, build the long, new waterway through dense primeval forests, over mountains, and across valleys for 363 miles. The canal would require 83 locks to lift large boats 675 feet up and then down as much as 625 feet *and* 18 aqueducts, one of which was over three city blocks long. Wood, then brick, and then stone were used to build the locks, thanks to the discovery in 1803 of a suitable limestone.

Lake Erie is 541 feet higher than the Hudson River and another 120 feet would be required to lift and lower boats going the full length of the canal. (With a width of 40 feet on the surface, tapering to 28 feet at the bottom, the canal had 4 feet of water.)

By the end of 1817, over 50 local clearing or construction contracts had been signed and over 1,000 men had been recruited at $12 a month— plus food. (Wisely, the commissioners had agreed to concentrate on the actual construction and have all financing decisions made by a separate group—all senior members of the state government.)

By contracting the work with many local people who knew their areas, the canal commissioners got expertise on each section, diversified their risk of dependence, and maintained control—since work would only be paid for when the particular section was completed and inspected. Meanwhile, out of pocket expenses for labor, food, and materials would be

---

[9] A major benefit of canals was the lower cost of power. Barges were usually pulled by horses or mules that could pull 25 times more weight on barges than they could pull in wagons over land. This meant less cost to buy horses for power, plus feed, gear, shoes, and so on.

covered. After clearing and digging the middle section, next would come a 59-mile section aptly called the *long level*, that was so flat that no locks would be required.

The hardest work was cutting down the many huge trees, cutting them into movable pieces, pulling out the roots, and carting all that wood out of the 60-foot wide pathway to be cleared. Only then could the canal be dug 4 feet deep and 40 feet wide.

Instead of cutting trees down, a large device was cleverly invented that *pulled* trees down. A cable connected the upper part of a tree to a 14-foot winch suspended between two larger 16-foot wheels on which it was rolled into place so the smaller wheel, with the cable, was free to rotate and rotate and rotate, steadily pulling the tree down. Next, a chain around the stump was wound around the inner wheel and connected by thick rope to a team of mules or horses. As the strong animals pulled steadily ahead, the winch put increasingly tremendous pressure on the stump until it was literally yanked out of the ground.

The time saving was immense. A team of seven men and four horses could remove 30 trees—stumps and all—in a single day. Then, instead of digging with picks and shovels, teams of mules with outsized heavy plows could break up the ground and haul away the dirt, saving both time and money.

Lack of the usual snows one year—which had favored the sleds hauling heavy loads to and from construction sites—was followed by too much snow the next year. In the spring, mosquitoes and what may have been malaria, caused over 1,000 men to have serious fevers. These and other challenges were steadily overcome, and the overall progress was good enough for the commissioners to authorize expanding out from the middle section in both directions.

More unusual weather—deep snows and heavy rains the next year— slowed down progress. To make up lost time, 4,000 men and 1,500 horses and mules were put to work. Then, they had some bad luck: the quicklime being used to seal the spaces between stones in the walls of locks deteriorated under pressure all too quickly. Fortunately, Clinton discovered, in his wide-ranging reading, a cement the Romans had once used. Unfortunately, importing it would be far too expensive. However, an engineer had heard about a local limestone near the village of Chittenango that would not disintegrate when wet, and tests proved him right. Over 500,000 bushels of this limestone would be used by the canal—and still more in other locations.[10]

Even more impressive, the longest stone structure ever built in America—with 11 giant arches and a total length of 802 feet—was constructed near Rochester to carry the Erie Canal *over* the Genesee River.[11] The aqueduct had to be three city blocks long—with seven tall arches to allow the water to flow under it. It would support 2,000 *tons* of canal water. When completed in September 1823, costs had gone over budget by $83,000 and the work was 11 months behind schedule.[12] But the power of the Genesee Falls would drive the mills that made Rochester famous as "the Flour City."[13]

MORE CHALLENGES

Still, major engineering challenges lay ahead. Between Little Falls and Schenectady, 13 locks were needed, and then, from Schenectady to Troy, a distance of 16 miles, another 27 locks were needed. After Troy, two major aqueducts were required—one was 748 feet long and 30 feet above the raging river—and the other even longer at 1,188 feet in length and requiring 26 piers.

---

[10] Ironically, the engineer who developed this crucial limestone got nothing but praises for his salient development.

[11] Rochester's population surged in just 25 years from 8,000 to 36,000.

[12] By 1833, a new bridge was needed to replace it.

[13] Between 1820 and 1830, Rochester's population increased 421% and Buffalo's by 314%. Rochester became the largest flour-producing center in the *world*. (The repeal of England's Corn Laws was likely caused by the importation of low-cost grain from America, which was a direct result of the canal.) The canal had a major role in making New York City the nation's leading commercial and financial center and would convert upstate family subsistence farming into a profitable commercial enterprise.

At Cohoes Falls, the challenge was daunting: cutting through solid rock high above the river. A British engineer estimated it would take two full years. However, in the end it was done in just 80 days. The total construction achievement was extraordinary, and the commissioners were ecstatic with expectations of completion in the coming year.

Fortunately, tolls on the middle section were increasing so the required money could be borrowed on increasingly favorable terms. In April 1819, the commissioners committed to complete the entire canal. In 1821, the labor force at work on the canal was over 9,000.

The Canal Fund was able to borrow $2 million between 1822 and 1824. Investor appetite for canal bonds was particularly strong in London. By 1829, overseas investors would own over half of the canal debt. New York State's own debts of $2.7 million when construction began were now fully paid off. With strong revenues—well above expectation—the canal was highly profitable. Canal bonds were repaid well ahead of schedule and tolls were abolished in 1882.

Below Schenectady, the land drops 200 feet over the 16 miles to Troy. This would require 27 different locks. Crossing the Mohawk River twice would require two major aqueducts. To cross from south to north, the aqueduct would be 748 feet long and 30 feet above the powerful river with 16 piers to allow the water to cascade below. Crossing back again later required an aqueduct 1,188 feet long supported by 26 stone piers. (This was the longest of 18 aqueducts required for the canal.) The route over the Mohawk and back saved $75,000 so it was well worth the great effort.

Still ahead was completion of the Rochester to Lake Erie section. Seventeen miles east of Niagara Falls, there was an unavoidable and nearly vertical wall of hard rock. Several engineers were invited by the commissioners to propose solutions to the daunting challenge of a nearly 70-foot vertical climb of the solid rock wall. The accepted solution came from a staff engineer named Nathan Roberts. He proposed a "flight of locks" set, not at 8-feet 4-inch rises, but at 12 feet apiece and in pairs—one going up and the other down—so traffic could flow in both directions to the height of a six-story building.

Instead of a sixth or even a seventh lock, Roberts decided to cut through the rock—by as much as 30 feet. This meant taking the boats up and over the huge stone Niagara escarpment *and* overcoming a bitter political fight. The toughness of the rock could be measured by the number of ruined drills, even when a special new steel was developed for this task. The cut took three long years to complete.

Crossing the Irondequoit Creek (a serious misnomer for a river that carried 30-ton boats) required another aqueduct that would flow some 70 feet above the "creek" *and* would extend nearly one mile from one side of the valley to the other. Geddes had proposed an enormous embankment to carry the 40-foot-wide canal filled with water from one side of the Irondequoit Valley to the other. However, engineers decided the soil was too porous to be strong enough for stone, so they began thinking of a wooden aqueduct. But, the risk was great that such a top-heavy structure might be pushed over by the strong winter winds coming off Lake Ontario. So, the engineers went back to building a massive embankment with a large culvert 25 feet high, 30 feet wide, and 100 feet long and carefully arched to support the weight of the embankment. To keep it from "spreading" and collapsing, 900 large pilings had to be sunk into more stable dirt that would be hauled in from other areas. Nearly 3,000 workers labored for two years to get it done. In late autumn 1821, water was brought in to fill that last section of the canal.

Even fully packed with 50 tons of freight, barges took only six days to travel the Erie Canal from end to end. Boats were typically 77 feet long and 14 feet 3 inches in beam, allowing just 4.5 feet of clearance on each side.

Completed in 1825, the canal would produce tolls over the next 57 years of $121 million or four times its total cost. The bonds issued to finance the canal had long since been paid off. (Tonnage carried on the Erie Canal rose steadily to a peak in 1880.)

CELEBRATION

On October 26, 1825, a flotilla of boats towed by mules left Buffalo. Nine days and 363 miles later, they arrived at seven in the morning in Albany. The great occasion marking the completion of the canal was magnificent and centered on Governor Clinton. He, of course, gave the keynote address and then led the cotillion that evening after a procession led by a well-decorated packet boat suitably named *The DeWitt Clinton.*

Celebrations were spectacular. The *Seneca Chief* led a procession of boats and yachts down the banner-bedecked canal from western New York to a ceremony off Sandy Hook.

As the first act of the ceremony, Clinton filled several bottles—each noted as "made in America"—with the water from Lake Erie. Dr. Samuel Mitchill added water from a dozen of the world's greatest rivers. Then Clinton placed them all in a cedar box specially designed for the occasion by the famous woodworker Duncan Phyfe, to be transported to France as a gift to the Marquis de Lafayette from the people of New York.

Celebrating the completion of the canal in just eight years, cannons were fired in series from Buffalo on the shore of Lake Erie. The "relay of sound" carried over a distance of 500 miles until the series of booms— which took 90 minutes—reached the harbor of New York City.

The Albany basin was jammed with canal boats and a huge gathering of cheering spectators massed along the wharves, the bridges, and the shoreline. After the line of boats reached the southernmost bridge across the basin, the Clinton contingent went ashore to be received by a welcoming committee that included every available local official and delegates from the national government, including Secretary of State Henry Clay, Chief Justice John Marshall of the Supreme Court, Attorney General William Wirt, and several high-ranking military men.

The Erie Canal was described as the greatest achievement of the age, second only to American Independence. William Stone celebrated the canal planners and builders with a poem that ended "America can never forget to acknowledge that they have built the longest canal in the world in the least time with the least experience for the least money and to the greatest public benefit."

FUTURE CHANGES

In 1826, 7,000 boats, up from 2,000 the prior year, were operating on the canal and revenues were over $500,000 or five *times* the interest due on the bonds. In 1836, work began to rebuild the canal to dimensions twice as wide as the original. By 1837, all of the debt had been retired.

The population of the west more than tripled in just 25 years from 2.5 million to 7.5 million.

The canal was enlarged in the 1840s and an even greater expansion was done at the turn of the century—at a cost of over $100 million (today's equivalent of $3.5 billion) to accommodate barges that were 25 feet wide and 250 feet long and pulled by steam powered tug boats.

The Erie Canal tied the Midwest to the East, bringing increasing prosperity to both. It was vital to the great growth of New York City and led to the repeal of the Corn Laws in the United Kingdom. However, canals could not compete with another major innovation: railroads.

The first steam railway in the United States, the Mohawk and Albany—its coal car ironically named *DeWitt Clinton*—offered to take passengers 16 miles in one hour as opposed to a full day to move through the many locks on the Erie Canal, signaling the future technological confrontation.

* * *

Readers may well wonder why there is no chapter on the railroads. After all, the railroads overwhelmed the canals as the preferred means of low-cost, long-distance travel, particularly for freight. They bound the West to the East, making our ever-expanding and increasingly diverse country more definitely one nation with a single, integrated economy and society.

Many lessons were learned from the railroads' experience: how to manage geographically dispersed operations, how to raise huge amounts of capital, how to organize workers' unions, how to simplify time zones, and how to promulgate a great many corporate laws and regulations.

The dominant reason for not having a chapter on the exciting adventures of the great railroad titans—Huntington, Hopkins, Crocker, and the others—is that they were, as is also the case with most great investments made in America, made by private people seeking personal gain. Readers interested in the "what might have been" can enjoy the whole story by reading Richard White's fascinating history, *Railroaded*, published by W. W. Norton in 2011.

Long distance train travel by rail was arduous. In 1860, Abraham Lincoln traveled by train from Springfield to New York City—825 miles "as a crow flies" or 1,700 miles by rail. The trip took five different trains and four days and three nights.

On September 6, 1869 the golden spike was driven into place with a silver hammer by Leland Stanford, president of the Central Pacific Railroad Co., at Promontory Summit in Utah. The 1,912 mile Overland Route then connected the eastern railroads at Omaha to Oakland, California. The railroads collectively made great contributions to the nation's economy and to its self-concept.

It might have been different. For example, imagine what might have happened if the federal government had, at public expense and for public purpose, designed and laid the optimal trackage and then assessed a moderate charge for that system's use by railroad companies who provided the rolling stock and engines—as did happen with trucking and the interstate highway system. That would have been a far better solution to the "railroad problem" and offered a strong chapter filled with interesting stories about colorful personalities. But that's not what happened.

* * *

The following are the primary sources for this chapter:

- Peter L. Bernstein, *Wedding of the Waters* (New York: W. W. Norton, 2006).

- Ronald E. Shaw, *Erie Waters West: A History of the Erie Canal, 1792–1854* (Lexington: University Press of Kentucky, 1990).

- David Hosack, *Memoir of DeWitt Clinton* (Sydney, Australia: Wentworth Press, 2016).

3

LOUISIANA PURCHASE

The Louisiana Purchase transformed America in scale and ended Napoleon's plans to establish an empire in North America. The financing of this major transaction marked the shift in global financial leadership from Amsterdam to London. The Purchase would also show the advantages of leverage on a remarkably successful investment.

The essence of any highly successful purchase is a favorable purchase price, and the two most important factors in such a price are a highly motivated seller and unexpectedly favorable future developments. Both came together with the 1804 purchase of Louisiana.

Napoleon, a master strategist, had extraordinary vision and an unusual capacity for bold action. He also understood the great importance of concentrating resources toward his most important objective: domination of Europe—which he knew required defeating England, France's most powerful adversary.

France and England had fought the Seven Years War. One result: France lost its Canadian possessions. Then came a pause. Nevertheless,

Napoleon was still scheming to find ways to counter England in North America—and the world. The center of his attention was the Caribbean Sea and the islands where slaves cut the cane to produce sugar, the much-in-demand sweetener that had been making so many fortunes. Napoleon concluded that taking control of those islands and building up the French colony at New Orleans were ways both to weaken England and to strengthen France. (Napoleon similarly decided to wrest India from England by first invading Egypt, which is why Nelson's great victory over Napoleon's fleet at the Battle of the Nile was so important to England.)

CHANGING STRATEGIES

Aiming to reestablish France in North America, Napoleon and his chief diplomat Charles-Maurice de Talleyrand-Périgord saw the first step as the capture of Santo Domingo. With success in Santo Domingo and a strong base established there, Napoleon would be able to drive the British out of the Caribbean and expand up the Mississippi Valley from New Orleans toward Quebec, in French Canada. That would reestablish France as the great power in the large area served by the many rivers that combine to make the mighty Mississippi River.

With Florida added and further expansion in the richly rewarding islands of the Caribbean, Napoleon envisioned a commercial bloc in the Caribbean Basin that consisted of multiple West Indian islands. France would export its manufactured goods to the islands, and the islands, in turn, would produce sugar, molasses, rum, coffee, and cotton for France. Louisiana would supply the islands and those troops stationed there with the resources they needed, such as grain, timber, and salted meat. New Orleans would also, in turn, be a market to the many settlers of the Mississippi Valley. In this context, it would be important to retake Louisiana—which Louis XV had given to Spain as recompense for losses it had suffered as France's ally in the Seven Years War. With control of the North American heartland, France could compel the United States to be a vassal to France as were Belgium, Switzerland, the Netherlands, and many of Austria and Germany's principalities. Then, Napoleon could focus on conquering England.

The first step would be to take control of Santo Domingo, where a slave rebellion had been led by Francois Dominique Toussaint L'Ouverture. Napoleon sent his brother-in-law, General Charles Leclerc, with 20,000 highly trained troops to put down the revolt. (Leclerc's wife, Napoleon's sister, went with him.) President Jefferson had, Leclerc believed, agreed to starve Toussaint out, apparently to discourage a slave rebellion in America.[1] (The full story of all the maneuvers made during this period would be more than complicated.)

Jefferson and Madison, his Secretary of State, had a long and successful history of working closely and effectively together. They now agreed to send a minister plenipotentiary to Paris to get clarification of the situation. They chose Robert R. Livingston, a wealthy New York landowner—with over 160,000 acres—who had a distinguished ancestry, a long history of friendship with France, a first-class mind, and great ambition. His mission was to determine if rumors were true that Spain might transfer New Orleans back to France.

Livingston—proud of having been Chancellor of New York State and having administered the oath of office to George Washington when inaugurated as president—had demonstrated advanced practices in farming and animal husbandry and been active in revolutionary politics since serving as a delegate to the Second Continental Congress in 1775. However, he was not part of the close-knit group of Virginians—and he knew it.

---

[1] The entire US Government, including all three branches, numbered only 293 people.

Livingston arrived in Paris in October, 1801, and was warmly welcomed by his old friend, the Marquis de Lafayette. He met Napoleon briefly in a public setting in the Tuileries Palace. Livingston soon initiated what would later develop into the Louisiana Purchase with an inquiry about buying New Orleans and western Florida. He was turned down. Then, he asked about acquiring the Louisiana Territory north of the Arkansas River. This would leave France with Saint-Domingue and the port of New Orleans and act as a buffer between its holdings and England's domain in Canada. However, Talleyrand rebuffed that idea, too.

Livingston analyzed the situation as an experienced economic developer. His analysis showed that the financial capital required to reestablish the sugar plantations on the islands *and* make New Orleans prosperous would be enormous and far too great for France. Then, he showed how destructive and inevitable conflict—and almost certainly war between America and France—would be. He had all this translated into French and gave copies of his analysis to 20 influential people in Paris, hoping to persuade the French government. However, Livingston's analysis had no impact on Napoleon.

Two weeks later, General Leclerc and his large army sailed from Brest, France, to Saint-Domingue, arriving in January. Leclerc landed and called on L'Ouverture's general to surrender the city. He refused. Then Leclerc attacked. The defenders torched the city, killed many whites, and disappeared into the countryside.

Leclerc, relying on what he believed had been Jefferson's prior assurance of help with food and provisions, was outraged by the prices he was going to be charged. Then, unable to borrow money in New York—since the French Revolution had destroyed France's credit with North American lenders—Leclerc decided to seize the necessary stores and then set the prices he would pay. Meanwhile, the fighting went well for the French, and in just 10 days, all the major ports had been captured.

While early French engagements on Saint-Domingue were successful, after a few months, the battles were nearly even, and in early February 1802, a truce was called. General Leclerc offered large bribes to officers who would switch sides. When several did, he was increasingly confident of prevailing when fighting resumed.

A strange disease—yellow fever—began killing French soldiers in increasing numbers. Believing it would get worse during the summer, Leclerc sent a message to Napoleon estimating that his original force of 20,000 would be reduced to just 4,000 by October.

Suddenly, in what was a disaster for Leclerc, Napoleon decided to reinstate slavery. Then, on November 2, 1802, Leclerc died of yellow fever. L'Ouverture was captured in a ruse and sent to a prison on the Swiss border, where he died within a year.

FOCUS ON LOUISIANA

On April 18, 1802, President Jefferson wrote a long letter to Robert Livingston, expressing his views:

Of all nations of any consideration, France is the one which, hitherto, has offered the fewest points on which we could have any conflict of right and the most points of communion of interests. Her growth, therefore, we viewed as our own, her misfortunes, ours.

There is on the globe one spot, the possessor of which is our natural and habitual enemy. It is New Orleans, through which the produce of three-eighths of our territory must pass to market, and from its fertility it will ere long yield more than half of our inhabitants. France, placing herself in that door, assumes to us the attitude of defiance. The impetuosity of her temper, the energy and restlessness of her character, place her in a point of eternal conflict with us.

Jefferson was clear: The fading Spanish empire had been one thing, but expansionist Napoleonic France was quite another. He was convinced that if France controlled New Orleans, America must ally with England and "marry the British fleet." With such national interests at stake, Jefferson was willing to shift his sympathies from Paris to London—or at least be seen that way—to improve America's negotiating power.

NAPOLEON DECIDES

Napoleon decided that defending lands so far away was too expensive. He needed to concentrate his resources for campaigns in Europe since his main goal was to control Europe. Once this priority was established, it was better to reduce or eliminate distraction in order to concentrate on that great objective.

With this framing, selling Louisiana for a decent price became an obvious move. However, to get a good price, it would be important to convince the Americans that the necessary amount must be substantial *and*, if only barely, within their ability to pay.

Napoleon was in his bath on Monday, April 11, 1803, when his brothers tried to change his mind. He refused. "I repeat: there will be no debate, for the reason that the project conceived by me and negotiated by me, shall be ratified and executed by me alone. Do you comprehend me? It is not only New Orleans that I will cede, it is the whole colony without any reservation. I know the price of what I abandon, I renounce it with the greatest regret. But, to attempt obstinately to retain it would be folly."

Within hours, Talleyrand was enquiring whether the United States would be interested in the entire territory. (Newspapers had recently carried reports of a decision by Congress passed on February 28, 1803, to build 15 gunboats to patrol the Mississippi River, and a resolution to raise

50,000 troops was being discussed. Also, Jefferson had obtained Cabinet approval for an alliance with England.)

GOOD ADVICE GETS TAKEN

Pierre Samuel du Pont de Nemours had emigrated from France to America in 1799 and launched several businesses, one of which would become the great explosives manufacturer, E. I. du Pont. He also enjoyed regular access to President Jefferson *and* kept his access to Napoleon. Jefferson allowed du Pont to read his letter to Livingston. (Jefferson made a practice of enlisting private citizens in government missions, so it was not surprising when he chose to share his thoughts with du Pont.)

Jefferson first hoped to convince du Pont to communicate the risk of war to Napoleon, but du Pont responded by suggesting force was not the best way. A purchase would be wiser and far less costly. His recommendation: "Consider what the most successful war with France and Spain would cost you. And contract for a part—a half let's say. The two countries will have made a good bargain. You will have Louisiana and probably the Floridas for the least expenditure possible and this conquest will be neither encumbered by hatreds nor sullied by human blood."

Then, because he understood that Napoleon needed cash and would need more if war with England broke out, du Pont made the same basic case to Napoleon in Paris.

* * *

"It is something larger than the whole U.S., probably containing 500 millions of acres, the U.S. containing 434 million," Jefferson wrote, seemingly thinking aloud as his mind took in what might happen. "This removes from us the greatest source of danger to our peace."

On May 1, 1802, Secretary of State Madison wrote to Livingston, urging him to be more assertive in his discussions with Talleyrand. He was to renew his efforts to buy the Floridas and New Orleans. No price was given. Livingston continued his probing to see if the French would sell and at what price. Time and time again, over the next several months, Livingston would ask for instructions on how much might be paid. But Madison would not give him a specific response.

On January 11, 1803, Jefferson nominated James Monroe, a devoted follower, as envoy extraordinary to the French government. He was to join with Livingston in persuading the French to sell New Orleans and the Floridas, which, he emphasized, were crucial to the future of the United States. Monroe was authorized to pay as much as Ff 50 million or $9,375,000 for Florida and New Orleans. If he could not make the purchase, he was to obtain guarantees of America's rights to deposit cargo for trans-Atlantic shipment.[2] (A week later, on January 18, Jefferson sent a secret message to Congress requesting $2,500 to explore the West from the Missouri River in hopes of locating a possible pathway to the Pacific. It was to be led by his private secretary, Captain Meriwether Lewis, and Lieutenant William Clark.)

Jefferson told Monroe that the maximum he could offer France was Ff 50 million or just over $9 million—which was over four *times* what Congress had indicated it might agree to. With Monroe appointed to a higher ranked position in early 1803, Livingston realized he had only a few weeks to achieve his goal of making a deal before the younger man's arrival in April. Talleyrand invited Livingston to meet and, for the first time, seemed interested in the sale of New Orleans.

---

[2] To avoid provoking partisan politics, Monroe would have to pay for his and his wife's and their two daughters' passage on a merchant ship. But he was short on cash. So, Madison bought from Monroe 200 pieces of silver flatware, 36 Sèvres plates, and a tea set that had cost Monroe $4,000 to ship from France after a previous mission.

Talleyrand had surprised Livingston with a question, asking if he might want to buy Louisiana. Livingston countered, "You might want to sell"—with the implication that that was the governing reality. Livingston wrote and gave to Talleyrand an analysis of why France should want to sell: Colonies are best for countries with surplus populations and lacking in the ability to manufacture fine products for export to other countries—neither of which applied to France. Besides, with renewed American friendship, France could easily win a substantial share of the trade with America that England was then enjoying.

GETTING SPECIFIC

Talleyrand invited Livingston to his office on April 11 and dropped an amazing proposition on the table. "Would you Americans wish to have the whole of Louisiana?"

Livingston cautiously said, "No. Our interest is only in New Orleans and the Floridas," but he went on to suggest that "France should give us the country above the Arkansas River as a buffer between yourselves and Canada."

Talleyrand's response: "But, if we gave you New Orleans, the rest would be of little value so I would like to know what you would give for the whole." Livingston suggested Ff 20 million or about $3 million dollars, but Talleyrand quickly said that price was far too low.

A few days later, Livingston was given an informal offer by Talleyrand of Ff 100 million or less than $20 million—which he immediately declared was too much. But, by then, the outer price limits had been set and both sides had clearly shown their interest in a transaction if only a specific price could be agreed.

France came back with a final offer of Ff 80 million or $15 million of which $3,750,000 would resolve valid claims against France for ships, crews, and cargoes seized. That set of claims would be taken over and paid by the United States and the other $11,250,000 would be paid via long-term bonds.

But did Jefferson, the "strict constructionist," have the power to make such a purchase? If not, should he seek a Constitutional amendment? This, of course, would take substantial time and with delays and uncertainties, France might decide not to go ahead with the deal. Or England might make a competing offer. After a week or so of inner turmoil, Jefferson resolved to seek Congressional approval—and on October 20, 1803, he got it.

As Madison stated, "It was a truly noble acquisition." Using a lawyer's analogy Jefferson made his point: "It is the case of a guardian investing the money of his ward in purchasing an important adjacent territory." When the guardian came of age, he might write, "I did this for your good, but I pretend to no right to bind you. You may disavow me, and I must get out of the scrape as I can. I thought it my duty to risk myself for you."

On Sunday July 3, 1803, Rufus King arrived in New York with the crucial document, a letter from Livingston and Monroe. They had signed a treaty with France on April 30 ceding to the United States the island of New Orleans and all of Louisiana as it had been held by Spain. The price was not mentioned.

On November 30, 1803, France took back formal possession of Louisiana and a month later, turned Louisiana over to the United States.

FINANCING THE PURCHASE

International finance and capital markets had both been developing rapidly in the prior decades and would play a vital role in the Louisiana Purchase. The price agreed was Ff 80 million or $15 million. But nobody paid or received that amount.

First, the agreed settlement was in two parts: $11.25 million in U.S. Government bonds and the rest ($3.75 million) by the United States accepting responsibility for that amount of payments owed by France to US citizens.

Second, the payment was not in cash, but in U.S. Government bonds with interest payable at the above market rate of 6% every six months and maturity of principal beginning only *after* 15 long years. This was, in effect, a 100% "margin" loan to finance the purchase on remarkably generous terms.

While 6% was a relatively high rate of interest at that time, the United States was a new and unproven borrower. Adding to the complexity, the American government was financed by a loan from two leading merchant banks—Hope & Co in Amsterdam and Baring Brothers in London. The bankers bought the American debt from France at a 13.3% discount and then sold the bonds to investors, presumably at par (or a mark-up of nearly 15%—a gross profit of almost $3 million).

This was the first major debt issue sold in London. (France and England had been at war with each other since 1793—and were at war again just two weeks later.) Henry Hope observed, "It is an operation of the utmost magnitude and importance and might stagger us in ordinary times." Agreeing, Francis Baring said, "We all tremble at the magnitude of the American account."[3]

---

[3] Based on information provided by ING and Fortis, today's successors, respectively, to Hope & Co and Baring Brothers. Senator William Bingham, said to be the wealthiest man in America then, had two daughters who married two Baring brothers, Alexander and Henry.

AFTER

du Pont wrote to Jefferson: "Let me congratulate the United States and yourself on the wisdom through which, avoiding a war that would have thrown you into the arms of a redoubtable ally, you have acquired without shedding blood, territory ten times in extent and in fertility as the one you desired."

Napoleon went on to achieve some of his greatest victories, including Austerlitz, the battle that secured for his empire most of the European continent.

In 1803, the British bombarded and blockaded Saint-Domingue and on January 1, 1804, it became independent with the Arawak name, Haiti.

At the time of the purchase, the population of New Orleans was about 10,000 and the population of the whole Louisiana territory was less than 100,000. New Orleans had no painted buildings and no paved streets—only dirt roads littered with trash.

On July 5, 1803, Lewis and Clarke left Washington with their party of 40 explorers.

Jefferson may have had doubts about the constitutionality of his decision to commit to the Louisiana Purchase, but his decision was central to what became Manifest Destiny and the American nation's development as a world power.

4

ALASKA PURCHASE

The purchase of Alaska involved a highly motivated seller and added an enormous territory to the American nation. Powerful leaders, particularly Secretary of State Seward and Senator Sumner, performed key roles.

In the mid-19th century, Alaskan commerce was under the nominal jurisdiction of the Russian-American Company, a Russian enterprise granted exclusive trading control by the Tsar in the late 1700s. Since then, the incorporation of California and Oregon territories into the United States and the mid-century Gold Rush demonstrated the unstoppable power of America's westward expansion and Manifest Destiny.[1] The increasing commercial value to Americans interested in whaling,[2] furs, fishing, and importing ice to California was sure to be disruptive and could all too easily lead to conflict and even war.

---

[1] The discovery of oil in Pennsylvania in 1859 signaled the switch from whale oil to kerosene and the steady decline of whaling.

[2] In the 1850s, over 100 Yankee ships hunted whales in the area and in the 1860s, over 300 whalers worked in Alaska.

Tsar Nicholas wanted to transfer responsibility for Russian America, as it was then known, to the United States. An enormous territory of 375 million acres, Russian America was on the other side of Siberia, thousands of miles from St. Petersburg. Moreover, it had a sparse population of almost entirely Inuit people in numerous isolated areas. It was of little importance to the Tsar and difficult to govern.

While the Civil War had precluded negotiating the acquisition of the Tsar's colony, Secretary of State William H. Seward had been planning the prospective purchase of Russian America. At 4 a.m. Saturday March 30, 1867, with the Civil War finally over, Seward signed the Treaty of Cession with Baron de Stoeckl, the Russian government's chief diplomat in Washington.

Telegraph was the new technology of the era. The Collins Overland Telegraph Company—with financial support authorized by Seward as Secretary of State—won a contract to string telegraph lines to Russian America. The Imperial Government insisted on a 40% "rebate." During the negotiations, the Americans said that if the British government had not allowed the line to pass through British Columbia, they would have bought the Hudson Bay Company, which had a British Crown charter in that area, to achieve the objective.

When Seward made his initial purchase offer, Foreign Minister Alexander Gorchakov countered that the Russian government would be willing to sell its entire North American colony.

While commercial interest waxed and waned—and Perry Collins's telegraph venture eventually failed—the clarity of the logic of Russia selling increased steadily. The Crimean War proved the importance of concentrating imperial strength near Moscow and St. Petersburg. "The United States of America, following the natural order of things," declared the Tsar's brother, "is bound to aim at the possession of the whole of North America and therefore there will be a time when we should meet them. No doubt they will take possession of our colonies without much cost or effort and we shall never be in a position to regain them."

INCENTIVES

After the 1846–1848 Mexican-American War, more than half of that nation's territory was gained by the United States.

The Trent Affair in November 1861 and the North's increase in tariffs to finance the Civil War led to tensions between the United States and Great Britain. Still, their commercial interdependence was great: America supplied some 80% of British cotton needs for mills that employed nearly one million people, and either directly or indirectly employed nearly four million more, about a fifth of the British population. Producing cotton textiles made up nearly 40% of the nation's exports. After the repeal of the Corn Laws, the United States eventually provided nearly 40% of British grain or corn requirements.

While Queen Victoria's government recognized the Confederacy and the United States as belligerents, Britain was officially neutral in the American Civil War, allowing the British to trade with both sides, selling military equipment and importing corn and cotton. This enabled the South to raise money in London and use British ports. Seward's angry reaction: "God damn them! I'll give them hell!"

Seward had ambitions to achieve a great expansion of his country and so make his mark on history. At age 60, he had a strong political base, was skillful as a lawyer, and had traveled extensively in Europe and the Middle East. In 1853, Seward projected a vision of an American Empire—all by free choice—that would extend from the tropics to the Arctic Circle. Success of the North in the Civil War and the elimination of slavery would create an opportunity to realize his vision.

Seward made clear his reason for advancing the Alaska purchase: "The nation that draws the most materials from the earth, fabricates the most, and sells the most of its products and fabrics to foreign nations, must be and will be the greatest power on earth."

Meanwhile, the Russian-American Company's fur trade was rapidly declining. The value of its shares fell from 500 rubles in 1854 to less than 75 just 10 years later. The company was drifting toward bankruptcy, and the Russian government had no interest in taking over the failing company.

NEGOTIATIONS

In a meeting in 1857 with President Buchanan, Stoeckl asked about Brigham Young's plans for the Mormons: Would they settle in the territory of the Hudson Bay Company and would they be colonists or conquerors? Buchanan laughed that he didn't care so long as he got rid of them.

Stoeckl's report concerned the Tsar. When he went home to Russia in 1858, Stoeckl and Gorchakov agreed that if America showed any interest in purchasing the Alaska territory, it should be given serious consideration. California's Senator William Gwin approached Stoeckl on January 4, 1860, and assured him that Buchanan *was* interested and ready to buy—for as much as $5 million. Unless the Americans paid more than $5 million, Gorchakov declared the Tsar could not be convinced. Meanwhile, so long as the remarkably unpopular Buchanan was in office, Congress would never entertain a costly purchase of Alaskan territory.

Serious Russians noted that the 20 million Americans believed in the strategy articulated in Manifest Destiny and the Monroe Doctrine and that their expansion into California and Oregon would inevitably lead on to include Russian America. Since that was inevitable, yielding with good grace and ceding the colony to America—and keeping it away from expansionist Great Britain—was a demonstration of long-term wisdom.

Gorchakov gathered opinions that were easily summarized: The Russian American Company was failing, and the Russian government could not afford to take over the colony. Moreover, Russian America was a sure source of trouble with America. The sooner it was sold, the better. Stoeckl was assigned responsibility for arranging the sale.

On March 8, 1867, Stoeckl met with Seward and began a diplomatic dance. His specific purpose was to advise Seward that the California Fur Company would not be authorized to set up a trading company. Seward raised the possibility of Americans being allowed to fish in Alaskan waters and was told this would not be possible. Seward then suggested that Russia might sell the colony. This was just the opening Stoeckl was looking for.

A few days later, the Secretary of State reported that the President was not particularly interested but would leave the matter to the Cabinet. After consulting with other Cabinet members, Seward agreed to negotiate terms.

Seward offered $5 million but seeing the expression on Stoeckl's face, quickly revised that to $5.5 million as the highest he could go. Stoeckl shook his head: $7 million would be necessary. Meanwhile, Stoeckl told Gorchakov that he hoped to get $6 million[3] or, perhaps, $6.5 million.

Stoeckl held firm at $7 million as Seward gradually raised his "final" offer. In the end, Seward returned to the table—over the objections of the Russian-American Company—but did not agree to raise his offer by more than $200,000 to cover currency exchange losses. The two men then agreed on the final price. The treaty was signed at 4 a.m. on March 30, 1867—the last day of the Congressional session. Only then were the negotiations made public.

---

[3] The difference between $6 million and $7 million may have led to the belief by some that Stoeckl got $7 million, but reported only $6 million—keeping $1 million for himself.

EXPANSIONIST AMBITIONS

Seward's purchase of Alaska—with its long chain of Aleutian Islands—positioned the United States on three sides of British Columbia, an isolated British colony with less than 10,000 inhabitants who generally felt annexation to the United States was "the only hope for our colony." Seward had given thought to accepting British Columbia instead of the $15 million cash settlement to resolve claims against Britain for building Confederate raiders like the *Alabama*, which, over 22 months, had captured 65 merchant ships as prizes.

When Parliament passed the North America Act in 1867 to create the Canadian Confederation, Canada agreed to assume British Columbia's debts and build an intercontinental railroad to connect all the Canadian provinces.

In 1867, the United States also took possession of what was then renamed Midway Island. Seward also wanted to annex the Sandwich Islands, now known as Hawai, but that did not happen until 1898. Also in 1867, Seward arranged for the United States to acquire the Dutch colonies of St. Thomas and St. John for $7.5 million, but Congress resisted. (The purchase was later completed in 1917 for $25 million.) Seward also tried to buy Greenland and Iceland and negotiated with Columbia to do a survey for what would become the Panama Canal.

SUMNER MAKES THE CASE

Senator Charles Sumner was called to Seward's home where he heard of the purchase for the first time. Sumner was at the peak of his power as the Radical Republican in the post–Civil War period and was chairman of the Committee on Foreign Relations. He could easily have quashed the purchase because President Johnson was so unpopular, and senators were offended by the "backroom" secretive process that had been followed by Seward.

Fortunately, Sumner saw himself as a grand strategist and as a future president. So, he took a constructive view: Rejection of the Tsar's offer was sure to offend the Russian Court, while acceptance would remove another European power from North America. He not only decided to take the long view and enthusiastically support the purchase, but would also make his case for the Senate's approval by demonstrating his expertise on the colony's economy. He has only nine days to prepare what would be a three-hour tour de force case for the purchase.

To marshal the evidence he needed, Sumner required help from an expert. Conveniently, one was working at the Smithsonian Institution—Professor Spencer Baird,[4] a famous naturalist. He and Sumner met almost daily to develop compelling documentation of the case for the acquisition.

As he approached the close of his long address to the Senate, Sumner turned to the question of naming the Russian territory:

As these extensive possessions, constituting a corner of the continent, pass from the Imperial Government of Russia, they will naturally receive a new name. They will be no longer Russian America. How shall they be called? Clearly, any name borrowed from classical antiquity or from individual invention will be little better than a misnomer or a nickname unworthy of such an occasion. Even if taken from our own annals, it will be of doubtful taste. The name should come from the country itself. It should be indigenous, aboriginal, one of the autochthons of the soil.

Happily such a name exists, as proper in sound as in origin. It appears from the 1778 report of Captain James Cook, the illustrious navigator, to whom I have so often referred. The euphonious designation now applied to the peninsula which is the continental link of the Aleutian

---

[4] While Baird never went to Alaska, he had done five years of research on the region.

chain was the sole word used originally by the native islanders, when speaking of the American continent in general, which they knew perfectly well to be a great land.[5] It only remains, that, following these natives, whose places are now ours, we, too, should call this great land Alaska.

There were many difficulties in getting the necessary money appropriated by the House of Representatives. Federal debt had ballooned during the Civil War. President Johnson's impeachment trial was pending, the House leadership had not been consulted on the acquisition, and Sumner was considered personally arrogant. Besides, with so much underdeveloped territory in the country, who needed 375 million more acres? However, Alaska did have potential. If America did not take it, Great Britain might. Also, spurning the agreement at such a late stage was sure to offend the Russian Tsar and people. The appropriation bill was passed on July 14, 1868—15 months after the Senate confirmation—by a vote of 92 to 48 (and 77 not voting).[6]

Few envisioned the mineral and oil wealth that would come to America with the addition of Alaska. In the 1860s, "Seward's icebox" was ridiculed as wasteful and foolish. However, many years later, the purchase proved to be a fortunate investment. Over the next century, the sale of Alaska's output—even before Alaska's vast oil deposits were discovered—including gold, lumber, and fish, would pay for the purchase many times over.

---

[5] The word *Alaska* was not improved when spelled *Alashka*, and the dropping of the letter *h* in *Oonalaska* seemed a more natural spelling.

[6] An amendment asserted the House of Representatives' right to be "primarily consulted" on any future purchase of territory.

5

NATIONAL PARKS

America's national parks (and the even more numerous state parks) are a splendid and hugely popular cluster of national treasures that attract millions of visitors each year. Most began without any capital investment, but they now require a continuing investment of billions of dollars a year to protect these treasures for future generations. America has, by far, more parks and more visitors to those parks than any other nation.

Our national parks are often called "America's best idea" and that may well be true. Our national parks are wonderful treasures of great beauty that attract nearly 300 million visits each year and are vicariously enjoyed by many more millions through stunning pictures.[1] We all marvel at Old Faithful and El Capitan.

Yellowstone, Yosemite, Glacier, Everglades, Bad Lands, Shenandoah, Grand Canyon, Death Valley, Great Smoky Mountains, and many others

---

[1] In 2010, park visitors spent an estimated $12.1 billion in gateway communities, and local jobs due to the park service were estimated at 189,000.

are as central to the concept of America as big cities such as Los Angeles, New York, Chicago, Houston, Boston, and Washington.

The national park system is the world's largest, both in terms of land area and number of units—423. There are 21 different types of parks, and they differ greatly in purpose and history. Some are remarkably large and others quite small. Franklin D. Roosevelt, famous for his casually improvising ways, used the term *system*, and when he did, it stuck.

Widely loved for preserving large parts of our beautiful country in their original state for us and future generations, America's national park system has changed over the years and was not developed systemically. Far from it. There has been no single plan. The process, like legislation in a democracy, has been one of many improvisations. In 1933, FDR nearly doubled the number of parks by transferring a slew of 64 military parks, battle sites, and memorials from the War Department to the National Parks Service. Many of the units, particularly the smaller ones, were sponsored by small groups of dedicated individuals and specific members of Congress. According to park service director Conrad Wirth, he saw to it that most congressional districts were touched by the effort to ensure success. The number and variety of parks increased so significantly in the 1970s that it looked like, "a park in every congressional district."

Time and again, controversy after controversy has developed around the national parks movement. Not all the resolutions to these controversies made sense to later observers. When a 2,222-year-old Sequoia was leaning dangerously over a group of cabins in Sequoia National Park, the decision was made not to move the cabins, but to remove the ancient tree, an unfortunate triumph of visitation over preservation—just the tip of the iceberg of controversy.

EARLY PARKS

Yosemite would be the first to be preserved, but not the first to be designated a national park. (That honor goes to Yellowstone, still the largest in the lower 48 states.) Yosemite began as a California state park, and it was influenced by a devoted naturalist and skillful activist with a remarkable ability to capture readers' imaginations and emotions: John Muir.

In June 1864, Abraham Lincoln signed the Yosemite Grant Act into law. A mere 56 acres of Yosemite Valley and its surrounding mountains were included in the original park. Then, the federal government granted the state of California 39,000 acres and charged the state with preserving the land "for public use, resort, and recreation," and to keep it "unalienable for all time."

California's governor appointed Frederick Law Olmsted, America's outstanding landscape architect, to head its governing board. Olmsted promptly dispatched two surveyors to map the boundaries of Yosemite Valley. He then wrote a 52-page text celebrating the beauty of the valley, the economic value of attracting tourists, and the capacity of the park to enhance a citizen's "pursuit of happiness."

Olmsted declared, "It is a scientific fact that the occasional contemplation of natural scenes of an impressive character, particularly if this contemplation occurs in connection with relief from ordinary care, change of air and change of habits, is favorable to the health and vigor of men and especially to the health and vigor of their intellect."

The national parks concept was first realized on a grand scale by President Ulysses S. Grant, who established Yellowstone as the first national park in 1872. Covering 3,468 square miles, it contains half the world's geysers, over 1,700 native flora, and several hundred species of animals, most being birds—and attracts over a million visitors each year. Congress was encouraged that no financial appropriation was called for *and* by assurances that the entire area was not suitable for cultivation. Also, given an average altitude of over 6,000 feet, the winters were too severe for stock raising.[2]

At the time, almost no one had visited the park's enormous acreage, and nearly no one expected to go. The high expense and slow speed of travel by horse and buggy was prohibitive to most Americans, and too little of the great park was within reach after visitors' arrival. Visiting Yellowstone could also be dangerous. In an incident in 1877, Chief Joseph and his Nimiipuu tribe would go through part of the park when pursued by the military. In a tragic series of events, 25 tourists encountered the desperate tribe; some were taken hostage, and two were killed.

NATIONAL PARKS MOVEMENT

The national parks movement has had three principal forces. First was disgust with an ugly visual disaster: Niagara Falls had been surrounded and inundated with tawdry commercial structures that spoiled the view for visitors.[3] Next was luck: Settlers who moved west seeking farmland had no interest in tall mountains, deep valleys, or deserts that, in later years, comprised the national parks' magnificent scenery. Third was national pride in these scenic wonders—in harmony with preservation and education.

Everglades National Park was authorized in 1934 but was not established until 1947. At 1.5 million acres, it is the third largest park in the

---

[2] National forests—long an alternative concept to the national parks—came into prominence with President Benjamin Harrison designating over 17.5 million acres, an amount increased to 47.2 million acres by 1901. In 1909, Teddy Roosevelt increased the total to 151 million acres. The U.S. Forest Service, under Gifford Pinchot, managed the extensive forests by leasing mineral sites, developing water power, and ensuring a perpetual supply of timber to the nation by harvesting mature forests.

[3] Olmsted was appointed to direct a survey of the area around Niagara Falls. His report on the disfigured area in 1878 gathered together a large and distributed group of supporters, and in 1883, the New York State Reservation at Niagara Falls was established. All the buildings and fences in the new park's boundaries were removed and no manufactured objects were allowed.

lower 48 states and the first without mountains or waterfalls. Native plants and animals are the main attractions—the last vestiges of primitive America.

In 1919, Mount Desert Island on the coast of Maine became the nucleus of Acadia National Park (then called Lafayette National Park) thanks to major grants by John D. Rockefeller Jr. He also contributed generously to help establish Great Smokey Mountain and Shenandoah National Parks, and later, Grand Teton National Park in Wyoming.

Cape Cod National Seashore was established in 1961 and eight more followed in the next 15 years. Similar moves were made along the Great Lakes, and a series of major trails were made part of the system.

In 1980, the several Alaska parks collectively added 43.6 million acres, 13.2 million of which now comprise Wrangell-St. Elias National Park. Possessing many magnificent mountains, glaciers, and volcanic areas—more than the total in the lower 48 states—Alaskan land offered both monumental scenery and an abundance of plants and animals. Preservationists were delighted that they would not need to compromise their values when establishing wilderness parks. (Enthusiasm for their agenda was, of course, primarily from people *not* living in Alaska.) In a compromise, 43.6 million acres would become part of the national park system, doubling the total acreage the system covered. The issue of whether priority would be given to monumental topography and views versus biological significance surfaced in vigorous form with the discovery of oil in Prudhoe Bay in 1968.

JOHN MUIR

The story of the national parks would be incomplete without reference to John Muir. His life story could not have been better suited to represent the values of preserving the wilderness for all. An independently minded Scottish American, he was called the *bard of Yosemite* and served as an eloquent advocate for the national parks concept. In 1892, Muir also helped found the Sierra Club. (With 3.5 million members, it continues to celebrate and work to preserve the wilderness.) Born in a small Scottish town to a strict Presbyterian family, Muir emigrated with his father and brother to Wisconsin. He went on to write 12 books and dozens of articles about the majesty of nature and wilderness in the High Sierras, Yosemite Valley, and his 1,000 mile walk down the eastern states.

Often called the *father of our national parks*, Muir changed the way Americans think of nature, conservation, and the importance of access to the wilderness he loved and celebrated so well. By reading his lyrical prose, many people saw the wonders of nature through Muir's eyes, and developed a strong respect for the wilderness, particularly as society became increasingly urban and removed from the great spiritual powers of nature.

John Muir spoke powerfully for the preservationists saying, "Any fool can destroy trees. They cannot run away; and if they could, they would still be destroyed—chased and hunted down as long as fun or a dollar could be got out of their dark hides, branching horns, or magnificent old backbones. Through all the wonderful, eventful centuries since Christ's time—and long before that—God has cared for these trees, saved them from drought, avalanches, disease, and a thousand straining, leveling tempests and floods, but He cannot save them from fools. Only Uncle Sam can do that."

Later in life, Muir wrote, "Wilderness was ever sounding in our ears, and nature saw to it that besides school lessons and church lessons, some of her own lessons should be learned, perhaps with a view to the time when we should be called to wander in wilderness to our heart's content." He was a romantic, but also anchored to the reality of his encyclopedic knowledge and exactingly keen powers of observation. Fortunately, his gifts as a writer enabled Muir to share the results of his explorations with a wide and appreciative audience.

Having decided not to become a physician, Muir's career decision settled on one of two disparate interests: inventing and his love of the outdoors. Taking two of his wooden clocks and a thermometer, he went to the

Wisconsin State Fair at Madison. He asked the price of a ticket, and was told that as an exhibiter, he needed none. His all-wood devices would make a fine exhibit and he could locate it anywhere he thought best. Muir won a cash prize of $10.

On a visit to the state university campus, Muir lamented to a student that he could not afford to study in such a beautiful place. When told how inexpensive it could actually be, he met with the acting president and was soon admitted. Muir covered expenses by working each summer on his father's farm. He chose courses that would be most useful to him: chemistry, mathematics, and physics plus Greek and Latin and botany and geology—all the while continuing to invent. (One invention automatically lit the fire in his cold classroom each morning by dropping sulfuric acid into a mixture of powdered chlorate of potash and sugar placed next to wood shavings and kindling. It worked every day of the long winter.)

While repairing a belt on factory equipment, Muir's hand slipped and he poked one end of a file into his right eye. His left eye also went dark. A doctor said with rest and darkness, the vision of the left would come back, and that after a few months, his right eye would as well. As his eye slowly mended, Muir resolved, "I [bid] adieu to all my mechanical inventions, determined to devote the rest of my life to the study of the inventions of God."

Having enjoyed the study of plants in the upper Midwest, he decided to explore those of the South and on September 2, 1867, Muir left Wisconsin with only old clothes, a Bible, Burns's poems, Milton's *Paradise Lost*, and a small plant press. He crossed the Ohio River, heading for the Gulf of Mexico—1,000 miles away.

In Savannah, Muir was disappointed that the money his brother had promised to send had not yet arrived. Each day, he asked and was turned away. Finally, the money wire came through and the local agent asked for identification. Muir had none, but after answering a series of questions, his botany expertise was enough to identify him.[4]

MUIR TAKES UP WRITING

In the winter of 1870–1871, Muir began writing for publication. Three pieces appeared in the *New York Tribune*: "Yosemite in Winter," "Yosemite in Spring," and "Yosemite Glaciers." The last explained a theory of how glaciers were formed based on flow measurements Muir had made using simple stakes. (His theory was later accepted as proven.)

In 1892, friends and admirers urged him to join in the founding of a new organization, the Sierra Club. Muir became its first president. The club's mission was "to explore, enjoy, and render accessible the mountain regions of the Pacific Coast. To publish authentic information concerning them, and to enlist the support and cooperation of the people and government in preserving the forests and other natural features of the Sierra Nevada Mountains."

Muir wrote extensively about the national parks' beauty. He also spoke to power about the importance of preservation. In 1903, President Theodore Roosevelt expressed a keen interest in visiting Yosemite with Muir. They spent four days together camping in the open. Muir asked Roosevelt for one thing: "In your own interest and in the interest of all the country, keep this great wonder of nature as it now is. You cannot improve upon it. The ages have been at work on it, and man can only mar it. Keep it

---

[4] Going on to Cuba, Muir would embark for California in April 1868. He worked for a sheep rancher for a year and then agreed to go with him into the high Sierras. One day, the view was so magnificent that he burst into shouts of joy and waved his arms. When he got to Indian Canyon and Yosemite Falls, he burst out again. At the end of the summer, Muir worked the sheep back to their ranch and then returned for two years, where he wrote of his romance with nature in such an engaging way that readers felt he was sharing secrets. Later, Muir had more places to visit, and in his last years, he went around the world, down the Amazon, as far south as Cape Town in Africa, across Siberia, along the coast of China, and on to New Zealand.

for your children's children and all who come after you as one of the great sights for Americans to see." When Theodore Roosevelt entered the White House, there were less than 50 million acres of national forests and when he left, there were 145 million.

The cultural nationalism that developed in many countries during the early 20th century, led to an Act for the Preservation of American Antiquities. Roosevelt boldly interpreted this to include geographic wonders and, in 1906, applied it to preserve Devil's Tower, a stark monolith that rose 1,267 feet above the Belle Fourche River in Wyoming. Shortly after that, he added Petrified Forest and Mesa Verde. "He then declared all 800,000 acres of the Grand Canyon an 'object of unusual scientific interest' as the greatest eroded canyon within the United States."[5] He did the same for 600,000 acres surrounding Mount Olympus in Washington state. (Grand Canyon, Death Valley, Grand Teton, and Olympic Zion all began as monuments and were later upgraded to national parks.)

Preservationists quickly recognized the political efficiency of needing to convince just one person—the President—rather than the many members of Congress.

CHANGING PRIORITIES

Differences of opinion have often made agreement on policy decisions difficult for our national park leaders. One early confrontation came in 1908. The City of San Francisco wanted to develop a large reservoir inside Yosemite and, to create it, chose to dam the Hetch Hetchy Valley. Their argument centered on the enjoyment of a few hundred hikers each year versus the perpetual needs of a city's several hundred thousand citizens.

---

[5] The Grand Canyon is a mile deep, extends 277 river miles, and the distance across the gorge averages 10 miles. In 1965, only 547 people floated down the river. In 1972, visitors numbered 16,428.

While objective observers might well find the Hetch Hetchy Valley full of water just as beautiful as the empty valley, preservationists were opposed; their priorities were clear: Aesthetic value took precedence over utilitarian needs. This would be fundamental to the establishment of the National Park Service under Woodrow Wilson in 1916.

Railroad companies were important advocates of the early parks. Preservationists decided that an alliance with the railroads was key to success. When the Great Northern Railway launched an advertising campaign—"See America First"—a dozen groups, including the Sierra Club and the Appalachian Mountain Club, joined in the campaign. The popular reaction to the message was highly favorable to the national parks movement.

Stephen Maher, who had made a fortune mining borax and was a long-time member of the Sierra Club, became the first director of the National Park Service. He had no great interest in preserving or protecting the wilderness. His focus was on increasing the number of people who visited the parks. Since they had been established through national politics, Maher accepted that origin as the basis for his policies and moved to increase public access by automobiles and by providing overnight accommodations.

The National Parks Organic Act of 1916 declared the national parks purpose: "to conserve the scenery and the natural and historic objects and the wildlife therein and to provide for the enjoyment of the same in such manner as will leave them unimpaired for the enjoyment of future generations." This sounds clear, but in practice it was not.[6]

When Governor Ronald Reagan dismissively said, "A tree's a tree. How many more do you need to look at?" he offended members of the Sierra Club, who believed in the visual magic of seeing large numbers of giant sequoias together. As a Sierra Club publication put it, "History will think it strange that Americans [believed they] could afford going to the moon on

---

[6] The National Parks Organic Act is found at 16 U.S.C. §§ 1-18f; the Yellowstone Enabling Act is found at 16 U.S.C §§ 21-22.

a $4 billion airplane while acquiring a patch of Redwoods—not too big for a man to walk across in a single day—was considered beyond its means."

CHANGES IN ACCESS AND POLICY

Changes large and small have characterized the national parks experience over more than a century. Many early visitors were unaware that the designated wildernesses prohibited not only cars but also roads of any kind. Nor would they have heard of endangered species being protected in the parks. Congress did not distinguish between "preserving" and "enjoying the use" of the parks, which were increasingly called *the nation's playgrounds.* Education as a primary mission of the National Park Service was first featured in the visionary report: "Rethinking the National Parks for the 21st Century."[7]

In 1918, Interior Secretary Franklin Lane signed a document—the Lane Letter[8]—produced by Horace Albright, assistant to Stephen Mather. It set out the park service's basic mission in three parts: "First, that the national parks be maintained in absolutely unimpaired form for the use of future generations as well as those of our own time; second, that they are set apart for the use, observation, health, and pleasure of the people; and third, that the national interest must direct all decisions affecting private or public enterprise in the parks."

A major change—the automobile—would bring increasing visitors to the national parks: three million in 1929 and 17 million in 1940. In the decade following World War II, annual visits increased to almost 60 million, and continued to soar over the next half-century to nearly 300 million. This growth would soon bring other changes. In 1955, a major

---

[7]Under the leadership of Gifford Pinchot, the national forests were managed more like farms with regular harvests: personal enjoyment by citizens was clearly secondary.

[8]"Secretary Lane's Letter on National Park Service Management" (May 13, 1918) is in *America's National Park System: The Critical Documents*, ed. Lary M. Dilsaver (Lanham, MD: Rowman and Littlefield, 1994), 48–52.

program, "Mission 66," was organized to improve facilities, roads, and overnight accommodations. This resulted in 1,200 miles of new roads, 1,500 miles of repaired roads, 900 miles of new or upgraded trails, 570 new campgrounds, and 220 new administrative buildings.

Many, if not all, of our national parks have been forged in controversy over a long series of different priorities: recreation policy, endangered species, social justice, science, climate change, biodiversity, wildfire policies, tribal values, wilderness preservation, and the natural boundaries of ecosystems. (For many years, bears were fed to create an "interesting recreational experience" for visitors.) Following the Leopold Report in 1963, priority shifted to "offer a vignette of primitive America." Among other policy changes, this meant allowing wildfires and predators. The report demonstrated that a focus on scenic preservation short-changed the responsibilities for conservation and ecological science.

Wildfire policy exemplifies how differing conclusions develop from different perspectives. Most people without special knowledge about forests are dead set against fires. (We all have Smokey the Bear and Bambi in mind.) At the same time, experts saw fires as part of nature, usually caused by lightning, and so favored allowing most fires to burn themselves out.[9] By the 1960s, hikers protested that brush and young trees made the forests impassable, and professional foresters argued that under these conditions, fires were far more intensive and did longer lasting harm. (Small and moderate fires clear the litter or fallen branches and toppled trees, leaving the ground ready for the next year's growth.) In 1978, the park service reversed its long-standing position on suppressing fires by recognizing them as "natural phenomena" and allowing them to run their natural course.[10]

Wolf restoration in Yellowstone was grounded in studies that showed wolves preyed mostly on already weakened animals, particularly sheep,

---

[9] The first to recognize this was Captain G. H. C. Gale, commandant of the Fourth U.S. Calvary in 1874. Gale believed that preventing fires would, ironically, "lead eventually to disastrous results."

[10] Climate change has made most areas drier and subject to massive destructive fires, which has led to additional changes in park service policy.

and did no harm to the strong. In 1995, eight Canadian wolves were carefully released at Yellowstone. There are now nine packs and at least 108 wolves.[11]

A consistent challenge for the National Park Service has been whether to limit the number of visitors to protect the parks and ensure a quality experience. At Yosemite, rather than cap the number of visitors, the park has limited parking and campsites, and relocated many facilities outside the park.

Snowmobiles were first allowed in Yellowstone in the 1960s by a superintendent who was a snowmobiler. By 1993, they had increased to an all-time high of 77,000 a year, and complaints of noise and pollution rose even faster. In 2000, after an extensive ecological study, snowmobiles were banned. However, a Wisconsin Court ruled that the Clinton administration's decision was politically biased and had an adverse impact on the local economy. So, the park service compromised and set a daily limit of 800 snowmobiles in Yellowstone.[12] (The cost of protecting snowmobiles against frequent avalanches runs about $1 million annually.)

The Leopold Committee's report redirected concerns about the biological health of the parks. The report called for each national park to "preserve or restore a natural biotic scene." Recognizing that it was advocating intrusions in the present to reverse *past* intrusions, the report sought to restore missing species, eradicate exotic (i.e., imported) species, and reduce infrastructure for visitors. The impact of the resulting act was substantial.[13]

---

[11] Because elk fear wolves and so avoid groves of aspens, cottonwoods, and willows, those trees are also coming back.

[12] Regulations and engine improvements have reduced the offending noise levels and exhaust fumes.

[13] The Wilderness Act is found at 16 U.S.C. §§ 1131-36. The term *wilderness* is further defined in 16 U.S.C. § 1131 (c) as "an area of undeveloped Federal land retaining its primeval character and influence, without permanent improvements or human habitation, which is protected and managed so as to preserve its natural conditions." For more on the Wilderness Act and its passage, see Michael McCloskey, "The Wilderness Act of 1964: Its Background and Meaning," *Oregon Law Review* 45, 1966: 288–321; Roderick Frazier Nash, *Wilderness and the American Mind* (New Haven, CT: Yale University Press), 200–237.

However, on implementation, local differences have also been consequential. Should park boundaries be set by people or by the priorities of nature to accommodate large ecosystems or migratory patterns? Should science or scenery be the first priority? Local policies versus national? Ecology versus economics? Local communities versus visitors? Patrons of park A versus park B? Profit versus beauty? Gateway community economics versus national park policies? Tribal law versus federal government policy?

Of course, priorities have changed over time as new concepts gained acceptance, but as Alfred Runte concluded in his study, "After restraint, only humility can uphold their integrity, ensuring the timelessness of the National Parks as the best idea that America—and the world—ever shared."

As more and more people go to America's national parks, enjoying their rugged beauty as John Muir promised in his inspiring writing, the importance of these treasures gets increasing recognition. Today, most Americans intend to visit more parks than they have already seen and more and more visitors from other countries are joining them.

* * *

These books have made particularly valuable contributions to this chapter. Both provide extensive sources for anyone wanting to go deeper on virtually any aspect of the National Parks' history:

- Richard West Sellars, *Preserving Nature in the National Park* (New Haven, CT: Yale University Press, 2009).
- Robert B. Keiter, *To Conserve Unimpaired* (Washington, DC: Island Press, 2013).
- John Muir, *The Story of My Boyhood and Youth* (Madison: University of Wisconsin Press, 1965).

6

GI BILL

Lurking behind President Roosevelt's caution about a program of benefits for veterans after World War II was a long series of political difficulties with veterans' groups and an increasingly conservative Congress controlled by Republicans keen to reduce government and inclined toward Senator Robert Taft's isolationism.

Looking back, most Americans would declare the GI Bill a great success—a success that must have seemed obvious to everyone in a grateful nation in 1944. After all, the bill passed the Senate unanimously, and the House of Representatives by another unanimous 387–0 vote—and the consequences were a multidimensional public policy triumph.

A few years earlier, however, there had been substantial opposition, and, at one critical time, it almost failed to come up for a vote in Congress.

The GI Bill developed out of a widely based concern about the near-term problems expected with the return of 15 million men and women to civilian life after World War II. After one, two, three, or even four years away, the veterans would want to catch up on the years they had lost while in military service and would want good jobs. And they would not be alone. Another 10 million American workers had been employed in war-related defense contractor jobs. While some, mostly women, would choose to stop working and return to raising children and homemaking, with war contracts ending, most of the combined 25 million would be looking for jobs in the private sector.

The general expectation among economists was that, as usual after a war, the nation would experience recession or even depression. In 1943, the National Resources Planning Board predicted 8–9 million unemployed workers during the expected "readjustment period."[1]

The demobilization problem facing the American government was originally seen as a defense against a daunting social and political problem. With too few jobs to go around, sociologists anticipated serious social disruption. Political scientists expected a sharp shift from patriotism to selfishness and an equally strong movement to the political far right. As they pointed out, every industrial nation in Europe except Great Britain had experienced a political revolution during the decade following the First World War—particularly Germany and Italy. Nobody needed to be reminded how disastrously those revolutions had affected the world. History's lessons—the eruption of fascism, Nazism, and communism in the 1920s and 1930s—suggested how hard it would be to find well-paid jobs for so many millions of veterans during the much-anticipated post-war recession.

REGENERATION

There had been many doubts about specific provisions in early drafts of the GI Bill. Bankers worried about defaulted loans. Educators worried about veterans being lazy and disorderly "students." Union leaders worried about their members losing their jobs to veterans. Many worried about the ability of the federal government to manage the complex implementation

---

[1] "Demobilization and Readjustment" in NRPB, June 1943.

of such a large new program of matching millions of returning veterans with specific job training or college studies *and* keeping all the costs under control.

In the Deep South, many remembered the challenges of Black Doughboys returning to strict segregation after the First World War. So, they worried about the social disruption of large numbers of Black GIs who had enjoyed far greater personal freedom and social respect before returning to a rigorously segregated social system. They were certain it could not be positive, and many believed it could be dreadful. Congressman John E. Rankin was one of these. So he saw it as his duty to his constituency to block the vote in the next session, and then force Congress to make changes more acceptable to the strictly segregated South.[2]

One solution to the major demobilization problem of absorbing many millions of young workers would be to get as many as possible enrolled in educational programs—upgrading veterans' skills for careers in the future and diverting them for a few years from the workforce.

Some had suggested basic skills training could be provided by public high schools, but thoughtful observers explained that most high schools were already busy enough with their standard student population. Why would they want to change significantly for a small group of very different students who would not be a source of continuing demand? Others suggested using the same school buildings and facilities—but at night after the usual high schoolers had gone home—with reliance on the relatively few teachers who would be interested in innovation and in extra pay *and* who were willing to develop courses appropriately designed for this special cohort. For larger school systems, this seemed feasible, but it was, at best, only a partial solution.

---

[2] The benefits of the GI Bill went largely to whites and, as a result, the economic gap between whites and Blacks widened significantly in the post-war era. In 2017, the median income for white households was $68,145 versus $40,258 for Black households.

Colleges, particularly the residential colleges, would have more and larger challenges. Dormitory rooms were already filled, but two could bunk together in what had been a single and four in a double, and so on. Even so, crowding was sure to be a major problem.

Many GIs had been drafted before finishing high school and many had little interest in returning to the classroom. Education was not seen as nearly as important then as it is now. They wanted to get to work. The parts of the GI Bill that seemed most wanted and therefore most important were getting a loan to buy a house or start a small business, help in finding a decent job, and in the meantime, unemployment benefits. The most popular job for GIs: truck driver.

Most serious observers thought that education was one of the least important parts of Public Law 346, or The Servicemen's Readjustment Act and known today as the GI Bill. Early surveys of soldiers and sailors found that less than 10% planned to go to college.

Before the GI Bill, only 14% of Americans went to college: *after* the GI Bill, that proportion more than doubled to 30%—an amazing national transformation.[3] Of the 15.4 million who had served in uniform, 2.2 million went to college or graduate school or both and another 5.6 million pursued vocational training, on the job training, or other forms of education through the GI Bill. The veterans concentrated their enrollments at three dozen of our nation's best collegiate institutions: For example, 15,000 went to Yale and 17,773 went to Columbia.

Veterans also got home loans with a total valuation of $33 billion. The economic benefits substantially increased the number of Americans in the middle class, so the GI Bill was an obvious success—as seen in retrospect.

Yet, as mentioned, it would not have been expected just 10 years before, and it was not a success for everyone. Discouraged from applying by the

---

[3] *Collier's Weekly*, December 20, 1944.

leading northern universities, 95% of Black veterans went to the underfunded traditionally Black universities or decided to accept vocational training.

A CLOSE CALL

The GI Bill nearly failed to become a law at all. The reasons? Congressional rules of procedure, divisions over the expected costs, doubts about projected benefits—*and* deeply rooted racism.

The House and Senate bills differed significantly, so the differences between the two versions had to be resolved by a House-Senate committee. After three weeks of discussions, the seven-member committee was divided 3–3 with the committee chairman, Representative John Rankin of Mississippi, holding the proxy of Representative John Gibson of Georgia. This was key. Representative Gibson would have voted in favor of the bill, but he had been ill and had gone home to rural Georgia's backcountry and was out of touch.

The House and Senate needed to reconcile differences between their versions of the bill. While agreeing on Titles I, II, and III, they were deadlocked on Title IV, particularly on how employment services would be managed. If the reconciliations were not completed at the next day's 10 o'clock session, there would be no agreement in time for a vote on the bill, and it would have to be reintroduced the following year—after changes to please the South.

Rankin, as chair of the House Veterans Committee, had already made sure key parts of the GI Bill would be administered locally: state-by-state rather than nationally by the federal government. This would ensure all benefits would be aligned with the established Jim Crow laws of rigorous segregation. Chairman Rankin was a confirmed Mississippi segregationist and particularly opposed to the provision granting 12 months of unemployment benefits equally to both whites and Blacks. Rankin was convinced that Black veterans would exploit the unemployment benefits saying, "We have

50,000 Negroes in the service from our state and if the Bill should pass in its present form, the vast majority of them would be 'unemployed' for at least a year."

If Rankin lost at the level of drafting the legislation, he was now ready to make sure that local administration could cut off benefits if a veteran declined to accept *any* job offer, even a clearly inferior job offer. (Actually, as history would show, less than 20% of the money set aside for the 52-week unemployment provision was paid out because veterans found jobs long before the year was up.)

Rankin refused to cast Gibson's favorable vote. Rankin's tactical pocketing of Gibson's vote would keep the committee from reporting out the bill as that year's session of Congress was closing in on adjournment, leaving the bill to die in committee. (Ironically, that was on June 9, only three days after the massive landings at Normandy.)

The only solution to the immediate political impasse was to find and get Representative Gibson back to Washington—in less than 24 hours—in time to cast his vote himself. However, all Gibson's Washington office knew was that he was somewhere near his family home in rural southern Georgia.

NECESSARY ACTION

It was already dinner time when Warren Atherton, in many ways the hero of the GI Bill story as the National Commander of the American Legion, learned of the problem. He got right to work.

A phone call to Douglas, Georgia, would have to take its turn *after* a five-hour wait (common during WWII for calls to small towns like Douglas), but *The Atlanta Constitution* had priority telephone service and agreed to help. The local operator—whose husband had just landed at Normandy—said she would call Congressman Gibson's home—every five minutes—until she got him on the line.

Next need: a plane ride to Washington. An Army Air base was only 40 miles away—but no planes were available. Eastern Airlines had a plane leaving Jacksonville, Florida, at 2:30 a.m. Shortly after 11:00 a.m., Gibson got home and the every-five-minutes operator told him the situation.

An Army car would take Congressman Gibson 150 miles through heavy rain. The Army driver raced to Jacksonville at an average speed of nearly 50 miles an hour and top speeds of 90—with motorcycle police escorts. (Crossing streets were blocked by police and the main road was cleared of all traffic.)

The Eastern Airlines flight was held for Gibson who flew to Washington in time for the 10 o'clock meeting, pausing briefly to say to reporters, "Americans are dying in Normandy in the greatest invasion in history— and anyone who dares to cast a vote against this Bill should be publicized to all the world. I'm going to hold a press conference after the meeting and am going to expose anyone who doesn't vote for the GI Bill of Rights."

The committee approved the bill—by Gibson's one vote. It then went to the House and the Senate where it was made law by a unanimous vote in both houses of Congress. After the GI Bill passed, President Roosevelt quickly moved to share the credit, saying when signing the bill into law on June 22, 1944, that it "substantially carries out most of the recommendations made by me in a speech on July 28, 1943, and more specifically in messages to Congress dated October 26, 1943, and November 23, 1943." He concluded that the GI Bill gave "emphatic notice to the men and women in our armed forces that the American people do not intend to let them down."

COMPLEX POLITICAL HISTORY

The antecedents of the GI Bill made a long and complicated political history. Understanding that history makes it easy to understand Roosevelt's prior political caution and then his later verbal scramble to get aboard the movement to pass the GI Bill. The power and complexity of the history of veterans' benefits are important to understanding the political difficulties of the era.

The idea of compensating widows and disabled soldiers went back to the Revolutionary War and the Civil War. After the Civil War, the administration of soldiers' pensions and disability benefits was notoriously corrupt and caused many to oppose future benefits except for the most seriously disabled soldiers. The cost of veterans' historical benefits—largely from the Civil War—was then the largest single item in the federal budget.

The Veterans of Foreign Wars (VFW), an organization of veterans of the Spanish-American War and the Philippine Insurrection, was organized in 1889 and offered membership to soldiers serving in World War I. The American Legion was organized in 1919 and was open to all honorably discharged veterans of the Great War. The two groups were natural rivals for membership and consequent political power, so differences in policy developed, particularly on when to pay out the soldiers' bonus from World War I. After that war, Congress had agreed to pay veterans a bonus in "deferred interest certificates" based on $1 per day of service—or $1.25 per day for overseas veterans—and accruing interest of 4%—but the bonus certificates would not become collectable until 1947. In the depths of the Depression, that seemed much too long to wait for many, if not most, veterans.

The VFW focused on immediate payment of the bonus. With the 1929 crash and the beginning of the Depression, that cause gained political power, and the VFW gained strength in recruiting members as its demand for payment became increasingly vehement. The more conservative American Legion, which had previously prevailed in membership, began losing members—*and* their dues and political clout—to the VFW.

In 1930, Congress addressed veterans' issues other than the bonus, including reorganization of various agencies into the Veterans Administration and an expansion of some of the benefits. While President Hoover went to the VFW encampment in Baltimore, he did not speak, having no reason to explicitly oppose the VFW's support of the bonus. The American Legion was a different matter. Hoover's appeal to patriotism and to progress made on other issues enabled the American Legion's leadership to divert the internal drive among its members for paying out the bonus sooner. However, populist Congressman Wright Patman, sensing a major issue that could win political support and power, hoped to get the Legion membership to support paying the bonus immediately.[4]

On February 12, 1931, Congress compromised and voted in favor of the payment of 50% of each veteran's bonus, but President Hoover vetoed the bill, saying payment threatened the moral fiber of the nation by "weakening the virtues of self-reliance and self-support." Congress promptly overrode the veto and within one week, nearly one million veterans had taken their 50%, and by January of 1932, 2.5 million had done so.

The VFW, having led the campaign for payment while the American Legion stood back, quickly doubled its membership. Also, since it did not wait until after soldiers were discharged, the VFW had grown from 76,669 members in 1929, to 187,469 members in 1932. The two groups were soon engaged in a competition for political power with a voting bloc they both believed could dominate US politics for decades.[5]

In January 1931, 1,000 VFW veterans marched in Washington and delivered petitions for prompt payment to 124 congressmen on the steps of the Capitol. VFW Commander Paul Wolman argued that immediate payment would have three benefits: relieve veterans' suffering, stimulate the economy, and relieve the government of a debt by "transferring the obligation from the shoulders of veterans to the strong boxes of bond holders." Then, the American Legion's executive committee met and reversed the Legion's prior position and gave support for the immediate payment of the bonus.

---

[4] Patman's proposal to pay out the full face value of the bonus certificates would total $2.2 billion and so was obviously controversial.

[5] In 1931, 47 different bonus proposals circulated in Congress.

With enough support in Congress, the Patman Bill bypassed the Ways and Means Committee for a floor vote, and on June 15 was quickly passed, in part because of an assured veto and strong opposition in the Senate. On June 17, with thousands of veterans sitting on the Capitol steps, the Senate decisively voted no!

BONUS PROTESTS

On May 10 of the next year, a group of 300 veterans left Portland, Oregon, for Washington—riding the rails and attracting attention—arriving on May 29. Groups of veterans came from all over the country to join with them, and the sympathetic district superintendent of police called the group of veterans the Bonus Expeditionary Force or BEF. The name would stick.

Some 40,000 veterans, often coming with their families, gathered in Washington. Small groups took shelter in empty government buildings. The largest group of veterans encamped on the flats near the Anacostia River. Each day, groups of veterans went to the Capitol, hoping to convince Congress to convert their certificates into cash in 1932 instead of waiting 15 more years for 1947. They made no real gains.

Deflated, 5,000 veterans accepted advances on their bonuses to pay for train tickets home. Still, 35,000 remained in Washington. On July 28, 1932, the federal government decided to expel the remaining BEF from the city. The local police were not successful, so President Hoover turned to the Army and Chief of Staff General Douglas MacArthur who exceeded his orders and used tanks and cavalry and troops with bayonets to drive the BEF out of Washington. The symbolism of the Army forcefully driving the veterans away would endure politically for many years.

"We are sure to win this election now," smiled Franklin Delano Roosevelt when he first heard the news reports. While he avoided mentioning the BEF during the campaign, he spoke often of "the forgotten man," easily heard as the veterans.

NEW DEAL POLITICS

Roosevelt's celebrated hundred days of legislation had included as its second bill what became known as the Economy Act. That act included a $460 million *cut* in veterans' benefits and pensions. The VFW organized another coalition of veterans and fought hard against FDR's Economy Act, which the more conservative American Legion had accepted. The Legion lost 20% of its members while the VFW gained 40,000. (Later, Congress restored $100 million of the previous cuts.)

In October, Roosevelt addressed the American Legion's Chicago convention. Acknowledging the government's responsibilities toward service-connected disabilities and to descendants of those killed in action, he asserted, "No person, because he wore a uniform must thereafter be placed in a special class of beneficiaries over and above all other citizens. The fact of wearing a uniform does not mean that he can demand of his government a benefit no other citizen receives." Roosevelt's remarks helped the American Legion's conservative leadership reverse the prior year's demand for immediate payment of the bonus. However, it provoked the VFW to be even more insistent on paying the bonus early.

On March 12, 1934, the House took up the renewed Patman Bill. The VFW was alone and vigorous in support for the Bill. Bonus supporters, in raucous discord, passed the Bill with enough votes to override any veto. In the Senate, allied with the administration, the Senate Finance Committee report was in opposition to the Bill. It was combined with a Bill to monetize silver, a bill that got no traction. So Congress adjourned without action and no veto was needed.

While the VFW would continue its vigorous campaign, the American Legion, with help from Roosevelt, sidetracked the bonus advocates within its ranks. The final vote was an overwhelming majority in favor, but the American Legion had greatly softened the wording from *demand* to *recommend.*

Complexity rose to dominance again in veterans' politics after the 1934 election. Populist Huey Long,[6] the radical Father Conklin, and Wright Patman were each prominent variables. The American Legion was divided. So was the VFW. On May 17, FDR again vetoed the Veterans Benefits Bill and for the only time in history, appeared in person before Congress to state his reasons. In an effort to override the veto, the Senate came up short by just five votes.

FDR then refocused his Congressional strategy and passed a series of major laws: the Social Security Act, the National Labor Relations Act, the Revenue Act, the Banking Act, the Public Utilities Act, and a $5 billion package of public works projects.

ROOSEVELT IS CAUTIOUS

At the 1943 convention of the American Legion, the main issue was recruiting new members. Warren H. Atherton, who had been particularly effective at recruiting new members in California, was elected National Commander. (Atherton was unusually well-matched to the opportunity. After serving as a Doughboy, he became a lawyer and married the daughter of the CEO—and a large shareholder—of Caterpillar Tractor.) In addition,

---

[6] In September, Huey Long—the Louisiana populist advocate of "share the wealth" and a "chicken in every pot"—was shot dead.

$250,000 was committed to support aggressive recruiting to replicate Atherton's great recruiting success in California on a national scale. After recruiting only 42,000 new members in 1942, the American Legion was determined to out-recruit the VFW, its rival for membership and national influence. A special committee was established to formulate a package of veterans' welfare legislation.

With war raging in Europe and in the Pacific, Roosevelt had little trouble with deferring serious discussion of post-war plans for returning soldiers and sailors, but he would remember the veterans' groups' political power and behavior. "There will not be *any* post-war problems if we lose this war," was Roosevelt's response to those who pressed for an explicit commitment to a specific set of benefits for the veterans.

Mrs. Roosevelt spoke of the potential political disruption that could be driven by an effective organization of veterans: "It will be far greater than any similar organization in the past and might become a pressure group thinking only of its own interests and feeling keen resentment if they feel that others have forgotten that their group was expected to give even of their own lives for the preservation of the civilian population who, in return, did not safeguard the opportunities for a future in a world of peace."[7]

Roosevelt appointed the National Resources Board of 1934 under the leadership of his cousin Frederick Delano to study the overall situation and propose a program. The objective was to avoid the troubles and hostilities that had come after World War I in America, and, in Europe, which had led to a rise in fascist and Nazi power. When released, the board's report advocated expanded access to education, full employment, and equal living standards. The board's reports were castigated by journalists and conservative groups as "socialist" and "fascist," and in 1943, Congress terminated its funding.

In his July 28, 1943, fireside chat, President Roosevelt outlined a plan based on the Delano proposals and urged Congress to pass enabling

---

[7] *New York Times*, April 6, 1942.

legislation insisting that "we are laying plans for the return to civilian life of our gallant men and women in the armed services. They must not be demobilized into an environment of inflation and unemployment to a place on the breadline or on a corner selling apples."

Roosevelt had come a long way in 10 years from his 1933 address to the American Legion's national convention when he rebuffed the VFW's demands for veterans.

PROPOSALS

The VFW developed a set of proposals for "mustering out" pay, a bonus for time served, and education and medical benefits. Then, the American Legion responded with its own proposals, which were more generous on each dimension. The VFW leadership split away from and opposed the Legion's proposals, accusing the American Legion of an "attempted power grab."

On February 22, in a reconciliation meeting at Washington's Statler Hotel, the two groups agreed to work together after the American Legion's leaders had agreed to include some face-saving provisions on hospitalization sought by the VFW. The agreed benefits were substantial: unemployment pay of $20 for up to 52 weeks, low-interest loans for farms or businesses, and educational benefits with cash stipends of $50 a month for single students and $75 a month for married students. (Of veterans, 51% would eventually use one of the educational benefits.) "As these veterans have led in war, so they must lead in peace," said Warren Atherton.

Atherton was skilled as an organizer and publicist, making sure the grateful nation rose to the occasion as large numbers of veterans returned home. He was a man with a mission and knew how to capitalize on the latent strengths of the Legion with its large membership, substantial financial resources, hundreds of local posts, and engagement with local communities by making its facilities available to troops of Girl Scouts and Boy Scouts. After an Oval Office meeting with Commander Atherton, Roosevelt declared in a message to Congress, "This nation is morally obligated to provide this training and education."

LACK OF INTEREST

Academic leaders had been skeptical of the idea of sending soldiers to college. Not only were GI's older and more worldly, educators worried that they would not be willing to study hard enough to meet the high standards of college studies. Also, it was believed that they would cause trouble socially. Many were married (most colleges then prohibited married students from enrolling). Finally, it would disrupt the colleges with a short-term influx of students who would not keep coming.[8] Robert M. Hutchins, President of the University of Chicago, predicted universities would opportunistically take advantage of the financial scholarships and accept less capable and less motivated students with lower academic standards. Harvard's Dean Bender also expected a diminution of standards.

Of the 1.5 million who had previously been graduating from high school each year, typically only 300,000 had wanted to go on to college. The millions of veterans would clearly overload the colleges. In his 1945 annual report, Harvard President James Conant, wrote, "As in other colleges and universities with restricted facilities, our chief problem today is one of selection. We cannot increase appreciably either the size of our staff or our physical plant in order to take care of this great number of highly qualified candidates for admission; therefore, many must be rejected. This is unfortunate, but inevitable."

---

[8] Much to the surprise of early doomsayers who had expected veterans to perform poorly in an academic setting, the veterans got better grades and were serious students.

Finally, recent surveys indicated that only a few veterans initially expressed any real interest in taking advantage of the proposed educational opportunities. A feature article in *Look* magazine summarized the apparent reality: "It's a splendidly designed program, but it has one big problem: the soldiers and sailors are just not buying it."

A special committee operating under the auspices of the Navy and War Departments—the Armed Forces Committee on Postwar Educational Opportunities for Service Personnel—had also taken up the issue. Named the Osborn Committee after its chairman, Brigadier General Frederick H. Osborn, the committee advanced legislative proposals that featured a provision for one year of education or vocational training for veterans who had served more than six months, with only a limited 100,000 getting more than one year's help and that help to come as a combination of loans and grants.

AMERICAN LEGION LEADERSHIP

The American Legion, with three million members, strong finances, and Atherton's dedicated leadership, took the lead. Because it had been so conservative, the American Legion would not have been expected to take a bold leadership position, but it did.

John Stelle, former governor of Illinois and "a big, fighting, hulk of a man" received a letter from his son describing what his fellow service people wanted after the war: "All they wanted was an opportunity from their government when they returned to get education or training and to find work." Stelle took this and the core ideas of what would develop into the GI Bill to the Legion's executive committee in November 1943.

Harry W. Colmery, chairman of the Republican National Committee and a former national commander of the American Legion, produced the first draft of the GI Bill—on stationery at the Mayflower Hotel in Washington.

Building on the administration's Bill and on prior proposals, the Legion was able to formulate its proposed Bill in just three weeks, with Stelle at a blackboard writing, erasing, and writing some more. A former newspaper man named Jack Cejnar, coined the name as *a bill of rights for G.I. Joe and G.I. Jane.* The categories of GI Bill benefits were similar to prior proposals, but the terms were much more generous: four years of college or graduate school, not just one, and a shorter time needed in the service to qualify. It was introduced just two months later by Senator Joel B. Clark of Missouri as the GI Bill.

A particular success of Atherton's campaign to get authorizing legislation was enlisting the powerful help of William Randolph Hearst and his national chain of newspapers. Hearst also gave the Legion three of his top reporters for the duration of the battle. They surveyed members of Congress and tipped Legion members which senators and representatives were either undecided or opposed to the bill, so letters in favor of the GI Bill could focus on them. (Thousands of letters poured in from posts and legionnaires.) The Hearst reporters also wrote numerous feature articles for major newspapers and magazines. Over the next six months, using its membership, local units, and its public relations apparatus, the American Legion worked to build support, urging every local unit to write letters—templates were provided—to their congressional representatives with as many members signing as possible.

The American Legion headquarters sent packets of materials to every outpost to help members write articles for local papers and helped them know what to emphasize on radio programs. Short films were sent to local theaters and American Legion members flooded Congress with telegrams in support of the GI Bill of Rights. Headlines of "The National Legionnaire" tell the story of the Legion's accelerating impact:

February: RIGHTS BILL FOR WAR II VETS ENDANGERED

March: 79 SENATORS SPONSOR LEGION BILL OF RIGHTS

April: SENATE PASSES LEGION OMNIBUS BILL 50–0

May: HOUSE GROUP REPORTS AMENDED GI BILL

July: PRESIDENT SIGNS RIGHTS BILL

RISING DEMAND

Low numbers of enrollments seemed at first to confirm low expectations. In September 1945, 15 months *after* the legislation, only 15,000 veterans had enrolled in colleges. "The G.I.'s Reject Education" was the title of an August 18, 1945, article by Stanley Frank in the *Saturday Evening Post*, then one of America's favorite magazines. Only 10% of the soldiers Frank interviewed at two veterans' hospitals had any interest in further education, and, worse, most of those would soon drop out. Five million soldiers and sailors had not even graduated from high school and fully half had quit school by the 10th grade. Only 23.3% had finished high school and only 3.6% had finished college. As of February 1945, less than 1% of discharged veterans were attending school or college under the GI Bill.

Frank suggested in his article that the problem was "unchanging human nature" and explained that people "did not like to think very far ahead." Ominously, he concluded, "We are perhaps expecting too much of the tired, bewildered, embittered soldier, disassociated as he has been from civilian life, in asking him to plan his career. In normal times, most people have modest ambitions and are content to drift with the tide, evading responsibility if they can." Editorially, the *Saturday Evening Post* saw the education benefit as a giant waste of taxpayers' money.

However, a year after Stanley Frank's "rejection" article, *The Post* was telling a much-changed story. In 1946, an article titled "Crisis of the Colleges" reported that the "facilities of the country's adult education programs are creaking under the load as [veterans] enroll by the hundreds of thousands." And in its February 9, 1946, issue, Harold Titus wrote that "a Gallup poll last spring indicated that 34% of the adult population—25,000,000 folks—had the impulse to take advantage of part-time educational facilities after the war."

For a solution, many turned to the state universities, citing the substantial surpluses several states had accumulated during the war years. New York had a surplus of $163 million, California had $154 million, Illinois $98 million, and Pennsylvania $96 million.

Enrollments climbed rapidly as men came home and learned what benefits were being made available to them. Eventually, twice as many signed up for college as the highest estimates had forecast and 20 times as many as previously expected went for vocational training. In 1946, 200,000 were in college; in 1947, that number jumped to over one million. And by 1949, over two million. Meanwhile, two and a half million were in noncollegiate training programs. When the eligibility period had ended, over half of all veterans got either training or education: 2.2 million had gone to college and another 5.6 million had vocational training. The total cost to the nation was $14.5 billion.

As the *Saturday Evening Post* explained, "Heads of American colleges are confronted with a reality that has always been a Democratic dream: the opportunity to raise the educational attainments of a solid chunk of a whole generation. Because of the government subsidy, the opportunity is here: men who could never go to college under normal circumstances are enrolling or knocking at the doors."

Sociologists would emphasize how the impact of low-cost business loans and home mortgages plus the educational benefits combined to expand the middle class. During the 1950s and 1960s, civic engagement was much higher because the veterans took volunteer organizations seriously and saw active participation as both an opportunity and a responsibility. Veterans were also far more active in community service organizations like the PTA and the Lions, Rotary, and Elks. Expectations changed. College was now normal, not limited just to the wealthy. Religious and ethnic prejudices were down and headed even lower.

Yale's Dean William C. Devane declared the program "immensely successful." *Time* magazine called the GI Bill "the most ambitious educational experiment in the nation's history"[9] and *Fortune* published a study of the college class of 1949, which was 70% veterans, and declared, "To most of those who worked with it, from the professors and placement directors to the recruiters for industry, '49 is the best class the country has ever produced."[10]

MAJOR FLAW: RACIAL DIFFERENCES

As veteran applications flooded universities, Black students often found themselves left out. Northern universities dragged their feet when it came to admitting Black students, and Southern colleges barred Black students entirely. The local VA encouraged Black veterans to apply for vocational training instead of university admission and arbitrarily denied educational benefits to some students.

Many Black veterans returning home from the war didn't even try to take advantage of the GI Bill's educational benefits—they could not afford to spend time in school instead of working. But those who did try were at

---

[9] *Time,* "Beginning of the End," July 30, 1951.
[10] *Fortune,* "The Class of 1949," June 1949.

a considerable disadvantage compared to their white counterparts. Public education in segregated schools had provided poor preparation for Black students, and many lacked educational ambition due to poverty and social pressures.[11]

The original GI Bill ended in July 1956. By that time, nearly 8 million World War II veterans had received education or training, and 4.3 million home loans worth $33 billion had been handed out in mortgages at 4% (tax deductible and before inflation); five million (29% of the veterans) got financing to start or buy a business or farm.

But most Black veterans had been left behind. Segregated schools in the South and in large northern cities were clearly *not* equal. Redlining neighborhoods by banks and deed covenants aimed at excluding Blacks from housing developments were common practices across the nation.

As employment, college attendance, and wealth surged for whites, disparities with their Black counterparts not only continued, but widened. There was, wrote Ira Katznelson, "no greater instrument for widening an already huge racial gap in postwar America than the GI Bill." In 1947, only two of the more than 3,200 VA-guaranteed home loans in 13 Mississippi cities went to Black borrowers. "These impediments were not confined to the South," notes historian Katznelson. "In New York and the northern New Jersey suburbs, fewer than 100 of the 67,000 mortgages insured by the GI Bill supported home purchases by non-Whites."

Black veterans and civil rights groups protested their treatment, but the racial disparities in the implementation of the GI Bill had already been set into motion. As the years went on, white veterans flowed into newly created suburbs and began amassing wealth while working in skilled positions, but Black veterans lacked those options. The majority of skilled jobs went to white workers.

---

[11] Ira Katznelson, *When Affirmative Action Was White* (New York: W. W. Norton, 2006).

The postwar housing boom almost entirely excluded Black Americans, most of whom remained in cities that received less and less investment from businesses and banks. Though the GI Bill guaranteed low-interest mortgages and other loans, they were not administered by the VA itself. Thus, the VA could cosign, but not actually guarantee the loans. Lenders froze out poorer neighborhoods, ensuring that loan assistance and insurance would be denied. And new suburbs like Levittown often came with overtly racist covenants that denied entry to Black people.

> Looking back at the GI Bill as an investment, the results were remarkable for the individual beneficiaries and extraordinary for the nation. The much-anticipated economic recession never came to pass and the American people were advanced in profound ways: those going to college were doubled, the suburbs and home ownership were expanded from a minority to a majority of Americans, and the base was laid for an extraordinary expansion of the economy and the middle class—although not equitably for Black citizens.

* * *

Here are two particularly helpful sources on this topic:

- Stephen Ortiz, *Beyond the Bonus March and GI Bill* (New York: New York University Press, 2010).
- Suzanne Mettler, *Soldiers to Citizens* (New York: Oxford University Press, 2005).

7

INTERSTATE HIGHWAYS

The interstate highway system transformed the concept of family travel in America and brought the different regions closer together. President Eisenhower correctly envisioned the system as a way of advancing the economy. Politics were everywhere in the laborious process of getting the necessary approvals from interest groups and Congress.

n 1909, less than 10% of America's roads were rated "improved" and very few were paved. Only Russia and China had worse roads. If major improvements were not made, constricted transportation would constrain economic growth severely.[1]

The Federal-Aid Highway Act of 1944 had been proposed to be the largest highway act in history and authorized a 40,000-mile highway system to connect major metropolitan areas at a cost of $500 million per year. However, it had inadequate congressional support.

---

[1] Mass transit was ignored because that was considered a local responsibility.

HIGHWAY MAN

Thomas H. MacDonald had left his state road building post in Iowa to become the most powerful highway man in America. (He was devoted to science and engineering. Never smiling, always formal, and wearing three-piece suits in his teens, he had insisted his four younger siblings call him Sir.)

In July 1916, the first Federal Aid Road Act had given the future bureau MacDonald would lead $75 million and five years to pay for half of each state's most urgent road building and improvements. When MacDonald got to Washington in 1919, he found a toxic blend of inactivity, hostility, and confusion. Only $500,000 of the $75 million had been spent and only 17.6 miles of road had been built. MacDonald, a man of action, promptly arranged to send $130 million worth of surplus military trucks and equipment to state highway departments to win their cooperation and goodwill.

In addition to being decisive, MacDonald was committed to federal-state cooperation and technical expertise. For MacDonald, roads served four important constituencies: agriculture, commerce, defense, and recreation. He developed expertise through research in every aspect of road building from the size, lettering, color, and placement of signs, to the optimal sand in mixing cement and in curing time, as well as the most effective steel reinforcement for concrete. In addition, during his 15 years in Iowa, he had become convinced that central to success was an effective partnership between the state and national governments.

A joint board of federal and state highway men worked together and agreed on several policies. They agreed to number all highways and that east–west highways would get even numbers while north–south highways would get odd numbers, with the most important highways getting numbers ending in 0. They agreed to consistently use the now ubiquitous red-yellow-green light system, and the size and the shape of route markers.

They also agreed on the selection of 50,000 miles of roads that would be made into primary highways.[2]

The Federal Aid Highway Act of 1921 had provided the first overall plan for the country's roads. It called for a system of interstate highways that would connect every county seat. States would be responsible for specific route plans and the federal government for construction standards. This approach became the basis for today's interstate highway system.

The Chief, as all knew McDonald, got things done. Results were published in *Public Roads*—the magazine of the Federal Highway Administration, which the nation's road builders studied. MacDonald linked good roads and national defense and worked with General Pershing to chart good cross-country roads for military use. By late 1921, he could cite 5,000 miles of completed highways and 17,000 more in the process of being upgraded.

In 1937, FDR called MacDonald to the White House to show him a map of the 48 states of the United States. FDR drew a series of six lines—three across from coast to coast and three North to South. They could pay for themselves, thought Roosevelt, by charging tolls and by taking a mile-wide swath of land by eminent domain and then selling lots at a profit to hotels, gas stations, and other businesses.

A year after his meeting with FDR, MacDonald produced a book—*Toll Roads and Free Roads*—showing six major arteries crossing the country, much as the President had sketched out a year before. Roosevelt and many others saw toll roads—a charge directly to users for their use of the highways—as the only fair way to pay for the highways, but MacDonald's year-long analysis concluded that tolls would cover only 40% of the $2.9 billion of costs.

---

[2] Speed limits vary: 50 mph in New York City; 75 mph in northern Maine; and 80 mph in parts of Utah, Idaho, Montana, South Dakota, and Wyoming.

MacDonald opposed toll roads, believing that access to highways was a driver's right. On the other hand, MacDonald's plan would mean the destruction of low income and "rundown" parts of cities, taking homes through eminent domain to allow for highway construction through cities. To his credit, he was always open about this necessity, but spoke of the importance of taking care of people over all else. In a 1947 statement he said, "No matter how urgently a highway improvement may be needed, the homes of people who have nowhere to go should not be destroyed. Before dwellings are razed, new housing facilities should be provided for the dispossessed occupants. This question of housing should be accepted as one of the major planning problems when a city decides that it needs and wants an expressway." However, he was ignored, and future realities would see the displacement of many poor people, immigrants, and people of color as their neighborhoods and homes were stolen and destroyed.

FDR saw interstate highways primarily as a way to reduce congestion, but MacDonald focused on how they could promote transcontinental travel. However, few people were traveling cross country in those days, and many would not be able to afford the tolls. (Highway expansion in several eastern states went ahead in the late 1930s and early 1940s with toll roads built in Pennsylvania, New York, and New Jersey. World War II put off any other major work.)

When MacDonald turned 70 in 1951, his appointment was extended only one year at a time by the Truman administration. Then, after 34 years of service, MacDonald was not renewed: 58-year-old Francis V. DuPont, who had been deeply engaged in highways in Delaware, would be taking over.

DuPont had many attractive qualities: the longtime head of his state's Republican party, he was an experienced engineer with political savvy who understood and could readily document how building highways would benefit the whole national economy. Another attractive quality: being wealthy, he declined any salary or reimbursement of business expenses while serving the public. Dupont was particularly thoughtful to MacDonald, sending a long two-page telegram to the Chief saying that he was honored to succeed him and was going to keep his policies. Surprising everyone who expected major changes, DuPont made only a few changes: He brought a single lawyer with him, and he made efforts to get suggestions from his staff.

EISENHOWER TAKES COMMAND

Long before coming into office, Eisenhower had had a memorable and motivating experience in 1919: the Army's first automobile and truck caravan across America. Beginning in Washington on July 7, 258 soldiers and 24 officers—Lieutenant Dwight D. Eisenhower was one of the officers—crossed the country in a three-mile caravan of 81 vehicles that took 62 10-hour *days* to reach San Francisco at an average "speed" of five miles per hour.

Eisenhower's later experience in Germany with the Autobahn—which had proven almost impossible to stop with bombing during World War II—convinced him of the importance to America of a transcontinental system of roads.

When Dwight Eisenhower took office in 1952, the plan for today's Interstate Highway System existed—but only in concept and on paper—at MacDonald's Bureau of Public Roads.

Eisenhower was publicly committed to fiscal conservatism and to international military preparedness, yet he also believed that the enormous investment in the interstate highway system was important both for the economic future of the nation and as a somewhat flexible—because it could be accelerated or slowed—stimulus to the economy that was then experiencing rising unemployment.

Although interstate highways were an Eisenhower priority it had to be deferred until after the Korean War was over—partly because most participants in the inevitable give-and-take of the politics of democracy had begun the process without any expectation of success. Several factors added to the difficulty, particularly the President's heart attack and Democrats' winning control of both House and Senate in 1954. In 1954, Eisenhower brought the concept up again at a governors' conference at Lake George. Thanks in large part to MacDonald and a popular, determined President Eisenhower, the nation's highways would be transformed by the largest public works project in the nation's history. Described as the "largest public works program since the pyramids," the 42,800 mile system of roads enabled travelers to go coast to coast without ever stopping for a traffic light. The federal government covered 90% of the cost.[3] The land along the highways became the favored sites for suburban housing developments, shopping centers, and industrial parks.

Eisenhower believed in delegating operational authority to subordinates and in teamwork—the two concepts with which he had succeeded in organizing coalition warfare. That's how he was determined to succeed with the world's largest-ever investment in transportation.

Sherman Adams—decisive and politically quite powerful—was Eisenhower's Chief of Staff. He believed in the federal-state cooperation that MacDonald had established at the Bureau of Public Roads because he had seen it work well when serving as governor of New Hampshire. The mandate Eisenhower gave Francis DuPont, Sherman Adams, and John Brandon in 1953 was to devise a dramatic plan to build and brand $50 billion of self-regulating highways and not increase the federal debt. That would certainly not be easy.

Initially, Eisenhower expected the interstate highway system to be financed with bonds that would be paid off with income from tolls, which

---

[3] The highways are owned by the state in which they are located.

is how the new highways were being financed in Pennsylvania, New York, and New Jersey.

As Eisenhower charged Gabriel Hauge, his assistant for economic affairs, in February, 1953: "Our cities still conform too rigidly to the patterns, customs, and practices of 50 years ago. Each year, we add hundreds of thousands of new automobiles to our vehicular population, but our road systems do not keep pace with the need." Eisenhower went on to request an overall plan that could be implemented in parts that would eventually fit together logically and effectively into a whole system. To build momentum, Eisenhower appointed two committees. One under DuPont had key people from Treasury, Defense, Commerce, and the Budget Bureau. The other was called the President's Advisory Committee on National Highway Programs, headed by General Lucius Clay.

CLAY GETS TO WORK

Clay was a good choice. As President of Continental Can Corporation and a Director of General Motors, he had known Eisenhower since their days at West Point, led the post-war occupation and rebuilding of Germany with great success, and oversaw the Berlin airlift. Clay also played a key role in securing for Eisenhower the Republican nomination and in organizing Eisenhower's cabinet. Clay was made Executive Secretary of the Advisory Committee and given an office in the White House.

Francis Cutler Turner, a quiet and effective executive, then head of the Federal Highway Administration, which was successor to the Bureau of Public Roads, was experienced in building highways in Alaska and the Philippines. He knew engineering and the history of federal aid to highways. A MacDonald protege, and a teetotaler who took a heavy briefcase home each night, Turner was appointed head of the Clay Committee's staff. Turner's role was to get the facts, explain the background behind each challenge, and convert constructive ideas into proposals for Congress. He would be the main but invisible midwife to the interstate highway system.

General Clay had three enormous tasks: Determine what kind of highway system the nation needed, figure out how much it would cost, and decide how to pay for it. Clay's committee found that only 8,500 miles of the system would have enough traffic to pay for themselves via tolls and that all but 3,500 miles of those miles were already operating as toll roads. That finding closed out the toll road alternative.

Clay's formal report on January 11, 1955, recommended "the top national and defense priority" be to spend $101 billion over 10 years on an interstate highway system and the urban and rural roads that fed traffic into the system. Of that total, $23.2 billion would be for the interstate highway system with a "plug" number of $4 billion for the main connecting roads. The other three-quarters of the total would be needed to bring three million miles of other roads up to snuff. Some $47 billion would be collected from fees and taxes during construction, so new money of "only" $54 billion would be needed. (Clay frequently asserted that the hidden costs of inefficiency, lives lost, and "national insecurity" were much larger than that $54 billion.)

Clay consulted with leading banks and decided on the creation of a new Federal Highway Corporation that would issue 30-year bonds to pay the federal government's 90% share of the costs. The bonds would be retired via user fees—primarily federal taxes on fuel. Happily, since the new roads would increase traffic and fuel use, there would actually be no need to increase the rate of taxation.

However, Clay's report was doomed to fail because the chairman of the Senate Finance Committee, Harry F. Byrd of Virginia, was absolutely opposed to any borrowing. He insisted on "pay as you go"—raise the money first, then build.

To convert the financing to "pay as you go," higher taxes on gasoline, oil, and tires were proposed. Surprisingly, this got buried in Congress by

292 votes to 123 due to strong opposition from the nation's trucking industry. Then, the truckers realized they would not get the new highways unless they reversed their campaign and instead argued in favor of the user taxes. Treasury Secretary George Humphrey explained that the financing plan was similar to Social Security, with taxes going into a trust fund that would be used exclusively on roads so the payers—the truckers—would get *all* the benefits. With that understanding among the truckers, political pressures reversed and the bill would easily pass: The vote was 388 to 19.

On June 26, 1956, both the Senate and the House gave final approval to the compromise legislation authorizing $25 billion over 12 years to accelerate the interstate highway system, increasing the federal tax on fuel from two cents to three cents per gallon, and confirming the federal share at 90%. On June 29, Eisenhower, who was confined in Walter Reed Hospital for an intestinal ailment, signed it into law.

REMARKABLE RESULTS

The interstate system would extend 48,000 miles; open 16,000 entrances and exits; build 55,000 bridges, overpasses, and scores of tunnels; and engage some 60,000 local contractors in doing the work. By 1962, 12,500 miles were open to users and miles were being added at an average of 34 miles per week. Each billion dollars spent provided the equivalent of 48,000 people years of work, consumed 16 million barrels of cement, used 500,000 tons of steel, and moved enough earth to cover the state of New Jersey knee deep in dirt.

Long-distance driving benefitted greatly. The driving time from New York City to Los Angeles was cut by more than 20%, from 79 hours to 62.

Cost estimates kept rising: $46.8 billion in 1965 doubled the 1956 estimate. Then costs went up by $12.25 billion in 1970, by another $6 billion in 1972, and reached $90 billion in 1975—and rose even more beyond that.

The total grew to $130 billion (nearly $600 billion in current dollars), covered 47,000 miles of roads, and was the single largest investment in public works ever made by the American people. (The most costly single project—not part of the original program—has been "the Big Dig" in Boston: $22 billion, more than twice the cost, in comparable dollars, of the Panama Canal.)

The interstate highway system lumbered its way to completion, but that did not end the troubles. Graft and fraud were relatively minor in amounts. The gravest problem with the interstate system was that it was a highway system for cars and did not address directly the need for transporting the growing amount of manufactured production. Redesigning the nation's railroads would have achieved far more for far less in several areas such as the Boston–Washington corridor—but only highways were considered.

Even worse for a democracy, the new interstate arteries poured large numbers of vehicles into cities without redesigning the roads of those cities to accommodate the large "deliveries." Since access ramps had to go somewhere, they were usually deliberately aimed, in city after city, into lower income and politically less powerful neighborhoods where costs would be low and clearance of "slums" would be popular with most voters. Of course, this meant disrupting established neighborhoods, social life, and families *and* imposing both financial and nonfinancial costs on those least able to absorb those costs.

In Milwaukee, a 16 block community of 600 Black families was uprooted. In Cleveland, 19,000 people were displaced. The same happened in Montgomery, Alabama, where Ralph Abernathy's church was specifically targeted, and many other urban communities that looked rundown to others but were home and community to those who lived there. In St. Paul, I-94 cut through the Black community, displacing one-seventh of the city's Black population. In Los Angeles, 3,550 people and 117 businesses, parks, schools, and churches were pushed aside.

Over half a century later, cities are still striving to overcome these problems; however, Eisenhower's interstate system has long been considered a great success. For most of the nation, it made transportation and travel easier and less costly—and made the nation more connected—a priority that extends back to George Washington's farewell address.

> The Eisenhower interstate highway system, the largest-ever civil construction program, succeeded as the connection between cities and towns but left many lower-income communities in frustrating condition.

8

LAND-GRANT COLLEGES

America was an enormous agricultural nation in the 1860s with only 5% of young people going to college and many farmers feeling anxiously defensive about their children rejecting the lonely, hard, and not very rewarding life on a family farm. However, if farmers got more education in the science underlying promising new developments in agriculture, they could improve their productivity at work and have more time for further learning and enjoyment of life and make America an even stronger, richer, and more independent nation.

John Turner was a visionary and advocate who conceived and articulated the concept of the land-grant colleges. Justin Morrill was a powerful leader in Congress who devoted his energy, legislative skills, and stature to the long process of winning political support for what would become over 100 land-grant colleges and universities in America.

American politics have influenced higher education in different ways, particularly as political parties waxed and waned over the late 18th century and through the 19th century. George Washington proposed a national university. Federalists supported a strong central government using revenues from tariffs to finance roads, canals, banks, and such national educational institutions as West Point. However, antifederalists opposed "monarchical" institutions as they sought to devolve power to the states. Jacksonian Democrats had no interest in universities, so they had to develop on their own.

During the second half of the 19th century, industrialization surged, high school attendance increased rapidly—increasing even more rapidly in the earlier part of the 20th century—and the idea of going to college began to spread. Scientific farming and new farming practices were promoted through state fairs, agricultural society meetings, and journals—particularly in the Northeast where traditional agriculture was in decline. An increasing concern among farmers was that their children would be drawn away from farming and move into the rapidly growing cities. Behavior confirmed their concern. From 1870 to 1910, farm employment fell from 53% to 31% of the nation's workers.

TURNER'S CONCEPT

Justin Morrill never acknowledged—and never denied—that the concept, mission, and virtually all the specific details of the land-grant colleges had been worked out and made public by John B. Turner. Born and raised on a farm, Turner studied classics and mathematics and graduated with honors from Yale. He then took a position as a professor at Illinois College for 15 years before ill health obliged him to retire.

Turner was a change agent.[1] He brought the Osage orange to Illinois as a cheap hedging—before wire fencing became available—to restrain animals and enable farmers to live in communities and organize schools. He was an active champion of public schools and rode around Illinois urging others to adopt the public school concept. He wrote articles about crop rotation and soil analysis and was the first to use machinery to plant corn.

Turner was a bold campaigner on behalf of the 80% of people who then lived on farms. "It is said of farmers and mechanics, that they do not and will not read and that the agricultural classes have no practical congenial literature. But I say, give them the literature and education suited to their wants and see if it does not improve them as it has their professional brethren."

The concept of an industrial university was laid out by Turner to the Farmers Convention in Granville, Illinois, in 1851. "All civilized society is, necessarily, divided into two distinct cooperative, not antagonistic, classes: a small class, whose proper business it is to teach the true principles of religion, law, medicine, science, art, and literature; and a much larger class who are engaged in some form of labor in agriculture, commerce, and the arts."

Pointing out that only 5% would go into what he called the professional class, Turner explained that the requisite education for the professional class was not matched by comparably appropriate education for the

---

[1] Turner was active in the underground railway and a personal friend of Abraham Lincoln. *The Cultivator*, in its April 1832 issue, had said, "The art of agriculture in this country is generally understood as well as any other. Our farmers can do the work and do it well. But the science, the theory of agriculture is not so well understood; agriculture sciences embraces a number of other sciences." And then, the sciences of farming were listed: botany, chemistry, geology, entomology, and astronomy. "The importance of the sciences increases every day." The writer went on to report how much was then being spent by the leading nations in Europe. The differences were substantial. In October 1839, *The Cultivator* was still on the case, saying, "When we consider that agriculture is the great business of the nation—of mankind—and that its successful prosecution depends upon a knowledge of the principles of natural science, we cannot withhold our surprise and regret that we have not long established professional schools in which our youth might be taught the principles and practice of their future business of life."

other 95%. To bring that about would require, at every level, the institutions and professors needed for the industrial classes. Turner then asserted that the whole process of transformation must start at the highest level of education: colleges and universities.

Turner addressed the Granville convention with two major propositions: first that the children of farmers and industrial people were entitled to education that would fit them for life, and second that the various industries were entitled to the advancement and development that could only come from educated minds. Turner proposed using a grant of 30,000 acres of land for each state to be sold to finance such institutions.[2] Turner was a vigorous campaigner for his concept and sent letters advocating it widely. Horace Greeley, writing in the *New York Tribune*, picked up the idea and advocated it in early 1863.

JUSTIN MORRILL

Justin Morrill enjoyed school so much that he once thought of a career in teaching but was guided to business as a career more likely to achieve personal independence. Born on April 14, 1810, the son of a blacksmith, young Morrill was decisively upwardly mobile. As a member of the New England middle class, Morrill was a tough businessman who pursued debtors and worked at accumulating personal wealth. He worked in retailing, made a great success, and invested in stocks and bonds and in local banking and manufacturing businesses. Morrill became a major sheep breeder and wool producer. Egalitarian policies were not his focus. He worked for

---

[2] Turner's speech resulted in the establishment of the Industrial League and it sponsored Turner as an advocate who campaigned across the state. In 1850, Francis Wayland, President of Brown University, said there were in the country 120 colleges, 47 law schools, and 42 theological seminaries, but not one institution focused on agriculture or manufacturing.

a high tariff, fought against the 40-hour work week, the direct election of senators, and women's suffrage. He had no interest in education for women.

Morrill never went to college but saw what would become land-grant colleges—institutions financed in part by grants of federal lands—as a way to advance industry and agriculture through scientific discovery and to train scientists who could advance the practice of American industry and agriculture. At 34, he became chair of the local Whig committee in Vermont and then became a delegate to national Whig conventions. In 1854, he could retire at 38 and focus on politics. At age 44, he was elected to Congress with a plurality of only 59 votes. Having been a Whig, Justin Morrill easily became a Republican favoring internal improvements, economic development, and protecting American industry—specifically Vermont's wool industry—with tariffs. He also supported internal improvements in transportation. He won six more elections by increasingly large margins, and after 12 years in the House of Representatives, was elected senator in 1866. He served for another 32 years.

Morrill, as a delegate to the organizational meetings of the United States Agricultural Society in Washington in June 1852, heard about the presented Turner Plan. In 1857, Senator Lyman Trumbull endorsed the Turner concept, but recommended any legislation be introduced by a member from one of the older states since Congress had done so much for newer states in recent years that it might cause some resistance.

Senator Morrill became convinced that more could and should be done to put farming on a more scientific basis as several European nations had been doing. Morrill spoke on June 6, 1862, about France and England having quadrupled agricultural production while American farmers were doing less and less well. His commitment to improvements would include advancing strong federal support for what would become known as the land-grant colleges that focused on scientific agriculture.

Since the national Republican Party lacked the nationwide organizational strength to build support for the new land-grant colleges, that role was largely filled by the Grange and other agricultural societies. These agricultural societies would have a strong influence on the development of land-grant colleges and on restraining many of them from rising to become clearly academic institutions.

The Morrill Land Grant College Act of 1862 fit with the contemporary establishment of the Department of Agriculture in 1862 and federal funding of agricultural experiment stations through the Hatch Act of 1887. While funding from the original land grants provided less than 1% of the total budgets of the land-grant institutions, the Morrill Act is clearly the most important higher educational legislation ever passed in the United States.

GETTING LEGISLATION

The use of land grants to finance education was well-established by the 1850s.[3] So was the government's responsibility for supporting and sponsoring education. But, there was widespread disagreement over what sorts of education and at what levels.

In December 1857, Morrill introduced a bill that proposed "donating public lands to the several states" and exploring the "expediency of establishing one or more agricultural schools for the benefit of agriculture and mechanical arts." The bill passed in the House, but not in the Senate. While his first proposed resolution in favor of federal action was defeated, Morrill was gaining respect for his financial sagacity. So, after reelection, he made an alliance of shared interest in education with Thaddeus Stevens of

---

[3] When the first Morrill Bill proposed granting 20,000 acres per member of Congress in 1857, over 4,000,000 acres of land had already been donated to support higher education in 15 states. The grants totaled 11,360,000 acres—equal to half the state of Indiana. Eventually, 17.5 million acres were distributed.

Pennsylvania. In 1859, a similar bill passed narrowly in both houses of Congress, but President Buchanan vetoed it, arguing that it was unconstitutional and injurious to those colleges that would not be receiving federal aid.

The Morrill Land Grant Act of 1862 provided federal land to each state and territory to be sold to raise capital to maintain "at least one college where the leading objective shall be, without excluding other scientific and classical studies, to teach such branches of learning as are related to agriculture and mechanical arts, in such manner as the legislatures of the States may respectively prescribe, in order to promote the liberal and professional education of the industrial classes in the several pursuits and professions of life." This broad mission, of course, left ample room for experimentation and for differences of purpose. History would soon demonstrate how differently states would work to fulfill their individual interpretations of the new law.[4]

Three years later, Abraham Lincoln would sign a very similar bill into law, adding military training.[5] It provided 30,000 acres of land (increased from the original 20,000) or the equivalent per Congressional representative to each state not then in rebellion. To make sure that each state was seriously invested in such colleges, none of the funds could be used on buildings in any way, and only 10% of the capital raised by the act could be used for acquiring land. (This provision caused several eastern states to link their land-grant colleges to existing institutions such as Yale and what would become the Massachusetts Institute of Technology.)

---

[4] In early 1892, Cornell, Penn State, and the University of Illinois committed to the extension program using the Chautauqua concept to engage farmers. By 1907, at least 39 land-grant colleges were doing something with extension programs.

[5] Half of the commissioned officers in World War II came through ROTC programs at land-grant colleges. Northern members of Congress passed the Morrill Act when southern states had seceded during the Civil War.

STATE-BY-STATE REACTIONS

Daniel Coit Gilman had studied European manufacturing, mining, and farming back in the 1850s and discovered that all were more advanced than their counterparts in America. The reason: scientifically trained specialists with more expertise. Returning to Yale's Sheffield Scientific School, he advocated a strong response to the opportunity afforded by the Morrill Act. The school was the only Connecticut institution to respond to the Morrill opportunity. The state and school agreed that half of the endowment would be used to provide full scholarships for state-nominated students while the other half would finance three new professorships in the sciences. (Over a dinner in New Haven, Morrill praised the school's commitment "along the lines he greatly recommended."[6])

State after state responded differently to the land-grant opportunity. In Maine, Bowdoin was the early leading candidate, but the legislature rejected its application after a campaign launched by the editor of *The Maine Farmer* and the state agriculture society, and instead created the Maine Agricultural and Mechanical College.

In Massachusetts, Governor John Andrews tried to deliver the Morrill funds to Harvard, but the state agricultural society blocked that move. While advocates of the land-grant concept fought back against a "popular misconception," the presidents of both Princeton and Harvard expressed concerns about "trade schools" taking up too much of the available money. The town of Amherst was one of the cities that offered to pay the $75,000—made a requirement in Massachusetts to be considered—and Amherst College, having long advocated an agricultural college be located in

---

[6] Edward Alexander Bouchet's personal story became an example of embedded racial prejudice at work. He studied at Yale and was the first African American to earn a PhD there; he did so well that he was a member of Phi Beta Kappa. While land-grant colleges actively sought PhDs for their faculties, none would accept Bouchet and he was obliged to settle for teaching chemistry and physics at Philadelphia's School for Colored Youth.

Western Massachusetts, offered to make available both its library and teaching help from its faculty to keep costs down. Massachusetts decided to give one-third of its land grant to what later became MIT and two-thirds to support the new agricultural college—with leaders of the state agricultural society made trustees.

The New Jersey legislature chose Rutgers over Princeton in the 1860s.

Vermont's legislature proposed to combine Middlebury College with the Vermont State University and Norwich College, but then Middlebury balked. Edwin Hammond, a leader in the state agricultural society and, like Morrill, a major sheep breeder, proposed and the legislators endorsed a Vermont College of Agriculture and Industrial Arts to receive all of the land grant funding *if* the trustees raised $100,000 within one year. While Morrill pledged $5,000, other potential donors did not commit, so the legislature turned to the University of Vermont, which then recruited a professor of civil engineering from Yale's Sheffield Scientific School to organize a range of science courses to be bolted onto its main liberal arts commitments.

Brown was the only institution of higher learning in Rhode Island when the legislature voted to accept the land-grant proposal in early 1863. Despite populist efforts to use the money to launch a new institution, none developed. Brown proposed to extend its engineering and scientific programs, but the state legislature was not prepared to provide the necessary funding, so Brown remained largely as it had been.[7]

What would prove to be one of the most successful land grants began with Ezra Cornell, a State Senator, offering a 300 acre farm *and* $300,000 if the State of New York would agree to allocate part of its land-grant funding and locate in Ithaca. Senator Andrew Dickson White rejected the idea of

---

[7]Northern members of Congress passed the Morrill Act when southern states had seceded during the Civil War. After the war, the Second Morrill Act of 1890 provided funding for those states that offered "separate but equal" opportunities for African Americans. In 1994, land-grant status was provided to Native Americans via 33 tribal colleges.

dividing the grant, preferring that all of it go to one institution and naming it for Cornell. Resistance from populists was loud but not durable, and Cornell University was founded in 1862 as a "true liberal university." Ezra Cornell's philanthropy enabled White to recruit exceptional faculty and erect fine buildings. (After Cornell's death in 1874, the original commitment to assuring broad access and vocational training were both allowed to end quietly.)[8]

SUMMING UP

Justin Morrill was not a progressive champion of democracy, but he wanted to expand scientific discovery and advance farming and industry so American farmers and companies could compete internationally. Morrill opposed efforts by the Grange to increase access by lowering academic standards and emphasizing vocational programs. His legacy, over the decades, has been transformed into a happy story of higher education being brought to the broader American population.

The Morrill Act reshaped higher education in America, expanded access, enticed states to invest in higher education, increased the national investment in scientific education, and helped modernize agriculture and industry. By 1900, more engineers had graduated from land-grant institutions than from any other type, and graduates were advancing American industrial processes and products. The land-grant idea transformed higher education through the concept of service and direct links with industry

---

[8] In the early 1890s, Cornell, Penn State, and the University of Illinois were committed to extension programs using the Chautauqua concept to engage farmers. By 1907, at least 39 land-grant colleges were doing something with extension programs. In 1929, Ezra Cornell's "any person, any study" was tested by Ruth Peyton, an African American from Oleander, New York, who was denied residency in one of the dormitories because that "would cause more embarrassment than satisfaction."

and agriculture, and expanded access to higher education programs. Major expansion would come after the World War II, thanks to the GI Bill. (See Chapter 6.)

In a speech on October 10, 1888, Senator Morrill said, "The fundamental idea was to offer an opportunity in every state for a liberal and larger education, not merely to those destined to sedentary professions, but to those needing higher instruction for the world's business—for the industrial pursuits and professions of life."

The land-grant colleges, in concert with the GI Bill, changed the proportion of young Americans going to college from "unusual" and 5% to "normal" and 35%, and this transformed America's workforce as would be needed for the transformation of our economy and our society to succeed in the information economy of today. This great transformation is not complete and it is not over. African Americans were too often left out, and the needs for advanced education are continuing to accelerate. The rate of return on the over 100 land-grant colleges' investment has, of course, been extraordinary in qualitative measures. In financial measures, returns have been infinitely high because the land had been taken without compensation from Native Americans. These engines of prosperity, learning, research, and teaching are world renowned and are the open doorway for talented individuals from all backgrounds to participate fully in our democracy and its advancement.

9
NATIONAL INSTITUTES OF HEALTH

The National Institutes of Health (NIH), thanks to the historic support from Congress, has been by far the world's leading funder of biomedical research. That research is both intramural (i.e., done by the remarkably talented research staff at the NIH) and extramural (i.e., done by the best independent researchers at major universities). To ensure the most meritorious proposals get funded, the extramural research grant recipients are selected by outside panels of leading researchers in each field.

The NIH is, by far, the world's largest funder of biomedical research aimed at improving human health. Americans can take quiet pride that all new knowledge is traditionally shared with the world—immediately and without any charge—an extraordinary gift to the billions of people around the world.

Scale is only one measure of the NIH. Quality of process and salience of results matter much more. Here, the NIH is particularly strong. There are 174 scientists working in or for the NIH who have won Nobel Prizes. Millions of lives have been saved and the health improved for many millions more. The financial returns on the nation's investment in the NIH have been enormous. Without the health advances from the NIH research thousands on thousands would have died; by living and continuing to work, they have been able to work and pay taxes, likely far in excess of the investments in the NIH.

"The National Institutes of Health speak the universal language of humanitarianism. It has been devoted throughout its long and distinguished history to furthering the health of all mankind. In this service, it has recognized no limitations imposed by international boundaries and has recognized no distinctions based on race, creed, or color," declared President Franklin D. Roosevelt on October 31, 1940, at the dedication of the NIH campus at Bethesda, Maryland. He emphasized: "We cannot be a strong nation unless we are a healthy nation. So we must recruit knowledge and science in the service of national strength. And that is what we are doing here today." Over the next several decades, the NIH would grow rapidly in importance to America and to the world.

ORIGIN

The NIH traces back to its origin in 1887 as the Hygienic Laboratory[1] under the direction of Joseph James Kenyon as part of the Marine Health Service (MHS). (It became the National Institutes of Health in 1920.) At

---

[1] The legislative chronology of NIH began in 1798 with an act for the relief of sick and disabled seamen supported by a monthly deduction of 20 cents from the pay of merchant seamen, a practice that continued until 1943. (In 1870, the Marine Hospital Service was reorganized and the 20-cent charge was increased to 40 cents. In 1878, the first federal quarantine law was passed to prevent the introduction of infectious diseases into the United States.)

16, Kenyon had decided not to go to college so he could study medicine with his father. (He went to medical school later.) The MHS focused on diseases that might be brought to America by crews on ships, particularly foreign ships. The MHS relied on consular offices in seaports around the world to give warnings about suspicious ships and their crews who might be carriers of disease.

Over Kenyon's 16 years as director—happily in parallel with major advances in microbiology and epidemiology—the nation's commitment to the world of public health expanded. Particular focus was on causes of epidemics, particularly cholera, yellow fever, plague, and smallpox. The final quarter of the 19th century saw a revolution in microbiology that revealed the causes of such dreaded diseases as malaria, typhoid fever, tuberculosis, cholera, diphtheria, botulism, and the plague. Kenyon's laboratory contributed significantly to the research that led to control of cholera and developed a series of effective vaccines to combat infectious diseases. In the early part of the 20th century, smallpox and diphtheria were virtually eliminated and typhoid fever was greatly curtailed.

In 1901, the Hygienic Laboratory was provided with its own building. Eleven years later, the name was changed to the Public Health Service, and research was explicitly made a focus. In 1929, two hospitals were built to care for drug addicts, and in 1930, the name was changed again to National Institute of Health. In 1944, the name was changed further to the plural: National *Institutes* of Health.

The National Cancer Institute was established in 1937, setting the prototype for the many specialist institutes to follow.[2] Then, in 1948, another specific disease-centered institute was established to study heart disease. Over the next decades, a series of disease-centered institutes were established.

---

[2] Donald C. Swarm, "The Rise of a Research Empire," *Science* 138, no. 3546 (December 14, 1962): 1233–1235.

FUNDING RESEARCH

The power of research-based knowledge to change lives led Congress to provide the NIH with more funding than requested by one American president after another. During the years of World War II, dramatic medical achievements advanced the case for medical research. Between 1943 and 1952, improvements in medical care were credited with adding over five full years to the life expectancy of Americans. Death rates from influenza fell by 77%, from appendicitis by 69%, and from tuberculosis by 50%.

As Doctor Howard Rusk explained, "As a result of these and other advances, the lives of 845,000 Americans have been saved in the last six years. They earned $1,488 million in 1952 and paid taxes of $284 million, which could be compared to $37 million spent on research that same year." While some questioned the directness of causal connection, nobody doubted the powerful favorable implication, particularly in Congress, where funding was strongly motivated by an appreciation of the desires of the American people for better health and longer lives. Also, of course, the rate of return on investment has been enormous and politically compelling.[3]

In the 1930s, there were no vaccines for many common childhood diseases. Viral research was new, and there were no blood transfusions. Air and water pollution were increasing, and there was little or no public education about health issues. Polio epidemics were terrifying communities across the nation. Typhus, typhoid, influenza, and tuberculosis seemed unstoppable. Fortunately, the small NIH staff was producing significant results and there was a virtual explosion in medical research. In 1938,

---

[3] *New York Times*, August 22, 1954.

leprosy, malaria, and 29 other chronic diseases were being investigated. Improved therapies were developed for one disease after another.

In the 1940s, many people would be nearly toothless by age 45, but with the right amount of fluoride, significant reductions in cavities would be achieved, as shown by NIH's Henry Dean. Fluoridation was soon adopted across America.

Mercury poisoning was a persistent problem for the hat industry, at a time when most men wore hats regularly. Hat makers used mercury salts in the process of converting wool fibers into hat material. Exposure made workers suffer various reactions, including serious mental illness—hence the expression "mad as a hatter." Scientists at the NIH figured out the safe level of mercury salts.

In 1946, the Research Grants Office was established to coordinate the rapidly growing extramural research and the following year, $11.5 million was divided among 1,115 grants. Congress liked being in control of how funds were spent and this contributed to a steady proliferation of disease-oriented institutes.

The Mental Health Institute budget in 1954 was $14.1 million, which was small compared to the $1.2 billion spent on care for the mentally ill. Heart disease research cost an estimated $166 million each year versus $16.6 *billion* in costs for care—not to mention the loss of earnings and taxes, which, of course, leaves out the personal losses involved.

ROLE OF CONGRESS

Congress has been remarkably active in its relationship with the NIH in recent decades, passing an average of 10 new pieces of enabling legislation each year. Organized as a division of the NIH, the National

Cancer Institute became a leader in extramural research. In 1951, grants to various extramural research organizations exceeded $16 million out of a total budget of $60 million.[4]

With the leadership of Dr. James Shannon, who took the helm in 1955, the NIH expanded substantially. The institute's budget exploded from $81 million to $1 billion over 13 years and the staff went up from 6,300 to 13,300. Salaries at the professor level increased from about equal to university professors to clearly higher. During Shannon's tenure, the NIH was involved in virtually every major medical advance, and Shannon increased the national interest in research by having NIH do even more research.

Biostatistics and cost-benefit analysis became an important common language for setting priorities for both intramural and extramural research management at the NIH in the early 1960s. Robert McNamara at the Defense Department was engaging in quantitative management such as program planning and output budgeting. President Kennedy wanted the same rigor applied in the way the NIH did business. The "benevolent tyranny" of biomedical statistics[5] became an integral part of medical research during the 1960s. Operations research provided an objective, quantitative basis for managerial decisions on the appropriate budgets for extramural research projects. This was particularly important for an organization that was so often caught in pressures from senators and congressional representatives in favor of their pet projects.

---

[4] In 1955, the amounts allocated to particular Institutes were $21 million to mental health, $14 million to heart, $2 million to dental, $8 million to arthritis, $8 million to neurological disease, and $6 million to microbiology. These amounts seemed small when compared with the $630 million costs of tubercular hospitals to serve those actually suffering the disease.

[5] Sepal Patel, "The Benevolent Tyranny of Biostatistics," *Bulletin of Historical Medicine* 87, no. 4, 2013: 622–624.

MAJOR OPPORTUNITY

As is so often the case, structure drives strategy at the NIH at least as much as strategy drives structure. As World War II was coming to a conclusion, a powerful drive was led by former MIT President Vannevar Bush.[6] Bush campaigned unsuccessfully to consolidate all science under one umbrella organization. (Presumably, he hoped to lead it.) Bush's National Science Foundation would have included the NIH.

Real estate has had a major influence on the NIH over the years. The NIH had outgrown the substantial two-story brick building built in 1919. In addition, the NIH needed more space for the many animals required for testing serums and vaccines and for research.

The NIH moved to its large center in Bethesda, Maryland in 1938. However, that move almost didn't happen. Fortunately, high-minded stubbornness by Luke and Helen Wilson, owners of a 70-acre estate that they called *Tree Tops* in Bethesda, Maryland, just north of Washington, DC, combined with the imaginative, persistent efforts of Dr. Lewis Thompson, who was not part of the NIH at the time but would soon go from being chief of the Division of Scientific Research at the Public Health Service to head of the NIH.

Thompson was the only one in the whole government who picked up an unusual opportunity. The Wilsons were interested in fostering improved international relationships.[7] The Wilsons' first thought was to establish a diplomatic school. This was the beginning of seven long years of efforts to give the Bethesda property to the nation. Then, they thought of an international think tank, but the Depression made this unrealistic. Next, they offered their 70 acres as a park, but were refused when they stipulated

---

[6] He had written compelling papers on the strategic importance of research and had performed brilliantly as a strategist for military research on various vital technologies such as radar and proximity fuses that were widely believed to have shortened the war.

[7] Luke Wilson, as head of an importer of a men's clothing company, had visited Europe by ship 88 times.

being able to continue living in their home. Their last thought was to train teachers of adult education, but their proposal letter got no reply. Finally, in 1934, they wrote to President Roosevelt offering their property to the government. Roosevelt circulated the letter around his administration. A few indicated some interest, but only Lewis Thompson took the initiative to meet with the Wilsons. His visit began an active courtship, assuring the Wilsons that the property would never be resold and that the work of the NIH would be for the benefit of all mankind. Once the Wilsons were satisfied, Thompson had to convince the neighbors that the "animal farm" would not change the atmosphere of the neighborhood.[8] When the Wilsons transferred the first 45 acres in 1935, this provided ample room for the expansion of the NIH.

CONCEPTS OF STRATEGY

Two concepts of research strategy have been in continuous competition at the NIH. One strategy relies on the scientific community to identify the most promising areas of research across many fields and select, through rigorous competition, the most promising investigators with the most promising projects and then fund them. The other strategy concentrates on particular kinds of disease, ensures strong funding, and then draws in the scientists and research initiatives that seem most promising. The most creative and successful scientists understandably favor the former. The public and Congress, also understandably, favor the focus on a specific disease, which is far easier for non-researchers to understand.

---

[8] Helen Wilson made light of their concerns at a gathering of neighbors: "There are only three reasons anyone would want to own an estate: You can raise chickens, raise children, or raise hell. I think we are a little too close to the highway for any of these so I decided to give the land to the government for NIH."

The most dramatic example of the goal-oriented specific disease strategy has long been cancer research. The most effective advocates of this strategy were not scientists or elected politicians, but two wealthy women: Mary Lasker and Florence Mahoney. Mrs. Mahoney, whose husband was publisher of the Cox newspaper chain, focused on creating an institute on aging; Mrs. Lasker focused on cancer research.[9]

After World War II, Lasker and Mahoney began to lobby for government-subsidized research, which was then both small and controversial. The NIH had only one institute. Fifty years later, the NIH had 27 institutes and a budget of $23.4 billion.

Mrs. Mahoney described her approach simply: "I start at the top." And by that, she meant she focused her efforts on the President: Truman, Eisenhower, Kennedy, and Johnson. One measure of their effectiveness: when told that Lasker and Mahoney wanted to see him, Johnson groaned, "Oh, my God, these two women are going to bankrupt this country!"[10]

Mary Lasker created a potent political force on behalf of cancer research. Her objectives and Shannon's were almost always aligned. That's why the Cancer Institute could get special budget authorization. Congress liked the idea that mission advocates were working for all Americans versus advocating for only one company or industry.

Equally important, Mary Lasker understood and obviously enjoyed the "dirty" work of cloakroom politics and was committed to a long game of unrelenting persuasion. She understood the importance of deploying legions of lobbyists. Lasker and Mahoney understood electoral politics and how to back winners. For example, they backed Claude Pepper for the

---

[9] Albert Lasker, a formidable leader in the growth of the advertising industry, made a substantial fortune. He and his wife Mary created the Lasker Foundation with an initial contribution of $50,000 to fund medical research. Mary Lasker joined the board of what is now the American Cancer Society with an agreement that one-fourth of the money she could raise would go into research. A formidable fundraiser, she and her husband raised $4 million in 1945, five *times* as much as the organization had raised before. And that was just the beginning.

[10] *New York Times*, December 12, 2002 Section B, p. 10.

Senate because he agreed with their belief in major government funding for research. (Lasker was an unsuccessful advocate of national health insurance and was unable to get the Cancer Institute separated from the NIH, but in 1971, she was able to get a special bypass budget that went directly to the President.[11])

The National Cancer Center is the oldest and largest unit in the NIH and in 2024 made 7,567 grants to more than 70 cancer research centers that totaled $4.2 billion. The NIH's funding of scientific research, particularly in cellular and molecular biology, has been remarkably effective.

GROWTH OF THE NIH

Because of the remarkable continuing success of the NIH research, public support and Congressional enthusiasm for funding advances in health, and the extraordinary rates of return on NIH research expenditures—estimated at between 25% and 40% per annum—the budget of the NIH has risen substantially and consistently from a modest base of just $707,000 in 1940 to an astounding $42 *billion* in the modern day:

- $52.7 million in 1950
- $399.3 million in 1960
- $1 billion in 1970
- $3 billion in 1980
- $7 billion in 1990
- $17 billion in 2000
- $31 billion in 2010
- $42 billion in 2020

---

[11] Robert Cook Deegan and Michael McGeary, *The Jewel in the Federal Crown* (Rutgers, NJ: Rutgers University Press, 2006).

Competition for NIH grants by some 54,000 applicants in a typical year is extraordinary. With peer-review decisions made by experts in each field, about 20% of the carefully documented applications are funded each year. (A special effort is made to encourage younger scientists to compete in hopes of encouraging them to pursue research careers.)

SELECTION PROCESS

Roughly 80% of grants each year are extramural with 50,000 grants going to 325,000 researchers at 3,400 institutions with a total tab of over $7 billion. A powerful measure of the effectiveness of the process: Of the 210 FDA-approved drugs developed in the period between 2010 and 2016, every one originated with an NIH research grant.

The NIH is organized to achieve perpetual success by focusing on excellence. When evaluating research proposals, peer review committees use this set of criteria:

1. High quality science as determined by rigorous peer review
2. Great potential to yield new knowledge
3. Maintains a diverse research portfolio that will produce major discoveries in the future
4. Addresses public health issues according to disease burden measured by mortality and prevalence
5. Supports scientific infrastructure and research laboratories

The NIH has been a great success: tackling the most serious medical issues with extraordinary objectivity *and* creativity that make science and scientists so highly regarded. Equally salient, the NIH has led international science in the discovery of cures for a panoply of diseases—adding years to the lives of people all over the world and happily improving the health of the living. In addition to these important human and social benefits, the financial rate of return on the NIH's quite large investments in biomedical research has been superb.

At this moment, when government funding for scientific research is under attack by the White House, one hopes that Congress will continue to make the investments in the phenomenally successful NIH that have had a remarkable return on the health of our nation—and beyond.

10

FOUNDATIONS

The remarkable size and number of public foundations in America are unique.[1] No other nation has anywhere near as many important foundations. Of course, tax policies relating to charitable deductions have been an important incentive. Thus, the American people have had a large, implicit role in fostering both public and private foundations. Foundations, guided by thoughtful trustees, bring an independent public-spirited energy to solving major problems at home and abroad.

Well before the Industrial Age, Ben Franklin set an example with his gifts of £1,000 to both Boston and Philadelphia, saying, "I wish to be useful even after my death, if possible." He had intended the money to be lent at interest to married apprentices, but in less than 100 years, there were no apprentices, so the funds had to be directed toward other purposes.

What may have been the first formal foundation in America—the endowment of the Smithsonian Institution—began with the 1838 arrival of an English lawyer named Richard Rush. He brought with him 11 boxes of gold sovereign coins then worth over $500,000 (over $16 million in today's dollars) that had been bequeathed in 1829 to America by the illegitimate

---

[1] Note that the world's largest foundation is in Denmark—the Novo Nordisk Foundation—which owns a controlling share in that drugmaker.

son of the Duke of Northumberland, James Smithson. Smithson never visited America.

John Quincy Adams led a campaign in the House of Representatives to ensure that the United States government accepted the bequest, and that its principal would be preserved in perpetuity. For Adams, it was an opportunity to establish a national astronomical observatory. There was no public funding for such a project on hand, and he hoped the bequest would first be used to propagate what he called *lighthouses of the skies*.[2] Adams envisioned that the principal of the fund would be preserved; it could be held as a loan to the US Treasury and collect 6% interest per annum.[3]

"Of all the foundations of establishments for pious or charitable uses, which ever signalized the spirit of the age, or the comprehensive beneficence of the founder," Adams wrote, "none can be named more deserving of the approbation of mankind than this." It was the "greatness and simplicity of Smithson's design" to promote knowledge that set the gift apart.

Finally, in 1846, Congress passed an act to establish the Smithsonian Institution, which would function as a model for future foundations. In 1867, the first Secretary of the Smithsonian advised George Peabody on how to set up his Peabody Education Fund in Baltimore. In 1904, the first general purpose foundation, the Carnegie Institution of Washington, also based its charter on the Smithsonian's.

ANDREW CARNEGIE

At the end of a brief 15-minute conversation that would herald an extraordinary transaction, J. P. Morgan took Andrew Carnegie's hand and

---

[2] *Memoirs of John Quincy Adams*, ed. Charles Francis Adams (Philadelphia: J. B. Lippincott, 1969), 789.
[3] John Quincy Adams to John Forsyth, October 8, 1838, *Memoirs of John Quincy Adam*, 842; Smithsonian Institution's charter: 29th Congress, 1st session, August 10, 1846.

said, "Mr. Carnegie, I want to congratulate you on being the richest man in the world."

Morgan had just agreed to meet Carnegie's price for his steel company, which would be the core of the United States Steel Corporation, the biggest company in America. Carnegie personally received $226 million—nearly $8 *billion* in today's dollars—in 5% gold mortgage bonds.

Carnegie was as active as a philanthropist as he was a pioneering businessperson. In both, he was a leader. Carnegie had decided to switch from accumulating wealth to wealth distribution. The former was not easy, but Carnegie had been unusually successful. The work of distribution would not be much easier, but Carnegie proved to excel at that, too.

Carnegie developed an interest in libraries years before his great transition and helped build one for the workers at the Homestead Works. Shortly after the major transaction with Morgan, Carnegie set up a relief fund for dependents of injured workers and established three libraries. In New York City during the early 1900s, Carnegie established 65 branches for its public library system. He declared his belief in facilitating self-improvement through reading and learning.

When word got out about the many New York libraries, "me too" requests came pouring in. So, Carnegie organized a system for responding positively to the many petitions. His process began with a series of relevant qualifying questions *and* a requirement that the municipality provide the land and commit to cover the costs of future operations. (While a third of the libraries incorporated the Carnegie name, this was not a requirement.) In 1901, he gave 132 library grants, in 1902, 128, and in 1903, 203. When Philadelphia requested funds for 30 branch libraries, Carnegie suggested the request should be augmented to provide for lecture rooms. Over his lifetime, Carnegie would give 1,419 grants totaling $60 million for libraries in the United States, 660 in Britain and Ireland, and 125 in Canada, 17 in New Zealand, and 12 in South Africa.

Believing workers and their families were more likely to be introduced to classical music in church, Carnegie also gave 7,689 organs to churches: 4,092 in the United States, 2,119 in England, and 1,005 in Scotland. Again, he organized and staffed a process to crank out the specific decisions within policy guidelines.

Andrew Carnegie's 11 Largest Philanthropic Initiatives		
Carnegie Corporation of New York	Support for higher education, libraries, research, and other Carnegie foundations	$125,000,000
Libraries	Provision of 2,811 public libraries	$60,365,000
Carnegie Foundation for the Advancement of Teaching	Pensions for teachers in higher education	$29,250,000
Carnegie Institution of Washington	Support for scientific research	$22,300,000
Colleges	Support for building and endowments of over 500 universities and colleges	$20,363,000
Carnegie Institute of Technology (Carnegie Mellon University)	Provision of applied technological education	$13,531,000
Carnegie Institute of Pittsburgh	Promotions of learning, scientific knowledge, and cultural activities	$13,188,000
Carnegie Hero Fund Commissions and other hero funds	Honor and reward citizens who risk their lives to save others in the United States and Europe	$10,540,000
Carnegie Trust for the Universities of Scotland	Support for Scottish universities and students	$10,000,000
Carnegie Endowment for International Peace	Advancement of understanding between nations to promote peace	$10,000,000
Carnegie United Kingdom Trust	Support for educational and social welfare provisions in UK	$10,000,000

Table based on Carnegie Endowment for International Peace, *A Manual of the Public Benefactions of Andrew Carnegie* (Berkeley, CA University of California Libraries, 1919). The total expenditure of $350.1 million, inflated by the United States consumer price index with 1901 (the year Carnegie cashed in his fortune) as base year, equated to $9.12 billion in 2009 prices. ("Purchasing Power of Money in the United States from 1774 to 2010," Measuring Worth, 2009. http://measuringworth.com/ppowerus.)

Carnegie certainly did not limit his activities to systemic philanthropy. He was a frequent speaker and wrote numerous articles and several books advancing his views. He also engaged vigorously with political leaders such as Benjamin Gladstone, particularly in his unrelenting campaign for peace, and for advocating arbitration of political issues.

Carnegie was born in Dunfermline, Scotland, in 1835, and sailed with his mother to America at age 13 after only two years of formal schooling. He mastered Morse code and started work at the Pennsylvania Railroad. At 30, he went into business and invested in railroads and bridges and capitalized on the Bessemer process for making steel for rails. He operated on an increasingly large scale because that reduced unit costs. Assertive leadership and acquisitions brought his company to industry dominance and the astronomical $492 million purchase by J. P. Morgan.

At age 33, Carnegie lamented, "To continue much longer overwhelmed by business cares and with my thoughts wholly upon the way to make more money in the shortest time, must degrade me beyond hope of permanent recovery." Spending only mornings on his business interests with the rest of his time and energy devoted to self-education, he developed personal connections with writers, politicians, and others—and wrote articles and books himself.

In "The Gospel of Wealth," Andrew Carnegie articulated his concept of how a wealthy person should, during his own lifetime, distribute that wealth. He was opposed to keeping it in the family and dubious about leaving a fortune for others to distribute. Carnegie explained his views:

The problem of our age is the proper administration of wealth, so that the ties of brotherhood may still bind together the rich and poor in a harmonious relationship. The conditions of human life have not only been changed, but revolutionized, within the past few hundred years. In former days there was little difference between the dwelling, dress, food, and environment of the chief and those of his retainers. The contrast between the palace of the millionaire and the cottage of the laborer with us today measures the change which has come with civilization. This change, however, is not to be deplored, but welcomed as highly beneficial. It is well, nay, essential for the progress of the race, that the houses of some should be homes for all that is highest and best in literature and the arts, and for all the refinements of civilization, rather than that none should be so. Much better is this great irregularity than universal squalor.

He continued:

The question then arises: What is the proper mode of administering wealth after the laws upon which civilization is founded have thrown it into the hands of the few? And it is of this great question that I believe I offer the true solution.

There are but three modes in which surplus wealth can be disposed of. It can be left to the families of the decedents; or it can be bequeathed for public purposes; or, finally, it can be administered during their lives by its possessors.

The question which forces itself upon thoughtful men in all lands is: Why should men leave great fortunes to their children? If this is done from affection, is it not misguided affection? Observation teaches that, it is not well for the children that they should be so burdened. The thoughtful man must shortly say, "I would as soon leave to my son a curse as the almighty dollar," and admit to himself that it is not the welfare of the children, but family pride, which inspires these enormous legacies.

As to the second mode, that of leaving wealth at death for public uses, it may be said that this is only a means for the disposal of wealth, provided a man is content to wait until he is dead before it becomes of much good in the world. Knowledge of the results of legacies bequeathed is not calculated to inspire the brightest hopes of much posthumous good being accomplished. Men who leave vast sums in this way may fairly be thought men who would not have left it at all, had they been able to take it with them. The man who dies leaving behind many millions of available wealth, which was his to administer during life, will pass away "unwept, unhonored, and unsung," no matter to what uses he leaves the dross which he cannot take with him. Of such as these the public verdict will then be: "*The man who dies thus rich, dies disgraced.*"

There remains, then, only one mode of using great fortunes; but in this we have the true antidote for the temporary unequal distribution of wealth, the reconciliation of the rich and the poor—a reign of harmony in which we shall have an ideal state, in which the surplus wealth of the few will become, in the best sense the property of the many, administered for the common good. This concentrated wealth can be made a much more potent force for the elevation of our race than if it had been distributed in small sums to the people themselves.

Rich men should be thankful for one inestimable boon. They have it in their power during their lives to busy themselves in organizing benefactions from which the masses of their fellows will derive lasting advantage, and thus dignify their own lives. In bestowing charity, the main consideration should be to help those who will help themselves; to provide part of the means by which those who desire to improve may do so. Neither the individual nor the race is improved by almsgiving.

Two examples of his work underscore the interest in helping those who would help themselves. First, the Carnegie Foundation for the Advancement of Teaching focused on university faculty members at a time when they didn't have pensions. His work benefitted not only those individuals but their academic institutions. It became the cornerstone of pension plans for faculty members, administered by TIAA and CREF. Second, his gift to four leading Scottish universities was centered on the novel concept of providing scholarships for fully half of their students.

ROCKEFELLER FOUNDATION

John D. Rockefeller, who at one time held the title of the world's richest man, had a hard time giving away a large part of his great fortune. A careful, patient, and deliberate man, Rockefeller had long given money to charities. In his teens, while earning $6 a month, he recorded giving 6% to Sunday school and to Baptist missions. As his earnings increased, so did his giving. Five years later, he gave, in addition to the Baptist church—to the Methodist church, a German Sunday school, and a church for African Americans. In 1865, when he was 26, his annual gifts were over $1,000, and four years later, they were nearly $6,000. As he explained years later, "From the beginning, I was trained to work, to save, and to give." As Rockefeller summed up his own creed, "A man should make all he can and give all he can."

He wrote a letter of congratulations to Andrew Carnegie when his "The Gospel of Wealth" was published in the *North American Review* in 1889. "I would that more men of wealth were doing as you are doing with your money, and the time will come when your example will bear fruits and men of wealth will more generally be willing to use it for the good of others."

On June 29, 1909, Rockefeller decided to give $50 million (today's equivalent of $1.6 billion) to establish the Rockefeller Foundation. Its mission was "to promote the well-being and to advance the civilization of the peoples of the United States—in the acquisition of knowledge, in the prevention and relief of suffering, and in the promotion of any and all of the elements of human progress."

Surely this was a major commitment to an inspiring purpose, but Congress would have none of it. Rockefeller sought, but was denied, a federal charter. The American people and their representatives in Congress did not trust Rockefeller. A storm of protest arose, and Rockefeller was publicly maligned. Over the next three years, a series of conditions were developed that reflected that distrust: The foundation couldn't own more than 10% of a company's stock: the selection of trustees would be subject to disapproval by holders of several specific federal offices; after 50 years, distribution of principal as well as income would be allowed and after 100 years required; income could not be accumulated; and the asset size of the foundation would be limited to $100 million.

Having failed to receive a federal charter, Rockefeller turned to New York State and got swift approval of all the accommodating changes he had made to mollify Congress. The declaration of mission was also simplified to "promote the wellbeing of mankind throughout the world."[4]

Immediately following the foundation's charter, Rockefeller contributed $35 million and a year later, another $65 million. (That combined $100 million would be $3.3 billion in today's dollars.) Over the next dozen years, he would give another $81 million and transfer to the foundation $59 million from the Laura Spellman Rockefeller Memorial. By 1929, Rockefeller's contributions totaled over $241 million—today's equivalent of roughly $8 billion. (The gifts were made in shares of stock with no obligation to retain them.)

When Frederick T. Gates, previously a Baptist minister—and for many years, the main adviser to Rockefeller in both business and philanthropy— wrote to say, "If any man's happiness in doing good depends on human gratitude or praise, that man's sun will go down at the end amid the clouds of disappointment and an embittered life." Rockefeller's swift response was, "Don't I *know* it!"

Gates declared that the foundation should "confine itself to projects of an important character, too large or otherwise unlikely to be undertaken by other agencies." As Rockefeller put it, "The best philanthropy involves a search for cause and an attempt to cure evils at their source." It was soon clear that the foundation itself should not be committed to managing programs, but focus on making enabling grants to those who had such expertise.

---

[4] Rockefeller had, as a matter of principle, refused to be a member of the governing board of the Rockefeller Institute or the General Education Board, and while he was formally a trustee of the Rockefeller Foundation for a few years, he never attended any meetings.

This led rather directly to a commitment of grants to eliminate hookworm, which was rampant in the American South. This great work was not easy to accomplish in 1910 due to lethargy within the medical profession and ignorance among the public. The cure, developed in Italy 25 years previously, was simple: capsules of thymol and salts taken over 18 hours and then wearing shoes.

Educating the public to recognize how widespread the debilitating disease had become was a critical challenge because the primary problem in combatting hookworm was an acute lack of knowledge. Only a minority of physicians knew about the disease and few of these recognized its importance. Among the few people who had heard of it, most thought it was something of a myth. However, Dr. Wickliffe Rose[5] and his associates found that 39% of the half a million children they examined suffered from the hookworm disease.[6]

Over time, Rose demonstrated that hookworm was rare beyond the wide belt between 36° north of the equator and 30° south *and* in regions with temperatures lower than 50° or less than 60 inches of rain. Rose also found that engaging governments rather than private agencies was important—an early example of the salience of public health. While the disease could never be entirely eliminated, it was brought down to such a low level of incidence that it was under control. Then, Dr. Rose and the Rockefeller Foundation went to work on yellow fever.

Yellow fever was first found in North America in 1668. Over the next 150 years, Philadelphia experienced 20 epidemics and New York 15. No preventive progress was achieved until the Spanish-American War, when Major Walter Reed demonstrated that yellow fever was distributed by the

---

[5] When the Rockefeller Sanitary Commission was merged into the foundation, it brought along Dr. Rose, who had already devoted five years to studying the disease.

[6] Hookworm larvae entered the body through bare feet, worked their way up through the blood stream to the intestines, multiplied and multiplied and then came out with stool to contaminate the soil where other barefoot kids would pick it up and the cycle would repeat and repeat. Victims' growth would be stunted, joints swollen, and lethargy would dominate their behavior.

Aedes aegypti mosquito. Vigorous use of anti-mosquito measures caused yellow fever virtually to disappear in Cuba. Three years later, similar measures were crucial to the construction of the Panama Canal. In the 1920s, yellow fever appeared to have been defeated and in 1925, only three cases were reported in the entire Western Hemisphere. Unfortunately, it came back. However, by 1937, the Rockefeller Foundation had succeeded in developing an effective vaccine and a year later, one million people were vaccinated. By the mid-1940s, 34 million doses of vaccine had been distributed and yellow fever was finally defeated.

Next, the foundation focused on malaria and increasing the wide use of mosquito netting and spraying. The Rockefeller Foundation then centered its efforts on developing the concepts of public health as an integral part of each major government's public service program.

These important successes in disease control led to a broad strategy of scientific research being used to achieve major advances in agriculture, the social sciences, and the humanities. The foundation's programs also expanded internationally—fulfilling the original "throughout the world" commitment. Over its first 40 years, the foundation was active in 93 different countries.[7]

At his last meeting as a trustee of the Rockefeller Foundation, Frederick T. Gates, who once described himself as "eager, imperious, insistent, and withal exacting and irritable" admonished the foundation's trustees, "When you die and approach the judgment of Almighty God, what do you think he will demand of you? Do you for an instant presume to think He will enquire into your petty failures or your trivial virtues? No! He will ask just one question: 'What did you do as a trustee of the Rockefeller Foundation?'"

---

[7] An interesting initiative of the Rockefeller Foundation was to sponsor, over many years, over 10,000 individual scholars who were recommended by their home institutions to do advanced research in their chosen fields.

FORD FOUNDATION

The Ford Foundation was created with Ford Motor Company stock, although the family retained all of the voting stock. In 1955, the foundation decided to sell Ford shares. Goldman Sachs, led by Sidney Weinberg, organized an enormous syndicate of 722 underwriters for the distribution of Ford stock. The share sale brought $643 million to the Ford Foundation. For comparison purposes, at the time only six other foundations had assets over $100 million and only 500 had over $1 million.

The Ford Foundation made an astounding commitment: to give out $500 million in just 18 months. The distribution was wholesale philanthropy: $210 million to help raise faculty pay at 615 liberal arts colleges and universities, $200 million to 3,500 nonprofit hospitals, and $90 million to 42 private medical schools.

In 1954, a staff of 240 at the Ford Foundation would dispense nearly $68 million—*four times* the grants of the Rockefeller Foundation and *10 times* those of the Carnegie Corporation—to 182 recipients.

BILL AND MELINDA GATES FOUNDATION

Microsoft cofounder Bill Gates took nearly everyone by surprise when he handed over the chief executive job to Steve Ballmer in early 2000, becoming the company's chairman and chief software architect. "I'm returning to what I love the most," Gates declared. (Skeptics suggested that a bruising antitrust battle Microsoft had just endured was a probable contributing factor.) Ten days later, Gates and his then-wife Melinda, gave an additional $5 billion to their namesake charitable foundation, making it the world's wealthiest.

In its first 25 years, the foundation has gave away more than $100 billion for global health, development, and education. It has supported vaccine development, malaria elimination, and many other causes. In May 2025, Bill Gates announced that the foundation will close in 2045—decades sooner than initially proposed—and intends to spend $200 billion over the next 20 years with an emphasis to "put the world on a path to ending preventable deaths of moms and babies."[8]

The Gates Foundation, with its large staff of experts, is one of the most deeply engaged in managing or guiding the programs to which it makes commitments. The Foundation's focus is on "primary problems that get too little attention." It seeks to address problems that are outside anyone's control and make it hard for individuals to reach their full potential—and seeks to give everyone an opportunity to lead healthy, productive lives. Of its charitable giving 90% is directed against disease, poverty, and inequity.

Relative to other foundations, the Gates Foundation is far more assertive or controlling. The traditional foundations allocate funds to the most promising applicants' proposals, expecting to select the "best of the best." The Gates Foundation goes the other way: It decides the problem it wants to attack and designs the action program; it then seeks the best subcontractors and manages them and the overall program closely.

Large foundations are an American phenomenon partly because wealthy people encourage other wealthy people to give. The best example may be the Giving Pledge, developed by Gates and Warren Buffett, where extraordinarily wealthy people publicly pledge to give 50% of their assets to charities. It has since established a model of lifetime giving as influential as Carnegie's "Gospel of Wealth."

Warren Buffett and Bill Gates met in 1991 and soon became friends and developed a remarkably close relationship with visits back and forth. In 2004, Gates agreed to serve on Berkshire Hathaway's board of directors. Buffett, who had always intended to give 99% of his wealth to charity, flew to New York City on June 26, 2006, to announce that he intended to make the Gates

---

[8] "Gates Doubles Down," *Financial Times*, May 9, 2025, 15.

Foundation the principal recipient of his personal fortune, which was then about $44 billion. (The three Buffett children each had a smaller foundation and Buffett also had a foundation named in honor of his deceased wife, Susan.)

Buffett had three requirements: Bill and Melinda Gates would continue to be active in the foundation (they divorced later and she left the foundation); that funds coming from Buffett each year would qualify as charitable dollars, not gifts; and that those contributions would be given away during the year. Between 2006 and 2023, Warren Buffett gave $39 billion to the foundation. Already the world's largest, the foundation had to scramble to keep up with its payout requirements of more than $3 billion each year.

After the Gates' divorce, Buffett left the board of the foundation, explaining that while he would continue his contributions during his lifetime, the foundation should not plan on a major testamentary addition.

With his assets rising above $100 billion, Buffett announced that he planned to entrust his three children with the responsibility to decide how his great fortune would be distributed. It is widely assumed that it will not go to the Gates Foundation.

MACKENZIE SCOTT

Great fortunes have been created through technology in the last 50 years. A new kind of philanthropy that is on a major institutional scale but clearly personal and private has been created by MacKenzie Scott, the former wife of Amazon founder Jeff Bezos. Scott distributed in only a few years $12.5 billion in 1,257 grants, of which the largest, $436 million, went to Habitat for Humanity. With personal assets of about $50 billion, Scott clearly has the financial capacity to continue being "a major force for good," as she puts it, "until the well runs dry."

Scott's approach is certainly unusual. Preservation of her privacy is important, and no grant applications are accepted. Thank you messages are not wanted. She dislikes the term *philanthropy* and what it implies about donors. To assure privacy, she works through donor-advised funds.

During her growing up years, she had experienced money troubles. Her stockbroker father went broke while she was at Hotchkiss, but she got a Princeton scholarship. As a creative writer, she bonded with and was encouraged by Toni Morrison, who was teaching at Princeton. After graduation, she worked at an investment firm where she met and then married Jeff Bezos who came up with the idea of selling books via the internet. They moved to Seattle to launch Amazon in 1994 and she published two novels: *Traps* and *The Testing of Luther Albright*.

As Amazon exploded in scale, scope, and, of course, profitability, the Bezos couple pledged funds to launch a Montessori preschool in 2018. A year later, they divorced. Within a year, Ms. Scott declared her intention to give not just the 50% of the Giving Pledge but "until the safe is empty."

Foundations are Great American Investments that have been propelled by federal tax incentives and by individuals' sense of improving society. With great fortunes being made in America, we must hope that new foundations will continue to be created. Many are on an enormous scale, and several are taking a vigorous and rigorously disciplined approach to their work. The consequences promise to be extraordinarily beneficial to our nation and the American people—and to the world.

* * *

These sources have been particularly helpful in this chapter:

- David Nasaw, *Andrew Carnegie* (New York: Penguin, 2006).
- Raymond B. Fosdick, *The Story of The Rockefeller Foundation* (New York: Harper Brothers, 1952).
- Dwight Macdonald, *The Ford Foundation* (New York: Reynal & Company, 1956).
- Alan J. Pifer, *Philanthropy in an Age of Transition* (New York: Foundation Center, 1984).

11

THE NATIONAL GALLERY OF ART

The National Gallery of Art is the result not of government but of one man's determination. Andrew Mellon, then one of the nation's richest men, created his fortune by imaginative investing in several companies that became leaders in the era's growth industries: oil and aluminum. Ironically, the core of this capitalist's collection came from the sale of art treasures by the communist leader of the Soviet Union, Joseph Stalin.

The National Gallery of Art is one of the best of the several dozen great art galleries that grace America and are complemented by well over 200 smaller regional or specialized or university art galleries. Taken together, they harbor over a million works of art recognized as among the world's best. So many other great paintings, sculptures, and portraits are still in private hands, but over time, many, if not most of them, will likely flow into the public galleries.

The National Gallery of Art in Washington, DC, is an example of this continuing phenomenon. It came into being at a small gathering featuring two remarkably powerful men who were traditionally direct opponents and had only one thing in common: They were both well known to the American public.

One had been Secretary of the Treasury under three successive presidents—widely celebrated as the greatest secretary since Alexander Hamilton—*and,* later, was the American ambassador to the Court of St. James. Andrew Mellon's public service came after he had built a great fortune in Gulf Oil, Alcoa, Koppers, and banking. A conservative Republican, he believed deeply that the nation's economic system had achieved well-deserved success after success and, while suffering in the Depression, would surely work out of its temporary problems if only left free to do so.

The other man—Franklin Delano Roosevelt—was wealthy by inheritance, widely celebrated as a master politician, and at the peak of his great powers as President. A vigorous New Deal Democrat, he was determined to experiment boldly to change the basic economic system he believed had been failing the American people.

While these two men did not know each other personally, both had had ample opportunity to develop strong views of each other—views of distrust, dislike, and disdain.

BUILDING A GREAT FORTUNE

Andrew Mellon was born in 1855 and, during an era of great growth in the American economy, was one of the nation's most successful industrialists. His father, known as Judge Mellon, had made a solid fortune in law and banking of $2.5 million (or $30 million in today's currency). From 1890 on, Andrew Mellon and his brother were responsible for the family's finances. The brothers worked closely together and had adjoining offices. Well into his forties, Andrew Mellon was "all business." Businessmen in

Pittsburgh recognized Andrew as the more skilled and more adventurous of the two Mellon Brothers, "If you want to borrow $5,000, see Dick: if you want to borrow $25,000, see Andy."

In the late 1890s, Andrew Mellon, groomed to be a private banker, saw the moment, seized the opportunity, and took his chance with an impressive combination of calculated aggression, right timing, and cool nerve that transformed him overnight into a leader in Pittsburgh. Backing inventive pioneers in converting bauxite into aluminum, Mellon became the major owner of Alcoa, the Aluminum Corporation of America. A venture into steel was a swift success in both Carborundum and Crucible Steel. He also made a bold move in coal that succeeded greatly.

Andrew Mellon and his brother got into the oil business almost by accident. They then got a lucky break with Spindletop, capitalized on a 400-mile pipeline, and bought out a floundering capitalist to become dominant shareholders in what would become Gulf Oil. Years later, Gulf would be earning $20 million a year. The Mellon brothers owned a comfortable majority of Gulf Oil and were major owners of Alcoa, Westinghouse, and other companies.

In May 1912, the federal government charged Alcoa with restraint of trade in its business practices. But when Alcoa agreed to "play fair" in the future, charges were dropped. This would not be the last confrontation between the government and Andrew Mellon.

GETTING STARTED IN ART

About this time, Knoedler & Company, the art dealers, opened an office in Pittsburgh and began decorating the walls of homes and offices of wealthy citizens, including the Mellon brothers. Andrew Mellon had shown no particular interest in art, but bought several paintings as gifts for members of his family.

By 1905, Mellon was worth $50 million, equal to $1.8 billion in today's currency. He was also beginning to buy more expensive paintings from Knoedler, including a Romney portrait of Miss Willoughby that would later be on display at the National Gallery.

As Mellon built his fortune, his interest in collecting great art grew even more rapidly. By 1915, Mellon would be worth $100 million or the equivalent today of $3.2 billion. He became an increasingly important client of Knoedler's and also began dealing with Joseph Duveen, as did his Pittsburgh friend Henry Clay Frick who introduced them and told Duveen that Mellon would be "the greatest collector of us all."

Duveen intended to make that happen, of course, and to make himself the primary helper. He would use his extraordinary personal charm, bribes to members of the Mellon household, and great theatrical pronouncements about what was great about specific paintings he was proud to be able to offer.

Mellon was poker-faced in negotiations and a hard bargainer on prices. He was also, as the years passed, gaining greater confidence in his own judgment of art and valuations.

PUBLIC SERVICE

As a loyal and generous Republican, Mellon was consequently a major power in Pennsylvania politics. With the election of Warren Harding, a movement developed to make Mellon, already America's leading financier, Secretary of the Treasury. Appointing a prominent businessman to that great office was certainly not the norm, but on March 5, 1921, Andrew Mellon became Treasury Secretary. He was 65 and on his first day as Secretary got to his office at eight—a full hour before his staff came in to work.

With wartime expenditures during World War I, the national debt had leaped from $2 billion to $26 billion, and with two million demobilized troops and a sharp drop in consumer demand, the post-war economy predictably fell into recession. The international situation was dire and clearing international debts would be a major focus of Mellon's work; he would continue as Treasury Secretary for three Presidents—all Republicans.

As the economy flourished in the 1920s, many saw Treasury Secretary Mellon as the principal guide to keeping "the good times rolling," and he was widely regarded as the administration's star. Honorary degrees from the nation's leading universities were one of many indicators of his national stature.

When Calvin Coolidge was President, Mellon's standing rose even higher. Budget surpluses enabled Mellon to reduce the federal debt significantly. Meanwhile, his income continued to rise and he was ranked third behind only John D. Rockefeller and Henry Ford in taxes paid.

Mellon introduced the smaller-sized dollar bill that is now familiar as an economy move: The smaller bills would be folded less often and so were replaced less frequently. This would save $2 million a year. He would also take responsibility for the design and construction of the large new government buildings that made up the commanding complex in Washington now known and admired as the Federal Triangle.

With Hoover's overwhelming election, Mellon, at 73, might have chosen to retire but he decided to stay on at the Treasury. Mellon was becoming a major buyer of art, but was changing his vision—with Duveen's strong encouragement—from creating a great *personal* collection to assembling a comprehensive *public* collection that would be well suited to his vision of a National Gallery for the country; 1928 was the peak year of his acquisitions.

The stock market crash and the Great Depression would change the nation and Mellon's reputation for good judgment and financial wisdom. He opposed the Bonus Bill and saw recessions as just an inevitable part of long-term economic growth. In 1931, Mellon's annual personal income peaked at $8.8 million.

A MAJOR OPPORTUNITY

The Hermitage collection of art—begun by Catherine the Great and then expanded considerably—was one of the greatest art collections in the world. In 1930, to raise the money Stalin needed to transform the Soviet economy, important parts of the collection would be for sale. Two major conditions were imposed: Absolute secrecy and only the best works would be sold. A third requirement would be particularly daunting for Mellon: The pictures could not be inspected—a cautious buyer's practice Mellon had always insisted on in his past acquisitions.

The enormous transaction would be from a "highly motivated" seller to a "motivated" buyer. In his first major transaction with Russia, Mellon acquired more than 20 fine paintings through Knoedler at a cost of over $2 million. In the end, Mellon acquired nearly all of the 50 greatest paintings in the Hermitage at a cost of nearly $7 million. (In current dollars *and* in today's art market, that would be close to $200 million.)

At this same time, Mellon's public reputation fell off sharply, second only to Hoover's. He was suddenly reviled widely in America. It was time to get away. Fortunately, Hoover appointed him to be ambassador to the Court of St. James's in 1932. Mellon knew the United Kingdom as a regular visitor over more than 30 years and was already on friendly terms with the royal family, the cabinet, and the business community.

LAWSUIT AND TAXES

Mellon left behind a rapidly falling public reputation, symbolized by a scathing, muckraking "expose," *Mellon's Millions*. FDR would publicly single out Mellon as "the mastermind among the malefactors of great wealth." The Internal Revenue Service (IRS) would open a major lawsuit, claiming that Mellon owed far more in taxes than he had paid. (The connection between FDR and the IRS suit was too obvious to ignore.)

FDR's government had been vigorously prosecuting Mellon for alleged fraud and evasion of large taxes. For Mellon, a financial leader who prized his reputation for probity and always kept meticulous records, this confrontation had been particularly upsetting. He had no reason to doubt that it was both political and personal.

Difficulties with the IRS increased as the amount due *plus* a 50% penalty charge rose to more than $100 million (in current dollars).[1] In addition to the increase in dollars, the formal legal charges were increased to deliberate fraud. This offended Mellon deeply. "I will spend the rest of my life in jail rather than admit to knowingly falsifying my tax return!"

Robert Jackson (later appointed to the Supreme Court and the lead prosecutor at the Nuremberg trials of Nazi war criminals) was in charge of the government's case. Jackson was inclined to agree with Mellon that private negotiations would be sensible, but FDR authorized the attorney general to press ahead with the public fraud charges. The long trial lasted from February 1935 to May 1936. Mellon was not convicted.

The two great men met by arrangement in the White House library where tea was served on December 31, 1936. Andrew Mellon's objective was to realize his ambition: to give his extraordinary collection of art to the American people and to do so on his own terms. Those terms he had developed thoughtfully and would insist on the name, the location, the design, the governance, and the mission.

If Andrew Mellon had his way, the National Gallery would be designed by John Russell Pope and built across the Mall from the complex of handsome government office buildings that Secretary Mellon had supervised during their construction. Mellon's gift to the nation would include a

---

[1] Only during the tax trial was Mellon's great plan of national benefaction made known. During the tax trial, Mellon's lawyer, Frank Hogan, made good use of the obvious dichotomy: "It is impossible to conceive of a man planning such benefactions and at the same time scheming to defraud his government."

substantial endowment so the great gallery would not be subject to the budgeting or short-term whims of politicians or economics.[2]

Franklin Roosevelt was loath to enable Mellon, whom he had attacked so vehemently and publicly, to achieve or attain a special status as an extraordinarily generous man of high standards who had done great good for his country and deserved the nation's respect and appreciation.

While Roosevelt was notorious for changing his mind and enabling various people to believe they knew his wishes, Mellon had an equally well-earned reputation for hard bargaining and holding others accountable for adhering to agreements he had made. For the meeting, Mellon brought with him a formal letter to FDR that presented the terms of his extraordinary gift to the nation.

The meeting took less than an hour. FDR agreed to every one of Andrew Mellon's terms. The National Gallery of Art would present Mellon's great collection and, in time, the collections of other future donors, particularly Chester Dale and Samuel Kress.[3]

> The National Gallery of Art is one of the many public art collections that grace America. Taken as a group, they equal all the other public collections of the rest of the world. We have to hope that a large part of the nation's private art collections will, in the years ahead, add substantially to the public collections.

* * *

---

[2] Mellon drove a hard bargain. By calling the building the National Gallery of Art, he was appropriating a name already attached to a bureau of the Smithsonian. He insisted that the funds and pictures come from the A. W. Mellon Educational & Charitable Trust, where he had already deposited them, rather than from his personal fortune, even though the Roosevelt administration was still contesting the bona fides of the trust. And in seeking to establish a board of nine trustees, five of whom would be private citizens and "general trustees," all initially to be appointed by Mellon, he ensured that overall operation of the gallery would be independent of the federal government, although it was technically part of the Smithsonian and dependent on Congress for its upkeep. On all these points, Mellon would eventually get his way, largely because, as Cummings informed FDR, his lawyers "assumed, and adhered to the position, that as Mr. Mellon was making the gift, he was entitled to dictate the terms thereof."

[3] David Finley was there at Mellon's request and Homer Cummings, the attorney general, was there at Roosevelt's.

The following sources were particularly helpful for this chapter:

- David Cannadine, *Mellon: An American Life* (New York: Vintage, 2021).
- Philip Love, *Andrew W. Mellon* (Baltimore: F. Heath Coggins, 1929).
- Harvey O'Connor, *Mellon's Millions* (New York: John Day Company, 1933).

12

NASA

The exploration of space, the moon, and the planets had been a fascination for millennia, but it was only in the last century that our country began to tackle it seriously. President Eisenhower, who enjoyed serious discussions with scientists, had favored unmanned exploration because of his concern for costs. President Kennedy, while originally a skeptic, saw manned space exploration as the most powerful way to demonstrate to the world the excitement of space exploration and America's leadership in technology.

WHAM!

In September 2022, at a speed over 14,000 miles per hour, the 1,300-pound DART—launched by NASA—slammed into the 523-foot wide asteroid named Dimorphos,[1] which was traveling at nearly 30,000 miles per hour seven million miles from earth.

---

[1] NASA chose its target because, while orbiting the sun, it also orbits a larger asteroid—Didymos—every 12 hours. NASA's initial calculations indicated that the impact would change the orbiting time by 10–15 minutes. The actual result achieved was a reduction of 32 minutes. The impact was measured by Hubble—*and* by 45 other telescopes around the world. The DART (Double Asteroid Redirection Test) cost $325 million.

NASA's goal: to see whether it could, if ever needed, deflect a life-threatening asteroid hundreds of miles from earth if it were heading toward us. While NASA said there is no chance of earth being hit in the next few hundred years by anything like the 10-kilometer-wide asteroid that had wiped out the dinosaurs 65 million years ago, thousands of "near earth" objects could be devastating to large areas of earth if they ever hit our planet.

While NASA's most publicized efforts were in its early decades, the agency continues to undertake important scientific work. On December 27, 2024, NASA announced another amazing achievement: Its Parker Solar Probe had passed the sun at a speed of 430,000 miles per hour, just 4% of the distance from sun to the earth of 93 million miles. This project sought to understand the solar winds and why the sun's atmosphere is hundreds of times hotter than its surface.

* * *

President Eisenhower and his scientific advisors believed unmanned exploration would be much cheaper and less challenging and therefore could move ahead faster. So, Eisenhower favored unmanned instruments when probing space.

President Kennedy came to see human space exploration differently. Accepting the costs and risks of the commitment, he challenged the nation to the dramatic goal of landing a person on the moon.

Kennedy believed America faced a formidable challenge from the Soviet Union. He recognized that his nation was in a multidimensional competition with a powerful and aggressive adversary. Specific events were, he believed, woven together into an overall fabric of competition for the confidence of the world's people. (A few months after Kennedy's inauguration, Soviet cosmonaut Yuri Gagarin had flown into space *and* the Bay of Pigs fiasco had occurred.)

Kennedy went in-person before Congress to deliver his challenge to America[2]:

> I believe that this nation should commit itself to achieving the goal, before this decade is out, of landing a man on the moon and returning him safely to the earth. No single space project in this period will be more impressive to mankind, or more important for the long-range exploration of space—and none will be so difficult or expensive to accomplish.
>
> Let it be clear—and this is a judgment which the Members of the Congress must finally make. Let it be clear that I am asking the Congress and the country to accept a firm commitment to a new course of action, a course which will last for many years and carry very heavy costs.

He went on to describe that it would entail $531 million in fiscal '62—and an estimated seven to nine billion dollars additional over the next five years.

On September 12, 1962, President Kennedy again challenged the nation in his speech at Rice University[3]:

> The exploration of space will go ahead, whether we join in it or not. It is one of the great adventures of all time, and no nation which expects to be the leader of other nations can expect to stay behind in the race for space.

---

[2] President John F. Kennedy before a joint session of Congress on May 25, 1961.

[3] Kennedy began with an analogy of time and history: "No man can fully grasp how far and how fast we have come, but condense the 50,000 years of man's recorded history in a time span of but a half century. Stated in these terms, we know very little about the first 40 years, except at the end of them advanced man had learned to use the skins of animals to cover them. Then, about 10 years ago, under this standard, man emerged from his caves to construct other kinds of shelter. Only five years ago, man learned to write and use a cart with wheels. Christianity began less than two years ago. The printing press came this year, and then less than two months ago, during this whole 50-year span of human history, the steam engine provided a new source of power. Newton explored the meaning of gravity. Last month, electric lights and telephones and automobiles and airplanes became available. Only last week did we develop penicillin and television and nuclear power, and now, if America's new spacecraft succeeds in reaching Venus, we will have literally reached the stars before midnight tonight.

This is a breathtaking pace, and such a pace cannot help but create new ills as it dispels old, new ignorance, new problems, new dangers. Surely, the opening vistas of space promise high costs and hardships, as well as high reward."

For space science, like nuclear science and all technology, has no conscience of its own. Whether it will become a force for good or ill depends on man, and only if the United States occupies a position of preeminence can we help decide whether this new ocean will be a sea of peace or a new, terrifying theater of war.

We choose to go to the moon. We choose to go to the moon in this decade and do the other things, not because they are easy, but because they are hard, because that goal will serve to organize and measure the best of our energies and skills, because that challenge is one that we are willing to accept, one we are unwilling to postpone, and one which we intend to win.

We shall send to the moon, 240,000 miles away from the control station in Houston, a giant rocket more than 300 feet tall, made of new metal alloys, some of which have not yet been invented, capable of standing heat and stresses several times more than have ever been experienced, to an unknown celestial body—and then return it safely to Earth, reentering the atmosphere at speeds of over 25,000 miles per hour, causing heat about half that of the temperature of the sun and do all this, and do it right, and do it first before this decade is out—then we must be bold.

Apollo—the name adopted for the moon project—was one of the most expensive American scientific programs ever undertaken. It cost $25.8 billion in 1960 dollars or an estimated $257 billion in present-day dollars. (In comparison, the Manhattan Project cost roughly $44.5 billion after accounting for inflation.) *Apollo* pushed NASA costs up over 5% of the federal budget, but since then, NASA has represented closer to 1%.

Since *Apollo*, NASA has launched over 1,000 uncrewed missions. *Viking* landed on Mars in 1976, and 20 years later a rover was landed on Mars by *Mars Pathfinder*. *New Horizons* was launched in 2006 and did a successful flyby of Pluto in 2015.

Calculating the economic returns on NASA's enormous investments would, of course, be difficult. Astronomers want to understand how and when galaxies were formed in the early universe. How this has led to tangible economic benefits is, at present, anyone's guess. Some of the perceived value of NASA's explorations of space includes wonderfully practical and priceless advances such as GPS. Some of the value has come to us as an ultra form of inspiration, such as Neil Armstrong's landing on the moon, an experience that those of us who witnessed the event via live television will never forget. Some of the value has come in "national prestige" for America as "the leader of the free world," and some has come in such unexpected ways as measuring the distance to the hole in golf. The concept of space travel has permeated American culture and society: media such as Star Wars, Star Trek, and expressions like *moonshot*.

For over half a century, the cost of NASA as a fraction of the national budget has declined as the American economy has grown substantially. In the years ahead, the competition in space will likely expand as the multiplicity of issues relating to space defense and global security grow. Still, the importance of space exploration and the scientific insights it produces deserve continuing support.

13

THE INTERNET

The internet began as an initiative within the Department of Defense. It is a classic example of the right action at the right time because the right people knew the right people and brought them together in the right way. Financial funding was only $1 million. The communication benefits—at extremely low cost—have certainly been enormous, both socially and economically.

n 1945, Vannevar Bush produced a report at Franklin D. Roosevelt's request that was delivered to Harry Truman with a deliberately compelling title: "Science, the Endless Frontier." His main message: Basic research provides the scientific capital from which the practical applications of knowledge can be drawn. By the end of his report, he was ready to conclude, "Advances in science when put to practical use mean more jobs, higher wages, shorter hours, more abundant crops, more leisure for recreation, for study, for learning how to live without the demeaning drudgery which has been the burden of the common man for years past."[1] The

---

[1] Establishing the National Science Foundation was the Congressional response to his report. By 2010, federal research was only half the amount spent by private industry.

commitment to basic science has helped produce many advances in technology. One advance is the internet.

The internet came into being in a way that is typical of major breakaway innovations: Changes in technology create a new possibility; extraordinarily talented pioneers are looking for and notice that possibility; they connect with a few other highly talented thought leaders they happen to know—or go looking for them; seed money is available; and one step leads to another in ways that seem logical in retrospect. In reality, however, the whole process depends on the creative determination of very specific people who connect with other specific people to drive the process of taking advantage of opportunities to advance toward an intuitively appreciated but as yet unknown or even unknowable direction based on hunches, experience, creative intuition, and, of course, the courage of all great explorers.

BACKGROUND

Before the beginning of the process that would develop the internet, computing in the early 1960s depended on punch cards—3½ × 5½-inch paper cards in which holes were punched as a way of recording data—and batch processing in which hundreds or even thousands of punch cards were processed at high speeds. Everyone involved in the field "knew" that batch processing was the only way to use a digital computer.

That, of course, meant that the very idea of a symbiotic human interaction with a computer was simply inconceivable. Another limiting reality was that each manufacturer had a different way of designing its computers so everybody "knew" computers of one manufacturer could not be made to communicate with those of any other manufacturer. Finally, there were capacity limits: The more advanced users of computers were using them all the time so their computers were fully booked—and any new and unproven use would be considered a threat to the agreed system. All these factors made for great stability and agreement on capacity limits *and* concepts of computing reality—but all this would change greatly.

LICK'S ASSERTION

Joseph Carl Robnett Licklider, widely known as *Lick*, was responsible for two of the important concepts on which the internet would be based. The first of those two concepts was that decentralized networks would facilitate the distribution of information to and from anywhere. This was the key technologically. The other vital key was the interface that would facilitate human-machine interaction in real time. Licklider also made a vital contribution by *not* agreeing with those who felt that as computers became increasingly powerful, the requirements for individuals would fade. Licklider believed correctly that the more powerful the computers, the more capable the people would need to be. Licklider was also important in obtaining federal funding—twice.

A cascade of changes would begin with the publication in March 1960 of an extraordinarily prescient article that Licklider[2] titled "Man-Computer Symbiosis." Licklider wrote that "man-computer symbiosis is an expected development of cooperative interaction between men and electronic computers. It will involve very close coupling between the human and the electronic members of the partnership. The main aims are: (1) to let computers facilitate formulative thinking as they now facilitate the solution of formulated problems and, (2) to enable men and computers to cooperate in making decisions and controlling complex situations without inflexible dependence on predetermined programs. In the anticipated symbiotic

---

[2] Joseph Licklider, "IRS Transactions on Human Factors," *Electronics* (March 1960): 4–11.

partnership, men will set the goals, formulate the hypotheses, determine the criteria, and perform the evaluations."

To clarify the symbiosis he envisioned, Licklider used the fig tree as an illustration: "The fig tree is pollinated only by the insect *Blastophaga grossorum*. The larva of the insect lives in the ovary of the fig tree, and there it gets its food. The tree and the insect are thus heavily interdependent: the tree cannot reproduce without the insect; the insect cannot eat without the tree; together, they constitute not only a viable, but a productive and thriving partnership. This cooperative 'living together in intimate association', or even close union, of two dissimilar organisms is called symbiosis."

Licklider anticipated his man-machine partnerships would perform intellectual operations much more effectively. He went on to say, "Prerequisites for this achievement of effective cooperative association include developments in computer time sharing, memory components, memory organization, programming languages, and in input and output equipment."

This, of course, was a daunting agenda of work to be done to keep up with and control the cascade of changes that Licklider assured his astonished readers were coming their way. Licklider continued: "Man-computer symbiosis is a subclass of man-machine systems. There are many man-machine systems. At present, however, there are no man-computer symbioses. If we focus on the human operator within the system, we see that, in some areas of technology, a fantastic change has taken place during the last few years. 'Mechanical extension' has given way to replacement of men—to automation—and the men who remain are there more to help than to be helped."

GETTING ORGANIZED

Licklider believed strongly in collaboration, particularly over long distances. He was a skillful searcher for raw talent, particularly when creativity was needed. He loved sharing ideas. Trained as a psychologist, he formulated theories about how symbiotic relationships could develop between people and machines and wrote about how human brains and computers could work in partnerships in ways nobody had ever conceived.

Licklider was recruited to the Advanced Research Project Agency or ARPA, in 1962.

Always humorous, he wrote another seminal paper deliberately titled all too grandly: "The Intergalactic Computer Network."[3] Licklider wrote, "Conceptually, it could be used simultaneously by many users doing many different things." This insight led numerous people to think differently about computers and networks.

Licklider thought of networks on three different levels: equipment networks, people networks, and information resources that could be focused on larger cognitive goals far beyond the capacity of individuals. As he explained: "Any present-day large-scale computer is too fast and too costly for real-time cooperative thinking with one man. Clearly, for the sake of efficiency and economy, the computer must divide its time among many users. Timesharing systems are currently under active development."

In 1962, Licklider was assigned to run a key program, which he saw as having two parts: (1) machine processing of information and (2) making that information useful for decisions.

In the early 1960s, Licklider and ARPA[4] got three research centers to start time sharing as an experiment and provided terminals to a few highly skilled individuals who were game to experiment. They connected with a few others in similar circumstances and all began to use their terminals to communicate with each other within their own workgroup. But they were limited to their particular geographic location: Nobody then imagined what would later be known as *distributed networks.*

---

[3] Eisenhower liked the rational thinking of scientists and frequently brought them together in the White House.

[4] In 1959, U-2 flights over the USSR showed that it was deploying ICBMs and ARPA was directed to determine how to deal with systems prone to instability such as the Cuban missile confrontation in 1962.

Paul Baran at RAND developed a distributed communications system based on message blocks. This was recognized by Len Kleinrock, who was then finishing his PhD at MIT and would help ARPA incorporate that capability into its strategy—a major advance toward Licklider's concept. They combined their thinking into a coherent concept that was then translated into a prototype network. By the end of the 1960s, a network was in operation with 16 nodes—and 7 more were added in early 1970. By 1974, 75% of the traffic was emails. Cooperative problem-solving became the main motivation for using the network, and the precursor to the internet was established!

An illustration of the importance of people-to-people connections was the linking of Licklider at NASA with Bob Taylor, who had just finished graduate school in psychoacoustics.[5] Taylor recognized Licklider as an expert in psychoacoustics. Licklider recognized Taylor's talent so he recruited Taylor as his "number 3" guy. When Licklider's "number 2" left soon after, Taylor, who was decisive on decisions based on rational analysis and recognized by his colleagues as consistently fair, advanced to lead the unit.

Taylor had three contractors he was working with, so he had three terminals at his office. One day, he wondered why he had to download information from one and upload that information to another instead of getting them to communicate directly with each other.

Nice abstract question, but Taylor got lots of resistance. So, he went to see Charlie Herzfeld who was heading ARPA and explained his idea in just 20 minutes—and immediately got the $1 million investment he needed. Taylor liked to emphasize the critical importance of Licklider going to ARPA and bringing with him all the connections that he had developed over the years with exceptionally talented people.

---

[5] In 1966, Taylor came up with the idea of developing a national network of computers.

In 1966, Taylor went after Larry Roberts, a leader in both electrical engineering and computers, but Roberts said he wasn't interested. He wanted to stay at Lincoln Labs where he was doing interesting work. Roberts couldn't find anyone as good, so he persisted until, in frustration, it dawned on him that more than half of Lincoln Lab's funding was coming from ARPA. So, he went to Herzfeld and got him to call his friend—who headed Lincoln Labs—and say that it was in Lincoln Lab's best interest *and* Larry Roberts's best interest if Roberts took the job at ARPA. Two weeks later, Roberts accepted. At about this stage in the development, "institutionalists" threatened to strangulate progress. Larry Roberts, fortunately, came to the rescue.

COMBINING KEY PARTS

Roberts was thinking of a major facility in the middle of the country.[6] Wesley Clark had a different concept: connecting smaller computers together to form the network and connecting the larger computers to these smaller nodes. In a cab ride to the airport after a conference, the two men connected, and Roberts saw the merits of distributed productivity.

Taylor had to overcome the strong reluctance to join a network and having valuable computer time taken away by network traffic. Roberts solved that problem by declaring that they would get no new funding for computers until they agreed to be part of the network. ARPA would provide each site with a small computer that would handle all the traffic. This had three benefits: ARPA could standardize the network, data would be widely distributed, and therefore network participants' mainframe computers would not be overloaded. The minicomputers would be called *routers*. The next step was to contract for producing them with Bolt, Beranek & Newman.

---

[6] The internet was really the work of a thousand people who believed in widely distributed credit. (When Leonard Kleinrock began taking credit for key developments, his colleagues rejected the proposition.) Most of the advanced work with computers was done along the West and East Coasts.

A major contributing factor to success was the development of the personal computer (PC) at about this same time. With lots of people using PCs, network effects became increasingly powerful, making today's internet virtually inevitable.

An important dimension to emphasize was the importance of brilliant young people who were curious, open to new ideas, had no vested interests, and were not at all set in their ways of thinking or working. As an illustration, Bob Taylor sponsored a series of multiday conferences or jamborees of outstanding people *under 30* (which excluded himself) to explore "spooked" new possibilities. He also believed in high turnover in managers, believing that after a few years, any individual would all too likely become resistant to new ways of thinking.[7]

THE INTERNET EMERGES

A universally standard 1,024 bits per message block could be sent over a "fishnet"-designed network. Breaking messages into small units called *packets* would use whatever routing had capacity to reach their destination and then get reassembled. Each node would have the ability to route the flow of data, the key characteristic of the internet and its predecessor the ARPANET.

In 1973, Robert Kahn and Vint Cerf jointly developed the internet protocol that specified a packet's destination and how it would get there *and* the translation control protocol that determined how it would be reassembled. This created the internet, but it was available only to insiders. It took nearly a decade before it was available to civilians and a full decade more

---

[7] Another origination story begins with the Soviet Union's detonation of an atomic bomb in August 1949, the Korean War in 1950, and Sputnik in 1957, and the creation of the Advanced Research Projects Agency, which became ARPA in February 1958. Small, freewheeling, and staffed entirely with young experts who were as good as the best outsiders, it had no set budget. It sought to redefine problems that were "ARPA hard."

before home users could connect and personal computers had been developed. This was, as Vannevar Bush had proposed in a 1945 article in *The Atlantic* entitled "As We May Think."[8]

The ARPANET, and later the internet, were deliberately open to tinkering by users. Both electronic mail (in 1973) and, much later the World Wide Web (in 1990) were added by users. The creative powers of millions of users is, of course, one of the internet's great strengths today.

Next came the challenges of crossing political boundaries to make the system function internationally and expunging any residual imperfections coming from its origins in cooperation with the military—and developing an appropriate system of governance.

User-driven contributions to the internet surged with the invention of the World Wide Web by Tim Berners-Lee at the European high-energy physics lab, CERN. Lee wanted to link computers around the world with a system that would provide multimedia data. By 1990, he had developed a system of web browsers and servers at CERN. In the internet's spirit of openness, he made it freely available to all users of the network.

> The internet has changed our concept of communication and has become a most welcome part of our daily lives. The great convenience and minimal cost of sending messages instantaneously and globally is nothing less than a revolution in communication.

---

[8] CEO of Digital Equipment Corp., Kenneth Olsen, 30 years earlier had declared, "I can't see *any* reason that *anyone* would want a computer of his own."

14

THE MARSHALL PLAN

The Marshall Plan is, in retrospect, a source of great pride for most Americans. While it was not an investment in improving America, it was an enormously large and highly successful investment in making the world safer and thus better for America and Americans. Several key people—George Marshall, Will Clayton, Dean Acheson, and Harry Truman—each performed vital roles in developing the national consensus in support of the extraordinary commitment.

The background of the Marshall Plan was the daunting change in the United States' relationship with the Soviet Union, from allies in war to adversaries in "peace"—and from optimism to pessimism. In this environment, Stalin and Molotov, over six long weeks of difficult and fruitless "negotiations" in Moscow, had convinced George Marshall that the chances for a favorable outcome through cooperation and negotiations were nil.[1]

---

[1] NATO would follow in 1949.

THE SPEECH

George Marshall, then one of the nation's most admired and respected Americans, went to Harvard University on June 5, 1947, to make a short speech about a gravely serious subject to an audience of 15,000. Never a compelling orator, only Marshall's great stature as the "organizer of victory"—and military commander of 15 million—would command the trust and attention being paid to his remarks by the Cambridge audience.

As he adjusted his reading glasses and began his 11-minute speech,[2] Secretary of State George C. Marshall, age 75, initiated the process of deliberation that would overcome a strong cost-cutting mood in Congress and result in the largest investment America ever made outside the United States: in today's dollars, $220 billion—nearly $1,000 for every man, woman, or child then living in America.[3]

In his flat voice, Marshall began: "The truth of the matter is that Europe's requirements for the next three or four years of foreign food and other essential products—principally from America—are so much greater than her present ability to pay that she must have substantial additional help or face economic, social, and political deterioration of a very grave character."

In 1948, fuel shortages in Europe were severe, the transportation system destroyed and food production—due to drought and severely cold winters— was down by one third. The particularly harsh winter had killed millions of animals and tuberculosis was again Europe's number one killer. Over five million homes and apartments had been destroyed in the war, and 12 million refugees had come from the East. Marshall continued: "It is logical that the

---

[2] The speech was crafted by Charles Bohlen to express concepts set out by Marshall with substantive contributions by Will Clayton and George Kennan.

[3] By mid-1947, our country had already provided over $15 billion in post-war relief. The role of economics in America's international policy traced back to Hay's Open Door policy, to Woodrow Wilson's 14 points, and to Cordell Hull's free trade aspirations.

United States should do whatever it is able to do to assist in the return of normal economic health in the world, without which there can be no political stability and no assured peace."

"Our policy is directed not against any country or doctrine but against hunger, poverty, desperation, and chaos. Its purpose should be the revival of a working economy in the world so as to permit the emergence of political and social conditions in which free institutions can exist."

The United States would provide the enormous resources required, but Europe must take the initiative and its purpose must be to restore health to European society and its economies—not just to block communism. Yes, self-interest was there, but another great driver was a sense of duty to protect the free world.

BACKGROUND

A few months before Marshall's speech at Harvard, President Truman had won approval from Congress for the so-called Truman Doctrine; it led to taking over the financial support for Greece and Turkey then being terminated by the United Kingdom. As President Truman had addressed a joint session of Congress on March 12, 1947, "When forces of liberation entered Greece they found that the retreating Germans had destroyed virtually all the railways, roads, port facilities, communications, and merchant marine. More than a thousand villages had been burned. Eighty-five percent of the children were tubercular. Livestock, poultry, and draft animals had almost disappeared. Inflation had wiped out practically all savings."

"As a result of these tragic conditions, a militant minority, exploiting human want and misery, was able to create political chaos which, until now, has made economic recovery impossible."

With Truman's urgency, Congress approved a $400 million investment and the Soviets seemed to have pulled back due to America's showing strength of commitment. (Later historians tended to agree that Stalin had decided to concentrate on Western Europe instead.)

Just weeks earlier, Stalin had been demanding huge amounts of reparations that would have crippled Germany's economy. Letting Germany and the rest of Europe drift into economic, social, and political chaos would have made those countries ripe for Soviet dominance. Given Stalin's intransigence—over many long weeks of what had begun as hopeful negotiations aimed at developing agreement on postwar policies, but never progressed constructively—Marshall had concluded that agreement was not possible and had come home deeply frustrated and despondent.

On his way home from Moscow, Marshall had stopped at Berlin's Tempelhof airport to meet with General Lucius Clay. Marshall gave Clay new instructions to rebuild the Anglo-American zone as a key part of what would later be called *containment*.[4]

THE PROPOSAL

As Marshall explained his proposal to the Harvard audience, all European countries were invited to join and receive help—a decision based on expert advice from George Kennan, diplomat and author of the 5,540-word "Long Telegram" to the State Department in which Kennan advocated a sustained policy of containment to block the Soviet Union's traditional strategy of expanding power incrementally outward at the perimeter of its empire. Kennan doubted the Soviets would accept the

---

[4] As a condition of receiving the money, France was obliged to merge its occupation zone with the UK and US zones, which became West Germany. As Truman observed, "For the first time in the history of the world, a victor was willing to restore the vanquished."

requirement that they cooperate with other nations and accept American leadership.

Taking a calculated risk, the invitation to participate was extended to the Soviet Union and to its satellite nations, but it was soon clear that Stalin would not accept. While the initial response of the communist countries seemed cooperative, Marshall returned from six weeks of frustrating negotiations with Stalin and Molotov convinced that early hopeful signs of cooperation were becoming increasingly unrealistic and that two separate blocs were forming in opposition to each other.

Knowing from his experience as a Yale trustee that scant attention would be paid to a mere graduation speech, Dean Acheson had arranged a luncheon with three British journalists—two from major newspapers and one from the BBC—on the day before Marshall's Harvard speech. Acheson urged them to get the text to Ernest Bevin, the British Foreign Secretary, immediately and at any hour.[5] Bevin recognized it as a lifeline and raced to get the French to join with him in responding positively and promptly. Without Acheson's initiative, it is hard to imagine how any of the great work over the next few years could possibly have been accomplished.

Then, Marshall made clear that the countries of Europe must agree on a plan of coordinated action and issued a warning: "Furthermore, governments, political parties, or groups which seek to perpetuate human misery in order to profit therefrom politically or otherwise will encounter the opposition of the United States."

"The free peoples of the world look to us for support in maintaining their freedoms. If we falter in our leadership, we may endanger the peace of the world. And we shall surely endanger the welfare of this nation."

* * *

---

[5] Marshall's speech was read by an English announcer on the BBC to be sure that his flat voice would not be misunderstood by the British people.

In just five weeks, with Bevin as chair and Bidault as host, 16 nations' ministers met at Le Quay d'Orsay. On July 12, 1947, six weeks later, a 690-page report was issued with a compilation of "wish list" components.

However, the Europeans' report was without clear recommendations or general agreement. To those most directly engaged, it must have been a profound disappointment. This unfortunate absence of initiative and action would have matched the grim political realities in America. Truman's popularity was low; Republicans controlled Congress; conservatives worried about inflation; and, with the war over, isolationist thinking was gaining strength.

DEVELOPING THE PLAN

Several exceptionally able people performed key roles in the time leading up to Marshall's short speech:

- George Kennan, having served with distinction in Moscow—and a great admirer of the Russian people and their culture, but *not* their government—had been brought to the State Department by Marshall to head a new Plans and Policy Unit—and told to "avoid trivia."
- Will Clayton, a 6'3" Assistant Secretary for Economic Affairs and the intellectual force behind the Marshall Plan, was a strong advocate of free trade and a self-made millionaire as a global cotton broker.[6] In his mid-sixties, he had toured Europe, gathering on the ground evidence to support his fervent view that the fabric of European economics and, therefore, society had been severely

---

[6] A 1936 *TIME* cover called him King Cotton.

disrupted and damaged. He was certain that America must take action decisively and swiftly.

Clayton documented the economic collapse affecting Europe and urged America's making a major commitment to prevent a disastrous collapse. "It is now obvious that we have grossly underestimated the destruction of the European economy." Clayton emphasized the dreadful damage done during the war to the social and political and psychological fabric of European society. "Millions of people in the cities are slowly starving."

Attacks on several countries' national integrity and independence were "feeding on hunger, economic misery, and frustration" and had already been successful in some countries. Clayton's conclusion: Prompt and effective aid for gravely affected countries was essential to America's own security. Government leaders ought to shock the American people into recognizing reality by sharing the full factual situation with them. Clayton was clear that the specific plans should come from the Europeans and recommended multinational integration comparable to what much later became the European Union.

Clayton, who worked harder and longer than anyone at the State Department, urged grants of $6–7 billion annually for at least three years. The grants, he believed, should be based on plans worked out by a confederation of the Europeans led by the United Kingdom, France, and Italy with the United States "running the show."

- General Lucius Clay, the stern military Governor of the American sector of Germany, had opposed the Morgenthau Plan to "pastoralize" Germany *and* the Soviet Union's aggressive use of reparations payments. As Clay put it, "between being for democracy on 1,000 calories and being a communist on 1,500 calories, there is no choice."

- Secretary of War Henry Stimson had called for cooperation among all European nations in the Continent's rehabilitation.
- Dean Acheson had worked effectively with President Truman to create the Truman Doctrine. As a political favor to Truman, Acheson had given an important speech at Delta State Teachers College in Greenville, Mississippi, a few weeks before and received a standing ovation when he spoke out against Communist expansionism. Acheson also emphasized the importance of Europeans taking the lead in responding to the important opportunity being presented.

When Clark Clifford urged it be called the Truman Plan, Truman scoffed at that idea: "If I send that plan with my name to the Hill, it will quiver a couple of times, go belly up, and die." Then, he added, "Even the worst Republican will vote for the plan if Marshall's name is on it."

CONVENING CONGRESS

Truman needed to convince Republicans that the Marshall Plan was an effective response to communism. In summer and fall 1947, over 200 Congressmen went to Europe on fact-finding tours. One group was led by Republican Christian A. Herter of Massachusetts. Its 18 members split into subcommittees that spent 45 days—without spouses since it was an "all work" tour of many nations—and returned with 17 trunks full of documentation.

A major public relations campaign for the Marshall Plan was organized and launched with Citizens Committees in all the major cities across the country. Polls found that nearly 80% of the American public had now heard of the Marshall Plan—up from under 50% in November 1947. Of those who had heard of it, favorable opinions outnumbered unfavorable ones by over three to one. These numbers were both a reflection of Republican Senator Arthur Vandenberg's assiduous shepherding of the legislation through the political process and a vindication of the personal risks he, as a presumed future presidential candidate, took in adopting Truman's policy as his own.[7]

Senator Vandenberg[8] had been carefully courted by Acheson and Marshall in a long series of private briefings, particularly those by Under Secretary Robert Lovett. Lovett met daily with the senator in his apartment for a cocktail and an hour of briefing on each day's classified cables that dwelt on the threats of communist political advances in France and Italy. At 64, Vandenberg, a former isolationist, an arch-conservative financially, *and* a noted orator, delivered a 9,000-word speech to Congress that he had personally retyped seven times.[9]

> This legislation, Mr. President, seeks peace and stability for free men in a free world. It seeks them by economic rather than by military means. It proposes to help our friends to help themselves in the pursuit of sound and successful liberty in the democratic pattern. The quest can mean as much to us as it does to them. It aims to preserve the victory against aggression and dictatorship which we thought we won in World War II. It strives to help stop World War III before it starts. It fights the economic chaos which would precipitate far-flung disintegration. It sustains western civilization.
>
> It means to take Western Europe completely off the American aid at the end of the adventure. It recognizes the grim truth—whether we like it or not—that American self-interest, national economy, and national security are inseparably linked with these objectives.
>
> [This Bill] is the final product of eight months of more intensive study by more devoted minds than I have ever known to concentrate upon any one objective in all my 20 years in Congress. It is a plan for peace, stability, and freedom. As such, it involves the clear self-interest of the

---

[7] Benn Steil, *The Marshall Plan: Dawn of the Cold War* (New York: Simon & Schuster, 2018), 249.

[8] Truman offered the position of Secretary of State to Vandenberg.

[9] "The Battle for World Peace and Stability," speech delivered by Senator Arthur H. Vandenberg, 80th Congress, 2D Session, March 1, 1948.

United States. It can be the turning point in history for 100 years to come. If it fails, we have done our final best. If it succeeds, our children and our children's children will call us blessed.

Vandenberg believed strongly that "partisan politics stops at the water's edge." "But for Vandenberg's leadership and coordination in the Senate," Marshall reflected several years later, "the plan would not have succeeded. I feel that he has never received full credit for his monumental efforts on behalf of the European Recovery Program, and that his name should have been associated with it."[10]

After Congress approved the Marshall Plan legislation, Vandenberg set out to gain approval for what would become NATO, and got it done on June 11, 1948, by a vote of 64 to 4.[11]

THE PLAN'S SPECIFICS

The Marshall Plan was in operation for four years, beginning on April 3, 1948. The goals: to help rebuild 16 countries destroyed by war, modernize European industry, increase productivity, encourage hope, and reverse the spread of communism. Over its four years, the Marshall Plan donated $17 billion[12]—equal to $220 billion today—not including $5 billion before April 3 nor $7.5 billion annually until 1961. By then, the movement toward European economic and political integration was well begun.

---

[10] Some acted as statesmen. But not all! The tobacco industry insisted on being included and being paid to send 40,000 tons of tobacco to Europe even though none had been requested. In another example of the serious imperfections of politics, 177 million pounds of inferior spaghetti was sent to Italy.

[11] The Berlin air lift averaged, in April, 7,850 tons daily. On April 15, a special coal airlift delivered 12,941 tons of coal in 24 hours via 1,398 planes landing nearly one every minute.

[12] The total federal budget in 1947 was $34.5 billion.

Then, in a major electoral surprise, voters reelected Truman and Democrats swept both houses of Congress. The success with the Berlin blockade and airlift helped clarify the confrontation with the Soviet Union and international communism.

Once again, Averell Harriman, who had done so much to shape the plan and push it through Congress, was called to serve, this time as the senior US administrator.

The Marshall Plan would help avoid another depression like the one that had hit the world in the 1930s, enabling Europe to afford goods from the United States and keeping down the tariff walls that had choked trade in the 1930s.

"You can't be vindictive after a war," Truman reflected years later. "I remember my grandmother telling me stories about the Yankee Red Legs who raided her farm and shot her chickens and butchered her pigs and set fire to the hay and the barns—my mother hated the Yankees till she died, and I didn't want hate to be this war's gift to the future."

The process of delivering the Marshall Plan aid was structured. Each participating nation aggregated the "shopping lists" of its companies. The United States delivered the goods and services—particularly transatlantic shipping—and businesses paid for them in local currency. The benefits were as follows:

- No need to pay in dollars—which were unavailable in Europe.
- Paying in local currencies retarded inflation.
- Funds could be used for longer-term investments (as in France and Germany) or paying off war debts (as in the United Kingdom).
- Each nation had a counterpart fund in its own currency. Counterpart funds were 60% invested in local industry. As loans were repaid, the funds were re-lent to other businesses.

- Marshall Plan money was administered by each national government and the European Economic Cooperation Administration. (The ECA was led by Paul Hoffman who had been CEO of Studebaker.) The major purpose was to buy goods from the United States since the European nations had little foreign exchange reserves and they needed to import food, machinery, feed, fertilizer, and fuel.
- Each nation had an ECA envoy—a prominent American business executive.

Of $13.2 billion in Marshall Plan aid, the 10 largest recipients were as follows:

• United Kingdom $3.2 billion	• Greece $694 million
• France $2.7 billion	• Austria $677 million
• West Germany $1.4 billion	• Belgium $555 million
• Italy $1.5 billion	• Denmark $271 million
• Netherlands $1.1 billion	• Norway $253 million

Increasing industrial productivity through know-how was a high priority. The Technical Assistance Program, which was authorized to spend $300 million—later $200 million—only cost Uncle Sam $31.4 million and was particularly effective. Tours of American factories and farms in small groups brought 4,700 French businesspeople to America. Hundreds of American technical advisors went to Europe, and 24,000 Europeans traveled to America. The cost effectiveness of these programs was great. The Bureau of Labor Statistics developed productivity data on many dimensions and then made specific recommendations that were a full generation ahead of European business practice and productivity. (American workers could earn enough to buy a car in 9 months versus 30 months in France.)

The European countries formed the Organization for European Economic Co-operation and Development in 1948 (becoming the Organization for Economic Co-operation and Development or OECD in 1961).

In the succeeding four years, the economies of Germany, France, the United Kingdom, and others grew at an average rate of over 35%. Instead of falling into depression and the political chaos of the early 1920s, they developed cooperative arrangements that would lead to the Common Market and the European Union—and peace.

The European Union and the World Trade Organization were developed during the Marshall Plan years.

* * *

Evaluations of the long-term consequences of the Marshall Plan are always debatable. Some economists have argued that the economic recovery of Europe did not really depend on the Marshall Plan; it was inevitable. Maybe so. More likely, the Marshall Plan was economically important in reducing the immediate harm and pain of adversity *and* in accelerating recovery. The Marshall Plan played a key role in developing NATO and European integration. The European Coal and Steel Community—which did not include the United Kingdom—eventually developed into the European Economic Community.

The Marshall Plan succeeded because it was both pragmatic and visionary. It helped Europe regain its self-confidence and contributed significantly to the integration of the economies and cooperation among European nations that led to the European Union. (Of course, it also contributed indirectly to the development of the Cold War and the continuing tension between Russia and the West.) While it did not necessarily make the United States stronger, the Marshall Plan made America safer, blocked the spread of communism, and helped establish America as the leader of the free world.[13]

* * *

Alistair Cooke, in his "Letter from America" dated October 16, 1959, told the story of a determined publisher persisting in his compelling offer to publish General Marshall's memoirs. Marshall declined, because his views had sometimes differed from Roosevelt's. Exasperated, the publisher bluntly said, "I will put it on the line, General. I am prepared to offer you $1 *million—after taxes*." To this, Marshall replied calmly "But sir, you don't seem to understand I am not interested in one million dollars."

> While latter-day observers have questioned whether the Marshall Plan was only a necessary stimulus to a recovery that was in the works anyway, the symbolism of the financial and technical and political commitment surely made a major difference to America's leadership in the free world, its standing, and the goodwill that we long received. May it be an object lesson to those in our nation's leadership today.

* * *

---

[13] The Berlin Airlift: In June 1948, the Soviets blockaded occupied Berlin by road, rail, and water from the Western powers. Berlin was deep in the Soviet quarter of Germany, and they meant to force Western Berlin into their control by depriving the people of resources. Left only with the air, the Western powers began an incredibly ambitious plan to supply West Berlin by flying in supplies. Within weeks, they were flying in 4,500 tons of goods—later upped to 5,000 tons—supplying West Berlin with much needed goods and resources; coal took up a significant amount of the tonnage to meet energy needs. Lasting just over a year, the airlift transported more than 1.5 million tons of coal, and over 500,000 tons of food. At its peak it transported nearly 13,000 tons in just 24 hours, and had nearly 1,400 flights in 24 hours. Turnaround times were very tight, averaging just 21 minutes to unload, refuel, and prepare to fly back out of Berlin.

The Berlin Airlift is perhaps one of the most notable moments during the Marshall Plan. The Western powers coming together to supply Berlin and halt Soviet aggression was the culmination of the West working together for a common goal of rebuilding and maintaining just one part of Europe, and the first true act of the coming Cold War that would define the rest of the century.

Sources that have been particularly helpful include the following:

- Ben Steil, *The Marshall Plan: Dawn of the Cold War* (New York: Simon & Schuster, 2018) has been by far the most useful. Beautifully written and well-balanced in its judgments, it is the definitive study of the Marshall Plan.
- Walter Isaacson and Evan Thomas, *The Wise Men* (New York: Simon & Schuster, 1986).
- Jeffrey Frank, *The Trial of Harry Truman* (New York: Simon & Schuster, 2022).
- Dean Acheson, *Present at the Creation* (New York: W. W. Norton & Company, 1969).

BIBLIOGRAPHY

Compiled by Maximillian T. Breed

CHAPTER 1: SOCIAL SECURITY

Downey, Kirstin. *The Woman Behind the New Deal: The Life of Frances Perkins, FDR's Secretary of Labor and His Moral Conscience.* New York: Nan A. Talese/ Doubleday, 2009. **Pages:** 5, 45, 101–105, 138, 142, 160, 235–236, 244, 387.

Frances Perkins Center. "Her Life." Frances Perkins Center. Accessed October 22, 2025. https://francesperkinscenter.org/learn/her-life/.

Henry P. Guzda, "Frances Perkins' Interest in a New Deal for Blacks," *Monthly Labor Review* 103, no. 4 (April 1980): 135.

Kheel Center. "'141 Men and Girls Die in Waist Factory Fire; Trapped High Up in Washington Place Building; Street Strewn with Bodies; Piles of Dead Inside.' *New York Times*, March 26, 1911, p. 1." *The Triangle Factory Fire.* Newspaper & Magazine Articles. Cornell University, ILR School. Accessed October 20, 2025. https://trianglefire.ilr.cornell.edu/primary/newspapersMagazines/nyt_032611 .html.

Martin, George. "How Miss Perkins Learned to Lobby." *American Heritage* 27, no. 3, 1976.

Martin, George Whitney. *Madam Secretary: Frances Perkins.* Boston: Houghton Miflin, 1976. **Pages:** VII, 206, 223–226, 237–238, 249–250, 306, 353–354, 378–379.

National Archives. "Frances Perkins: Champion of Workers' Rights." Accessed October 22, 2025. https://visit.archives.gov/whats-on/explore-exhibits/frances-perkins-champion-workers-rights.

American Foreign Service Administration. "Frances Perkins Leaves a Legacy." Accessed October 22, 2025. https://afsa.org/sites/default/files/francesPerkins-LeavesLegacy.pdf.

Perkins, Frances. *The Roosevelt I Knew.* New York: The Viking Press, 1946. **Pages:** 152, 153.

Graham, Rebecca Brenner. "Frances Perkins Breaking Glass Ceilings in the Cabinet." Last Modified October 23, 2024. Accessed October 23, 2025. https://www.whitehousehistory.org/frances-perkins.

U.S. Department of Labor. "Chapter 3: The Department in the New Deal and World War II (1933–1945)." Accessed October 23, 2025. https://beta.dol.gov/about/history/annals/1933–1945.

"The Reminiscences of Frances Perkins (1933–1934)." Oral History Research Office Collection of the Columbia University Libraries (OHRO/CUL), n.d. **Pages:** 214, 215, 216.

Social Security. "The Committee on Economic Security." Accessed October 23, 2025. https://www.ssa.gov/history/ces.html.

Social Security. "1935 Congressional Debates on Social Security." Accessed October 23, 2025. https://www.ssa.gov/history/tally.html.

Cohen, Wilbur J. "The Development of the Social Security Act of 1935: Reflections Some Fifty Years Later." *Minnesota Law Review* 68, no. 379, 1984: 379–408.

Flynn, Simone I. "Social Security." EBSCO, 2021. Accessed October 24, 2025. https://www.ebsco.com/research-starters/social-sciences-and-humanities/social-security#full-article.

Millen-Penn, Ken. "New Deal and the U.S. Supreme Court." EBSCO, 2022. Accessed October 24, 2025. https://www.ebsco.com/research-starters/law/new-deal-and-us-supreme-court.

Social Security. "A Tea Party That Changed History." Accessed October 24, 2025. https://www.ssa.gov/history/tea.htm.

Pushaw, Robert J. Jr "Analyzing Justice Cardozo's Opinions on the Constitutionality of the New Deal." *Touro Law Review* 34, no. 1, Article 20, 2018. Accessed October 24, 2025.

Roosevelt, Franklin D. "Address to Advisory Council of the Committee on Economic Security." Accessed October 24, 2025. https://www.presidency.ucsb.edu/documents/address-advisory-council-the-committee-economic-security.

"Roosevelt Heads List in Radio Appeal Poll; Johnson, Borah, Wallace, Perkins Are Next." *New York Times*, August 2, 1934.

Franklin D. Roosevelt Presidential Library and Museum. "Great Depression Facts." Accessed October 24, 2025. https://www.fdrlibrary.org/great-depression-facts.

Reiff, Nathan. "Historical U.S. Unemployment Rate by Year." Last Modified November 16, 2025. Accessed October 25, 2025. https://www.investopedia.com/historical-us-unemployment-rate-by-year-7495494.

Concord Historical Society. "John Gilbert Winant." Accessed October 25, 2025. https://concordhistoricalsociety.org/john-gilbert-winant/.

Bureau of Internal Revenue. *Statistics of Income for 1935*. Washington: United States Government Printing Office, 1938.

Nelson, Chris Ernest. "The Battle for Ham and Eggs." *San Diego Historical Society Quarterly*, 38, no. 4, 1992: 203–225.

United States Senate. "Huey Long Filibusters New Deal Legislation." Accessed October 25, 2025. https://www.senate.gov/about/powers-procedures/filibusters-cloture/huey-long-filibusters.htm.

"Winant Resigns So He Can Attack Landon and Defend Security Act; Board Chairman, a Republican, Declares His Party's Candidate Seeks to Substitute the Dole with a Means Test for Humanitarian Law—Congress Vote Cited. WINANT RESIGNS TO ATTACK LANDON." *New York Times*, September 29, 1936.

Social Security. "Social Security Act of 1935." Accessed October 25, 2025. https://www.ssa.gov/history/35acviii.html.

Jason Dawsey, "1936, a Year for the Worker: Labor Action and the Reelection of Franklin D. Roosevelt." The National WWII Museum. July 13, 2023. Accessed October 25, 2025. https://www.nationalww2museum.org/war/articles/1936-year-worker-labor-action-and-reelection-franklin-d-roosevelt.

Perkins, Frances. "The Roots of Social Security." Speech Delivered October 23, 1962. Accessed October 26, 2025. https://www.ssa.gov/history/perkins5.html.

Schlabach, Theron. "Rationality & Welfare: Public Discussion of Poverty and Social Insurance in the United States 1875–1935." Accessed October 26, 2025. https://www.ssa.gov/history/reports/schlabach4.html.

Social Security. "Life Expectancy for Social Security." Accessed October 26, 2025. https://www.ssa.gov/history/lifeexpect.html.

Kollmann, Geoffrey and Solomon-Fears, Carmen. "Major Decisions in the House and Senate on Social Security: 1935–2000." March 26, 2001. Accessed October 26, 2025. https://www.ssa.gov/history/reports/crsleghist3.html.

DeWitt, Larry. "The Development of Social Security in America." *Social Security Bulletin* 70, no. 3, 2010.

Social Security. "Frances Perkins." October 1979. Accessed October 26, 2025. https://www.ssa.gov/history/fpbiossa.html.

CHAPTER 2: ERIE CANAL

American Society of Civil Engineers. "Erie Canal." Accessed October 27, 2025. https://www.asce.org/about-civil-engineering/history-and-heritage/historic-landmarks/erie-canal.

Clark, John G. and Mannikko, Nancy Farm. "Construction of the National Road." EBSCO. 2023. Accessed October 27, 2025. https://www.ebsco.com/research-starters/history/construction-national-road.

Gallatin, Albert. *Report of the Secretary of the Treasury; on the Subject of Public Roads and Canals; Made in Pursuance of a Resolution of the Senate, of March 2, 1807.* Washington: R.C. Weightman, 1808.

Bernstein, Peter L. *Wedding of the Waters: The Erie Canal and the Making of a Great Nation.* New York: W. W. Norton & Company, 2005. **Pages:** 23–24, 27, 37–45, 89–95, 98–102, 106, 152, 157–159, 164–165, 169, 174–179, 194–196, 202, 205, 208–210, 220, 236–238, 257, 264–265, 267–270, 303, 311–313, 317–328, 330–333, 349–350, 356, 360.

Boston Society of Civil Engineers Section. "Historic New England Infrastructure: South Hadley Canal." December 8, 2020. Accessed October 27, 2025. https://www.bsces.org/news/historic-new-england-infrastructure-south-hadley-canal/.

Museum of our Industrial Heritage. "The Turners Falls Company." Accessed October 27, 2025. https://industrialhistory.org/p/1060/The-Turners-Falls-Company.

Shaeffer, Mathew. "Dismal Swamp Canal." Accessed October 27, 2025. https://northcarolinahistory.org/encyclopedia/dismal-swamp-canal/.

Hawley, Jesse. *Jesse Hawley's Erie Canal Essays.* New York: J. Seymour, John-Street, 1829.

Geddes, George. "Origin and History of the Measures that Led to the Construction of the Erie Canal." Syracuse: Summers & Co., 1866. https://www.eriecanal.org/texts/Geddes-1866/body.html.

Hosack, David. *Memoir of De Witt Clinton: With an Appendix, Containing Numerous Documents, Illustrative of the Principal Events of His Life.* New York: Printed by J. Seymour, 1829. **Pages:** 97–101, 347–348, 353, 378, 386, 406–407, 503.

Shaw, Ronald E. *Erie Water West: A History of the Erie Canal, 1792–1854.* Lexington: University Press of Kentucky, 1990. **Pages:** 33–39, 69, 75, 203, 241, 323, 406.

Safran, Franciska. "The Preservation of the Holland Land Company Records." *New York History* 69, no. 2, 1988: 163–183. http://www.jstor.org/stable/23178292.

New York Heritage. "Historical Context." Accessed October 28, 2025. https://nyheritage.org/node?page=74.

Digital History. "Agriculture." Accessed October 28, 2025. https://www.digitalhistory.uh.edu/disp_textbook.cfm?smtID=11&psid=3837.

Ransom, Roger L. "Canals and Development: A Discussion of the Issues." *The American Economic Review* 54, no. 3, 1964: 365–376. http://www.jstor.org/stable/1818521.

Larkin, F. Daniel. "Historical Context: Erie Canal Freight." Accessed November 1, 2025. https://considerthesourceny.org/using-primary-sources/erie-canal-new-yorks-gift-nation/chapter-5-freight-and-passenger-travel-erie-canal/historical-context-erie-canal-freight.

Erie Canalway National Heritage Corridor. "Historical Timeline." Accessed November 1, 2025. https://eriecanalway.org/learn/history-culture/timeline.

Erie Canalway National Heritage Corridor. "Fast Facts." Accessed November 1, 2025. https://eriecanalway.org/learn/history-culture/fast-facts.

Fagant, John. "Abraham Lincoln in Western New York." Last Modified 2010. Accessed November 2, 2025. https://buffaloah.com/h/fagant/linc.html.

Russell, Andrew J. "Official Photograph from the 'Golden Spike' Ceremony, 1869." Accessed November 2, 2025. https://www.gilderlehrman.org/history-resources/spotlight-primary-source/official-photograph-golden-spike-ceremony-1869.

Steam Locomotive. "Golden Spike: The Promontory Summit & the Birth of the Transcontinental Railroad." Accessed November 2, 2025. https://www.steamlocomotive.com/events/promontory/.

CHAPTER 3: LOUISIANA PURCHASE

Blakemore, Erin. "The Story of New France: The Cradle of Modern Canada." May 21, 2020. Accessed November 3, 2025. https://www.nationalgeographic.com/history/article/story-new-france-cradle-modern-canada.

Library of Congress. "Louisiana: European Explorations and the Louisiana Purchase a Special Presentation from the Geography and Map Division of the Library of Congress." Accessed November 3, 2025. https://www.loc.gov/static/collections/louisiana-european-explorations-and-the-louisiana-purchase/images/lapurchase.pdf.

Library of Congress. "The Louisiana Purchase." Accessed November 3, 2025. https://www.loc.gov/collections/louisiana-european-explorations-and-the-louisiana-purchase/articles-and-essays/the-louisiana-purchase/.

Historical Society of the New York Courts. "Robert R. Livingston." Accessed November 3, 2025. https://history.nycourts.gov/figure/robert-r-livingston/.

American Heritage. "Clermont State Historic Site." Accessed November 3, 2025. https://www.americanheritage.com/content/clermont-state-historic-site.

Livingston, Robert R. "*Robert R. Livingston to Thomas Jefferson, 14 April 1803.*" Letter from the National Archives. Original Source: *The Papers of Thomas Jefferson*, vol. 40, *4 March–10 July 1803*, ed. Barbara B. Oberg. Princeton: Princeton University Press, 2013. **Pages:** 198–203. Accessed November 3, 2025. https://founders.archives.gov/documents/Jefferson/01-40-02-0146.

Girard, Philippe. "The 1802 Expedition to Saint-Domingue (Haiti) and the Louisiana Purchase." December 2024. Accessed November 3, 2025. https://heritage.bnf.fr/france-ameriques/en/1802-expedition-saint-domingue-haiti-and-louisiana-purchase.

Crout, Robert Rhodes. "The Napoleonic Exclusif: Saint-Domingue and the Leclerc Expedition." *Proceedings of the Meeting of the French Colonial Historical Society* 1, 1976: 30–39. http://www.jstor.org/stable/45137164.

Forsdick, Charles and Christian Høgsbjerg. "The Harder They Come, The Harder They Fall . . . : 1801–1803." In *Toussaint Louverture: A Black Jacobin in the Age of Revolutions*. Pluto Press, 2017. **Pages:** 104–127. http://www.jstor.org/stable/j.ctt1pv89b9.11.

Humanities Texas. "René-Robert Cavelier, Sieur de La Salle." Accessed November 3, 2025. https://www.humanitiestexas.org/programs/tx-originals/list/ren%C3%A9-robert-la-salle.

Hylton, Raymond Pierre. "Treaty of Ryswick." EBSCO. 2022. Accessed November 3, 2025. https://www.ebsco.com/research-starters/history/treaty-ryswick.

Grill, Johnpeter Horst. "Seven Years' War." EBSCO. 2023. Accessed November 3, 2025. https://www.ebsco.com/research-starters/history/seven-years-war.

Neidenbach, Elizabeth Clark. "Treaty of Fontainebleau." Last Modified May 4, 2023. Accessed November 3, 2025. https://64parishes.org/entry/the-treaty-of-fontainebleau-2.

National Archives. "Treaty of Alliance with France (1778)." Accessed November 3, 2025. https://www.archives.gov/milestone-documents/treaty-of-alliance-with-france.

Leonard, Thomas M. "Jay-Gardoqui Treaty, 1785–1786." In *Encyclopedia of U.S.-Latin American Relations*. Washington, DC: CQ Press, 2012. **Page:** 520. https://doi.org/10.4135/9781608717613.n487.

Popkin, Jeremy D. "The Haitian Revolution: Symbol and Heritage." December 2022. Accessed November 3, 2025. https://heritage.bnf.fr/france-ameriques/en/node/6232.

Louisiana State Museum. "The Louisiana Purchase: A Medley of Cultures: Louisiana History, 1699–1877." Accessed November 3, 2025. https://louisianastatemuseum.org/louisiana-history-louisiana-purchase.

Dehler, Gregory J. "Neutrality Proclamation." Accessed November 3, 2025. https://www.mountvernon.org/library/digitalhistory/digital-encyclopedia/article/neutrality-proclamation.

American Philosophical Society Library. "Manuscript Subscription List Put Forward by Jefferson to Support a Proposed Scientific Expedition Under Andre Michaux, 1793." Accessed November 4, 2025. https://diglib.amphilsoc.org/islandora/object/graphics:4751.

Jefferson, Thomas. "*American Philosophical Society's Instructions to André Michaux, [ca. 30 April 1793].*" Letter from the National Archives. Original source: *The Papers of Thomas Jefferson*, vol. 25, *1 January–10 May 1793*, ed. John Catanzariti. Princeton: Princeton University Press, 1992. **Pages:** 624–626. https://founders.archives.gov/documents/Jefferson/01-25-02-0569.

Schaeffer, Wendell G. "The Delayed Cession of Spanish Santo Domingo to France, 1795–1801." *The Hispanic American Historical Review* 29, no. 1, 1949: 46–68. https://doi.org/10.2307/2508293.

USS Constitution Museum. "*Quasi War with France (1798–1801): U.S. Navy's First Naval Conflict.*" Accessed November 4, 2025. https://ussconstitutionmuseum.org/major-events/the-quasi-war-with-france/.

The Napoleon Series. "Treaty of San Ildefonso." Accessed November 4, 2025. https://www.napoleon-series.org/research/government/diplomatic/c_ilde-fonso.html.

Gates, David. *The Napoleonic wars, 1803–1815*. London: Pimlico, 1997. **Page:** 1.

Gordon, John Steele. "The Business of America: We Banked on Them." *American Heritage* 46, no. 4, 1995.

Jefferson, Thomas. "*Thomas Jefferson to Robert R. Livingston, 18 April 1802*." Letter from the National Archives. Original source: *The Papers of Thomas Jefferson*, vol. 37, *4 March–30 June 1802*, ed. Barbara B. Oberg. Princeton: Princeton University Press, 2010. **Pages:** 263–267. https://founders.archives.gov/documents/Jefferson/01-37-02-0220.

Harriss, Joseph A. "How the Louisiana Purchase Changed the World: When Thomas Jefferson Purchased the Louisiana Territory from France, He Altered the Shape of a Nation and the Course of History." April 2003. Accessed November 4, 2025. https://www.smithsonianmag.com/history/how-the-louisiana-purchase-changed-the-world-79715124/.

Smith, Robert. "*Robert Smith to Thomas Jefferson, with Jefferson's Note, 19 January 1803*." Letter from the National Archives. Original source: *The Papers of Thomas Jefferson*, vol. 39, *13 November 1802–3 March 1803*, ed. Barbara B. Oberg. Princeton: Princeton University Press, 2012. **Pages:** 366–367. https://founders.archives.gov/documents/Jefferson/01-39-02-0312.

Library of Congress. *Acts of the Seventh Congress of the United States*. Washington, DC, 1803. Accessed November 4, 2025. https://tile.loc.gov/storage-services/service/ll/llsl//llsl-c7/llsl-c7.pdf.

History of Economic Thought. "Pierre Samuel DuPont de Nemours, 1739–1817." Accessed November 4, 2025. https://www.hetwebsite.net/het/profiles/dupont.htm.

Nemours, Pierre Samuel Du Pont de. "*Pierre Samuel Du Pont de Nemours to Thomas Jefferson, 30 April 1802*." Letter from the National Archives. Original source: *The Papers of Thomas Jefferson*, vol. 37, *4 March–30 June 1802*, ed. Barbara B. Oberg. Princeton: Princeton University Press, 2010. **Pages:** 367–375. https://founders.archives.gov/documents/Jefferson/01-37-02-0295.

Jefferson, Thomas. "*Thomas Jefferson to Thomas Mann Randolph, 5 July 1803*." Letter from the National Archives. Original source: *The Papers of Thomas Jefferson*, vol. 40, *4 March–10 July 1803*, ed. Barbara B. Oberg. Princeton: Princeton University Press, 2013. **Pages:** 660–662. https://founders.archives.gov/documents/Jefferson/01-40-02-0505.

Madison, James. "*James Madison to Robert R. Livingston, 1 May 1802.*" Letter from the National Archives. Original source: *The Papers of James Madison*, Secretary of State Series, vol. 3, *1 March–6 October 1802*, ed. David B. Mattern, J. C. A. Stagg, Jeanne Kerr Cross, and Susan Holbrook Perdue. Charlottesville: University Press of Virginia, 1995. **Pages:** 174–177. https://founders.archives.gov/documents/Madison/02-03-02-0208.

Jefferson, Thomas. "*Thomas Jefferson to the Senate, 11 January 1803.*" Letter from the National Archives. Original source: *The Papers of Thomas Jefferson*, vol. 39, *13 November 1802–3 March 1803*, ed. Barbara B. Oberg. Princeton: Princeton University Press, 2012. **Pages:** 312–313. https://founders.archives.gov/documents/Jefferson/01-39-02-0269.

Mullen, Pierce. "The Louisiana Purchase." Accessed November 4, 2025. https://lewis-clark.org/louisianas-purchase/the-louisiana-purchase/.

National Archives. "Jefferson's Secret Message to Congress Regarding the Lewis & Clark Expedition (1803)." Accessed November 4, 2025. https://www.archives.gov/milestone-documents/jeffersons-secret-message-to-congress.

United States Senate. "The Senate Approves for Ratification the Louisiana Purchase Treaty." Accessed November 4, 2025. https://www.senate.gov/about/powers-procedures/treaties/senate-approves-louisiana-purchase-treaty.htm.

De Cesar, Wayne T. and Page, Susan. "Jefferson Buys Louisiana Territory, and the Nation Moves Westward." *Prologue Magazine* 35, no. 1, 2003. Accessed November 4, 2025. https://www.archives.gov/publications/prologue/2003/spring/louisiana-purchase.html.

Livingston, Robert R. "*Robert R. Livingston to Thomas Jefferson, 14 April 1803.*" Letter from the National Archives. Original source: *The Papers of Thomas Jefferson*, vol. 40, *4 March–10 July 1803*, ed. Barbara B. Oberg. Princeton: Princeton University Press, 2013. **Pages:** 198–203. https://founders.archives.gov/documents/Jefferson/01-40-02-0146.

Madison, James. "*James Madison to James Monroe, 30 July 1803.*" Letter from the National Archives. Original source: *The Papers of James Madison*, Secretary of State Series, vol. 5, *16 May–31 October 1803*, ed. David B. Mattern, J. C. A. Stagg, Ellen J. Barber, Anne Mandeville Colony, and Bradley J. Daigle. Charlottesville: University Press of Virginia, 2000. **Pages:** 248–250. https://founders.archives.gov/documents/Madison/02-05-02-0275.

Jefferson, Thomas. "*Thomas Jefferson to John Breckinridge, 12 August 1803.*" Letter from the National Archives. Original source: *The Papers of Thomas Jefferson*, vol. 41, *11 July–15 November 1803*, ed. Barbara B. Oberg. Princeton: Princeton

University Press, 2014. **Pages:** 184–186. https://founders.archives.gov/documents/Jefferson/01-41-02-0139.

Livingston, Robert R. "*Robert R. Livingston to Thomas Jefferson, 2 May 1803.*" Letter from the National Archives. Original source: *The Papers of Thomas Jefferson*, vol. 40, *4 March–10 July 1803*, ed. Barbara B. Oberg. Princeton: Princeton University Press, 2013. **Pages:** 301–304. https://founders.archives.gov/documents/Jefferson/01-40-02-0224.

National Park Service. "Louisiana Territory Officially Transferred." Accessed November 4, 2025. https://www.nps.gov/articles/000/louisiana-territory-officially-transferred.htm.

Howe & Rusling Team. "The Louisiana Purchase and the Birth of American High Finance." March 8, 2019. Accessed November 5, 2025. https://www.howeandrusling.com/the-louisiana-purchase-and-the-birth-of-american-high-finance/.

Martello Towers. "Wars with France 1793 to 1815." Accessed November 5, 2025. https://martellotowers.co.uk/frenchwars.

Nemours, Pierre Samuel Du Pont de. "*Pierre Samuel Du Pont de Nemours to Thomas Jefferson, 12 May 1803.*" Letter from the National Archives. Original source: *The Papers of Thomas Jefferson*, vol. 40, *4 March–10 July 1803*, ed. Barbara B. Oberg. Princeton: Princeton University Press, 2013. **Pages:** 357–361. https://founders.archives.gov/documents/Jefferson/01-40-02-0268.

Bradshaw, Jim. "Saint-Domingue Revolution." Last modified February 2, 2025. Accessed November 5, 2025. https://64parishes.org/entry/saint-domingue-revolution.

Thibodeaux, Ron. "Growing a Nation: New Orleans was the Centerpiece of the Louisiana Purchase." Last modified August 10, 2014. Accessed November 5, 2025. https://ronthibodeaux.com/2014/08/10/growing-a-nation-new-orleans-was-the-centerpiece-of-the-louisiana-purchase/.

Gauthier, Jason G. "History and the Census: The 1803 Louisiana Purchase." Last modified January 2, 2025. Accessed November 5, 2025. https://www.census.gov/about/history/stories/monthly/2023/april-2023.html.

Discover Lewis & Clark. "July 5, 1803 Lewis Sets Out." Accessed November 5, 2025. https://lewis-clark.org/day-by-day/5-jul-1803/.

CHAPTER 4: ALASKA PURCHASE

Greene, Jim. "Russian America (1799–1867)." EBSCO. 2023. Accessed November 5,2025.https://www.ebsco.com/research-starters/history/russian-america-1799-1867.

Library of Congress. "The Alaska Purchase." Accessed November 5, 2025. https://www.loc.gov/collections/meeting-of-frontiers/articles-and-essays/alaska/the-alaska-purchase/.

Alaska Department of Natural Resources. "Fact Sheet Title: Land Ownership in Alaska." Alaska. March 2000. Accessed November 5, 2025. https://www.middlebury.edu/institute/sites/default/files/2020-08/DNR%20Fact%20Sheet_Land%20Ownership.pdf.

Gustafson, Milton O. "Seward's Bargain: The Alaska Purchase from Russia." *Prologue Magazine* 26, no. 4, 1994. Accessed November 5, 2025, from the National Archives. https://www.archives.gov/publications/prologue/1994/winter/alaska-check.

Ault, Phillip H. "The (Almost) Russian-American Telegraph." *American Heritage* 26, no. 4, 1975. Accessed November 5, 2025, from the National Archives. https://www.americanheritage.com/almost-russian-american-telegraph.

Montana Trappers. "Hudson's Bay Company: The Most Important Industry in North America." Accessed November 5, 2025. https://www.montanatrappers.org/basics/history/hudsons.html.

Kushner, Howard I. *The United States, Russia, and Russian-America*. Montreal: Concordia University, 1979. Accessed November 5, 2025. https://www.wilsoncenter.org/sites/default/files/media/documents/publication/op71_us_russia_russian_america_kushner_1979.pdf.

National Archives. "Treaty of Guadalupe Hidalgo (1848)." Last modified September 20, 2022. Accessed November 5, 2025. https://www.archives.gov/milestone-documents/treaty-of-guadalupe-hidalgo.

National Museum of American Diplomacy. "The Trent Affair: Diplomacy, Britain, and the American Civil War." January 5, 2022. Accessed November 5, 2025. https://diplomacy.state.gov/stories/the-trent-affair-diplomacy-britain-and-the-american-civil-war/.

Lowcountry Digital History Initiative. "Impact on the British Cotton Trade." Accessed November 5, 2025. https://ldhi.library.cofc.edu/exhibits/show/liverpools-abercromby-square/britain-and-us-civil-war/impact-cotton-trade.

Narron, James and Morgan, Donald P. "Crisis Chronicles: The Cotton Famine of 1862–1863 and the U.S. One-Dollar Note." November 20, 2015. Accessed November 5, 2025. https://libertystreeteconomics.newyorkfed.org/2015/11/crisis-chronicles-the-cotton-famine-of-1862-63-and-the-us-one-dollar-note/.

Dattel, Eugene R. "Cotton in a Global Economy: Mississippi (1800–1860)." October 2006. Accessed November 5, 2025. https://www.mshistorynow.mdah.ms.gov/issue/cotton-in-a-global-economy-mississippi-1800-1860.

New World Encyclopedia. "Corn Laws." Accessed November 5, 2025. https://www.newworldencyclopedia.org/entry/Corn_Laws.

McPherson, James M. *Battle Cry of Freedom: The Civil War Era*. Oxford: Oxford University Press, 1988. **Page:** 44.

Ostrower, Gary B. "William H. Seward." EBSCO. 2023. Accessed November 5, 2025. https://www.ebsco.com/research-starters/history/william-h-seward.

Anderson, George W. *Coal: It's Development and Destiny*. Philadelphia: Inquirer Printing Office, 1857.

Gerus, Oleh W. "The Russian Withdrawal from Alaska: The Decision to Sell." *Revista de Historia de América*, no. 75/76, 1973: 157–178. http://www.jstor.org/stable/20139106.

Bradsher, Greg. "From Buchanan's Blunder to Seward's Folly, Sort Of." November 26, 2013. Accessed November 5, 2025. https://text-message.blogs.archives.gov/2013/11/26/from-buchanans-blunder-to-sewards-folly-sort-of/.

Witek, John Wayne. "The Purchase of Alaska: The Reasons Offered by Representative Nathaniel P. Banks Examined, with Special Emphasis on the Interest of William H. Seward in the Far East." Master's thesis. 1962. https://ecommons.luc.edu/cgi/viewcontent.cgi?article=2785&context=luc_theses.

Ireland, Willard E. "The Annexation Petition of 1869." *BC Historical Quarterly*, October 1940. Hosted by Hallmark Heritage Society. Last modified 2021. Accessed November 6, 2025. https://hallmarkheritagesociety.ca/archives/history-articles/the-annexation-petition-of-1869/.

Marvel, William. "CSS Alabama." Last modified February 7, 2024. Accessed November 6, 2025. https://encyclopediaofalabama.org/article/css-alabama/.

Campion, Edmund J. "British North America Act." EBSCO. 2023. Accessed November 6, 2025. https://www.ebsco.com/research-starters/politics-and-government/british-north-america-act.

Roy, Patricia E. "'The interests of Confederation demanded it': British Columbia and Confederation." Accessed November 6, 2025. https://ucp.manifoldapp.org/read/reconsidering-confederation/section/1caf29ec-c7eb-4227-90ba-ce6d9cf1bb13.

Scott, James Brown. "The Purchase of the Danish West Indies by the United States of America." *The American Journal of International Law* 10, no. 4, 1916: 853–859. https://doi.org/10.2307/2186936.

Schoonover, Bruce. "Acquisition of the Danish West Indies by the United States." March 8, 2005. Accessed November 6, 2025. https://stjohnhistoricalsociety.org/vol-vi-no-5-march-2005-acquisition-of-the-danish-west-indies-by-the-united-states-by-bruce-schoonover/.

Gissurarson, Hannes H. "Proposals to Sell, Annex or Evacuate Iceland, 1518–1868." October 2015. Accessed November 6, 2025. https://skemman.is/bitstream/1946/23162/1/Loka%C3%BAtg%C3%A1fa_STJ_hannes.pdf#.

Herber, Elmer C. "Spencer Fullerton Baird and the Purchase of Alaska." *Proceedings of the American Philosophical Society* 98, no. 2, 1954: 139–143. http://www.jstor.org/stable/3143644.

Sumner, Charles. *Speech of Hon. Charles Sumner, of Massachusetts, on the Cession of Russian America to the United States*. Washington, DC: Congressional Globe Office, 1867. **Page:** 48.

CHAPTER 5: NATIONAL PARKS

Dustin, Daniel L., Bricker, Kelly S, Brownlee, Matthew T. and Schwab, Keri A. "The National Parks: America's Best Idea?" August 1, 2016. Accessed November 6, 2025. https://www.nrpa.org/parks-recreation-magazine/2016/august/the-national-parks-americas-best-idea/.

National Park Service. "Annual Visitation Statistics Release." Accessed November 6, 2025. https://www.nps.gov/subjects/socialscience/visitor-use-statistics-dashboard.htm.

National Park Foundation. "How Many National Parks Are There?" Last modified November 14, 2024. Accessed November 6, 2025. https://www.nationalparks.org/connect/blog/how-many-national-parks-are-there.

National Park Service. "Quick History of the National Park Service." Last modified August 24, 2022. Accessed November 6, 2025. https://www.nps.gov/articles/quick-nps-history.htm.

Keiter, Robert B. *To Conserve Unimpaired: The Evolution of the National Park Idea*. Washington, DC: Island Press, 2013. **Pages:** 41–42, 48, 76–81, 92, 107, 148–152, 159–163, 236.

Richard West Sellars. *Preserving Nature in the National Parks: A History*. New Haven, CT: Yale University Press, 1997. **Pages:** 33–37, 182, 184, 124–216, 258.

National Park Service. "John Muir and President Roosevelt." Last modified December 19, 2024. Accessed November 6, 2025. https://www.nps.gov/jomu/learn/historyculture/john-muir-and-president-roosevelt.htm.

Eschner, Kat. "Lincoln's Signature Laid the Groundwork for the National Park System." June 30, 2017. Accessed November 6, 2025. https://www.smithsonian-mag.com/smart-news/lincolns-signature-laid-groundwork-national-park-system-180963826/.

Beveridge, Charles E. "Olmsted and Yosemite." *SiteLINES: A Journal of Place* 5, no. 1, 2009: 6–8. http://www.jstor.org/stable/24889349.

Hill, Jane F. "Conservation of Yosemite Valley." EBSCO. 2024. Accessed November 6, 2025. https://www.ebsco.com/research-starters/science/conservation-yosemite-valley.

National Park Service. "Park History Program." Last modified May 7, 2024. Accessed November 6, 2025. https://www.nps.gov/orgs/1220/index.htm.

Yellowstone Forever. "Yellowstone National Park Facts." Accessed November 6, 2025. https://www.yellowstone.org/experience/visitor-information/yellowstone-national-park-facts/.

Yellowstone Forever. "Winter in Yellowstone: Adapt or Die." Accessed November 6, 2025. https://www.yellowstone.org/winter-in-yellowstone-adapt-or-die/.

National Park Service. "Flight of the Nez Perce." Last modified April 18, 2025. Accessed November 6, 2025. https://www.nps.gov/yell/learn/historyculture/flightnezperce.htm.

National Park Service. "A Beginning for the Park." Last modified April 14, 2015. Accessed November 6, 2025. https://www.nps.gov/ever/learn/kidsyouth/a-beginning-for-the-park.htm.

National Park Service. "A History of Acadia." Last modified September 12, 2025. Accessed November 6, 2025. https://www.nps.gov/articles/000/acadia-history-brief.htm.

National Park Service. "Cape Cod National Seashore Marks 60th Anniversary on August 7." Last modified July 27, 2021. Accessed November 6, 2025. https://www.nps.gov/caco/learn/news/cape-cod-national-seashore-marks-60th-anniversary-on-august-7.htm.

Chesemore, David L. "U.S. Congress Protects Alaskan Lands and Wildlife." EBSCO. 2023. Accessed November 6, 2025. https://www.ebsco.com/research-starters/law/us-congress-protects-alaskan-lands-and-wildlife.

Ungvarsky, Janine. "Wrangell–St. Elias National Park and Preserve." EBSCO. 2024. Accessed November 6, 2025. https://www.ebsco.com/research-starters/history/wrangell-st-elias-national-park-and-preserve.

Benson, Alvin K. "Alaskan Oil Discovery Sparks Controversy." EBSCO. 2023. Accessed November 6, 2025. https://www.ebsco.com/research-starters/mining-and-mineral-resources/alaskan-oil-discovery-sparks-controversy.

Yosemite Online. "Old Yosemite Landmarks." Accessed November 6, 2025. https://www.yosemite.ca.us/library/lights_and_shadows/old_landmarks.html.

National Park Service. "John Muir." Accessed November 6, 2025. https://www.nps.gov/articles/john-muir.htm.

Wilderness Connect. "John Muir." Accessed November 6, 2025. https://wilderness.net/learn-about-wilderness/people/john-muir.php.

National Park Service. "John Muir's Books and Publications." Last modified September 10, 2024. Accessed November 6, 2025. https://www.nps.gov/jomu/learn/historyculture/john-muir-s-books-and-publications.htm.

National Park Service. "Influential People in John Muir's Life." Last modified December 19, 2024. Accessed November 6, 2025. https://www.nps.gov/jomu/learn/historyculture/people.htm.

Muir, John. "The American Forests." *The Atlantic*, August 1897: 145–157.

Muir, John. *The Story of My Boyhood and Youth*. Boston: Houghton Mifflin Company, 1913. **Pages:** 23–25, 98–99, 106–110.

Blakemore, Erin. "Conservationist John Muir's Youthful Hobby: Inventing Amazing Alarm Clocks." May 26, 2017. Accessed November 6, 2025. https://www.mentalfloss.com/article/501253/john-muir-youthful-hobby-amazing-alarm-clocks.

Muir, John. *A Thousand-Mile Walk to the Gulf*. Boston: Houghton Mifflin Company, 1916. **Pages:** IX, XVI–XVII, 1–2.

Yosemite Online. "John Muir Writings." Accessed November 6, 2025. https://www.yosemite.ca.us/john_muir_writings/.

Terrell, Ellen. "Roosevelt, Muir, and the Camping Trip." August 11, 2016. Accessed November 6, 2025. https://blogs.loc.gov/inside_adams/2016/08/roosevelt-muir-and-the-camping-trip/.

National Park Service. "American Antiquities Act of 1906: Overview." Last modified August 8, 2019. Accessed November 6, 2025. https://www.nps.gov/articles/american-antiquities-act-of-1906.htm.

National Park Service. "The Proclamation of National Monuments Under the Antiquities Act, 1906–1970." Last modified March 6, 2023. Accessed November 6, 2025. https://www.nps.gov/articles/lee-story-proclamation.htm.

National Archives. "Hetch Hetchy Environmental Debates." Last modified August 25, 2017. Accessed November 6, 2025. https://www.archives.gov/legislative/features/hetch-hetchy.

National Park Service. "Stephen Tyng Mather." Last modified August 2, 2024. Accessed November 6, 2025. https://www.nps.gov/people/stephen-tyng-mather.htm.

National Park Service. "NPS Organic Act of 1916." Last modified November 17, 2019. Accessed November 6, 2025. https://www.nps.gov/pipe/learn/management/nps-organic-act-of-1916.htm.

UPI Archives. "The Sierra Club Says Ronald Reagan Is Wrong When . . ." October 9, 1980. Accessed November 6, 2025. https://www.upi.com/Archives/1980/10/09/The-Sierra-Club-says-Ronald-Reagan-is-wrong-when/5945339912000/.

National Park Service. "National Park System Advisory Board Report 2001: Rethinking the National Parks for the 21st Century." 2001. https://www.nps.gov/subjects/policy/upload/Rethinking-the-National-Parks-for-the-21st-Century-2001.pdf.

National Park Service. "Visitation Statistics: Annual Visitation Statistics by Year." Last modified February 16, 2022. Accessed November 6, 2025. https://www.nps.gov/subjects/socialscience/highlights.htm.

National Park Service. "Mission 66 Background and History." Last modified September 1, 2023. Accessed November 6, 2025. https://www.nps.gov/articles/000/mission-66.htm.

National Park Service. "Wolf Management." Last modified September 9, 2025. Accessed November 6, 2025. https://www.nps.gov/yell/learn/management/wolf.htm.

National Park Service Air Resources Division. "Air Quality Concerns Related to Snowmobile Usage in National Parks." Denver, Colorado. 2000. Accessed November 6, 2025. https://npshistory.com/publications/air-quality/snowmobile-air-quality.pdf,

Runte, Alfred. *National Parks: The American Experience*. Lincoln: University of Nebraska Press, 1997. **Page:** XVII.

CHAPTER 6: GI BILL

Reagan, Patrick D. "Roosevelt Signs the G.I. Bill." EBSCO. 2023. Accessed November 7, 2025. https://www.ebsco.com/research-starters/history/roosevelt-signs-gi-bill.

National Archives. "Servicemen's Readjustment Act (1944)." Accessed November 7, 2025. https://www.archives.gov/milestone-documents/servicemens-readjustment-act.

Mettler, Suzanne. *Soldiers to Citizens: The G.I. Bill and the Making of the Greatest Generation.* Oxford: University Press, 2005. **Pages:** 7, 16–17, 20–22, 41–44, 64, 99–104, 107–108.

Sparrow, John C. *History of Personnel Demobilization in the United States Army.* Department of the Army, 1952. Accessed November 7, 2025. https://history.army.mil/portals/143/Images/Publications/catalog/104-8.pdf.

Ortiz, Stephen R. *Beyond the Bonus March and GI Bill: How Veteran Politics Shaped the New Deal Era.* New York: New York University Press, 2009. **Pages:** 27–31, 34–40, 48–58, 62, 66–67, 81–85, 91–92, 107–109, 114–115, 141–143, 188–200.

Liquid Trucking. "Veterans Are Driving America." November 10, 2023. Accessed November 7, 2025. https://liquidtrucking.com/veterans-are-driving-america/.

Clark, J. H. Cullum. "Raising Up the World's Best Educated Workforce Through Postsecondary Education." September 30, 2025. Accessed November 7, 2025. https://www.bushcenter.org/publications/raising-up-the-worlds-best-educated-workforce-through-postsecondary-education.

Hinnershitz, Stephanie. "The GI Bill and Planning for the Postwar." March 13, 2025. Accessed November 7, 2025. https://www.nationalww2museum.org/war/articles/gi-bill-and-planning-postwar.

Schmeling, J. & Maury, R. "Student Veterans: A Valuable Asset to Higher Education and the Workforce. Presentation to the Veterans Leadership Program." August 14, 2019. Accessed November 7, 2025. https://www.tamus.edu/veterans/wp-content/uploads/sites/12/2020/08/Business-Case-For-Student-Veterans_SVA_IVMF_Jared-Lyon.pdf#.

Schiff, Judith. "Yale After World War II: The Bushes Weren't the Only Family in Extremely Close Quarters." *Yale Alumni Magazine* LXXIX, no. 6, 2016.

Levinson, Robert. "Many Black World War II Veterans Were Denied Their GI Bill Benefits. Time to Fix That." September 11, 2020. Accessed November 7, 2025. https://warontherocks.com/2020/09/many-black-world-war-ii-veterans-were-denied-their-gi-bill-benefits-time-to-fix-that/.

Bolté, Charles G. and Harris, Louis. *"Our Negro Veterans."* Public Affairs Committee, Incorporated, 1947. **Page:** 15.

Hindley, Meredith. "How the GI Bill Became Law in Spite of Some Veterans' Groups." *Humanities* 35, no. 4, 2014: 71–85.

Smith, Jillian B. "The Performance of Change Through the G.I. Bill." *Swarthmore Undergraduate History Journal* 2, no. 1 2021: 71–85. https://doi.org/10.24968/ 2693-244X.2.1.6 https://works.swarthmore.edu/suhj/vol2/iss1/6.

Department of Veterans Affairs. "Born of Controversy: The GI Bill of Rights." Accessed November 7, 2025. https://www.va.gov/opa/publications/celebrate/ gi-bill.pdf#.

Strickland, Sandy. "Midnight Ride of John Gibson to Save GI Bill." Last modified April 21, 2019. Accessed November 7, 2025. https://www.jacksonville.com/ story/news/reason/call-box/2019/04/21/curious-jax-midnight-ride-of-john-gibson-to-save-gi-bill/4842131007/?gnt-cfr=1&gca-cat=p&gca-uir=true&gca-epti=z11xx02d00----v11xx02b00xxxxd11xx65&gca-ft=126&gca-ds=sophi.

DeWitt, Larry. "Research Note #19: Social Security Benefits as a Percentage of Total Federal Budget Expenditures." June 2003. Accessed November 7, 2025. https://www.ssa.gov/history/percent.html#.

American Presidency Project. "Fireside Chat." Accessed November 8, 2025. https://www.presidency.ucsb.edu/documents/fireside-chat-1.

American Presidency Project. "Message to Congress on the Education of War Veterans." Accessed November 8, 2025. https://www.presidency.ucsb.edu/doc-uments/message-congress-the-education-war-veterans.

Department of Veterans Affairs. "Object 46: Harry Colmery's Handwritten Draft of GI Bill." Accessed November 8, 2025. https://department.va.gov/history/100-objects/object-46-draft-of-gi-bill/.

Nilsson, Jeff. "A Hasty Prediction for the G.I. Bill." July 6, 2012. Accessed November 8, 2025. https://www.saturdayeveningpost.com/2012/07/hasty-prediction-gi-bill/.

DeVane, William Clyde. *Higher Education in Twentieth-Century America.* Cambridge, MA: Harvard University Press, 1965. **Page:** 124.

Olson, Keith W. "The G. I. Bill and Higher Education: Success and Surprise." *American Quarterly* 25, no. 5, 1973: 596–610. https://doi.org/10.2307/2711698.

Katznelson, Ira. *When Affirmative Action Was White: An Untold History of Racial Inequality in Twentieth-Century America.* New York: W. W. Norton & Company, 2005. **Page:** 140.

CHAPTER 7: INTERSTATE HIGHWAYS

Pennybacker, J. E. Jr. and Eldridge, Maurice O. *Mileage and Cost of Public Roads in the United States in 1909*. Washington: Government Printing Office, 1912. Accessed November 10, 2025. https://www.govinfo.gov/content/pkg/SERIALSET-06322_00_00-005-0582-0000/pdf/SERIALSET-06322_00_00-005-0582-0000.pdf.

Federal Highway Administration. "Interstate System: Dwight D. Eisenhower National System of Interstate and Defense Highways." Last modified September 19, 2023. Accessed November 10, 2025. https://www.fhwa.dot.gov/programadmin/interstate.cfm.

Weingroff, Richard F. "President Franklin D. Roosevelt and Excess Condemnation." Last modified February 25, 2025. Accessed November 10, 2025. https://highways.dot.gov/highway-history/general-highway-history/president-franklin-d-roosevelt-and-excess-condemnation.

Pedersen, Neil. "Franklin D. Roosevelt (1933–1945): We Continue to Benefit from His Transportation Legacy." November 22, 2024. Accessed November 10, 2025. https://enotrans.org/article/franklin-d-roosevelt-1933-1945-we-continue-to-benefit/.

Pfeiffer, David A. "Ike's Interstates at 50: Anniversary of the Highway System Recalls Eisenhower's Role as Catalyst." *Prologue Magazine* 38, no. 2, 2006. Accessed from the National Archives on November 10, 2025.

Weingroff, Richard F. "The Greatest Decade 1956–1966: Part 1 Essential to the National Interest." Last modified June 30, 2023. Accessed November 10, 2025. https://highways.dot.gov/highway-history/interstate-system/50th-anniversary/greatest-decade-1956-1966-part-1-essential.

Colorado Department of Transportation. "50th Anniversary of the National System of Interstate and Defense Highways." Accessed November 10, 2025. https://www.codot.gov/about/CDOTHistory/50th-anniversary.

Federal Highway Administration. "Part I – History." Accessed November 10, 2025. https://highways.dot.gov/highway-history/interstate-system/dwight-d-eisenhower-system-interstate-and-defense-highways/part-i.

Federal Highway Administration. "Stories from the Early Days of the Bureau." Last modified June 27, 2017. Accessed November 10, 2025. https://www.fhwa.dot.gov/highwayhistory/mcdonald.cfm.

Weingroff, Richard F. "Creation of a Landmark: The Federal Aid Road Act of 1916." Accessed November 10, 2025. https://highways.dot.gov/sites/fhwa.dot.gov/files/landmark.pdf.

Phelps, Hailey. "When Interstates Paved the Way: The Construction of the Interstate Highway System Helped to Develop the U.S. Economy." Second/Third Quarter 2021. Accessed November 10, 2025. https://www.richmondfed.org/publications/research/econ_focus/2021/q2-3/economic_history.

Weingroff, Richard F. "A Journey to Better Highways: 100 Years of Public Roads." Summer 2018. Accessed November 10, 2025. https://rosap.ntl.bts.gov/view/dot/76603.

Weingroff, Richard F. "From Names to Numbers: The Origins of the U.S. Numbered Highway System." Last modified June 27, 2017. Accessed November 10, 2025. https://www.fhwa.dot.gov/infrastructure/numbers.cfm.

Govinfo. *Sixty-Seventh Congress. Sess . I. Ch . 119. 1921.* Washington, DC: U.S. Government Printing Office, 1921. Accessed November 10, 2025. https://www.govinfo.gov/content/pkg/STATUTE-42/pdf/STATUTE-42-Pg212.pdf.

Sherwood, Martha. "Pershing Map." EBSCO. 2022. Accessed November 11, 2025. https://www.ebsco.com/research-starters/communication-and-mass-media/pershing-map.

Edwards, Amy H. "Hiding in Plain Sight: The FDR Interstate Highway Map." June 26, 2018. Accessed November 11, 2025. https://unwritten-record.blogs.archives.gov/2018/06/26/hiding-in-plain-sight-the-fdr-interstate-highway-map/.

Federal Highway Administration. "Thomas H. MacDonald on Toll Roads." Last modified June 27, 2017. Accessed November 11, 2025. https://www.fhwa.dot.gov/infrastructure/mcdonaldtoll.cfm.

Mohl, Raymond A. "The Interstates and the Cities: Highways, Housing, and the Freeway Revolt." Accessed November 11, 2025. https://www.prrac.org/pdf/mohl.pdf.

Weingroff, Richard F. "Firing Thomas H. MacDonald—Twice." Last modified June 27, 2017. Accessed November 11, 2025. https://www.fhwa.dot.gov/infrastructure/firing.cfm.

Weingroff, Richard F. "Before the Federal-Aid Highway Act of 1956: Francis V. Du Pont in Context." Accessed November 11, 2025. https://www.fhwa.dot.gov/highwayhistory/dupont.pdf.

"THE ADMINISTRATION: Man in the Storm." *Time Magazine*, June 30, 1958, Accessed November 11, 2025. https://time.com/archive/6826919/the-administration-man-in-the-storm/.

Weingroff, Richard F. "General Lucius D. Clay: The President's Man." Last modified June 30, 2023. Accessed November 11, 2025. https://highways.dot.gov/highway-history/interstate-system/general-lucius-d-clay-presidents-man.

Davis, Jeff. "Federal Highway Policy Under President Eisenhower, 1953–1954." Last modified September 9, 2020. Accessed November 11, 2025. https://enotrans.org/article/federal-highway-policy-under-president-eisenhower-1953-1954/.

ITE. "Francis (Frank) C. Turner." Accessed November 11, 2025. https://www.ite.org/about-ite/history/honorary-members/francis-c-turner/.

Weingroff, Richard F. "Senator Harry Flood Byrd of Virginia: The Pay-As-You-Go Man." Last modified June 27, 2017. Accessed November 11, 2025. https://www.fhwa.dot.gov/infrastructure/byrd.cfm.

Weingroff, Richard F. "Kill The Bill: Why the U.S. House of Representatives Rejected the Interstate System in 1955." Last modified June 30, 2023. Accessed November 11, 2025. https://highways.dot.gov/highway-history/interstate-system/kill-bill-why-us-house-representatives-rejected-interstate-system.

National Archives. "National Interstate and Defense Highways Act (1956)." Last modified February 8, 2022. Accessed November 11, 2025. https://www.archives.gov/milestone-documents/national-interstate-and-defense-highways-act.

Witcher, T. R. "How the Interstate Highway System Connected—and in Some Cases Segregated—America." July 15, 2021. Accessed November 11, 2025. https://www.asce.org/publications-and-news/civil-engineering-source/civil-engineering-magazine/article/2021/07/how-the-interstate-highway-system-connected--and-in-some-cases-segregated--america.

Weingroff, Richard F. "The Greatest Decade 1956–1966: Part 2; The Battle of Its Life." Last modified June 27, 2017. Accessed November 11, 2025. https://www.fhwa.dot.gov/infrastructure/50interstate2.cfm.

Federal Highway Administration. "The Size of the Job." Last modified June 30, 2023. Accessed November 12, 2025. https://highways.dot.gov/highway-history/interstate-system/50th-anniversary/size-job.

Cox, Wendell and Love, Jean. "40 Years of the US Interstate Highway System: An Analysis; the Best Investment a Nation Ever Made." June 1996. Accessed November 12, 2025. http://www.publicpurpose.com/freeway1.htm.

Federal Highway Administration. "The Dwight D. Eisenhower System of Interstate and Defense Highways: Part III; Cost." Last modified June 27, 2017. Accessed November 12, 2025. https://www.fhwa.dot.gov/highwayhistory/data/page03.cfm.

Haynes, Wendy. "Boston's Big Dig Project: A Cautionary Tale." *Bridgewater Review* 27, no. 1, 2008: 3–7. Accessed November 12, 2025. https://vc.bridgew.edu/cgi/viewcontent.cgi?article=1211&context=br_rev.

Bennett, James T. "Buttigieg's 'Reconnecting Communities' Program Will Solve Nothing." September 8, 2022. Accessed November 12, 2025. https://www.independent.org/article/2022/09/08/buttigiegs-reconnecting-communities-program-will-solve-nothing/.

University of Minnesota. "The Costs and Consequences of Progress." September 15, 2021. Accessed November 12, 2025. https://twin-cities.umn.edu/news-events/costs-and-consequences-progress.

Yawn, Andrew J. "Cleaved by Concrete: The Legacy of Montgomery's Interstates and the Neighborhoods They Destroyed." Last modified February 1, 2022. Accessed November 12, 2025. https://www.montgomeryadvertiser.com/story/news/2018/03/07/cleaved-concrete/395087002/.

Dillon, Liam. and Poston, Ben. "The Racist History of America's Interstate Highway Boom." November 11, 2021. Accessed November 12, 2025. https://www.latimes.com/homeless-housing/story/2021-11-11/the-racist-history-of-americas-interstate-highway-boom.

CHAPTER 8: LAND GRANT COLLEGES

National Center for Education Statistics. *120 Years of American Education: A Statistical Portrait.* 1993. Accessed November 12, 2025. https://vincentfamily.org/Ancestors/05_Oakley_Vincent/photos_&_documents/National_Center_for_Education_Statistics_120_years.pdf.

Mintz, Steven. "Statistics: Trends in American Farming." Accessed November 12, 2025. https://www.gilderlehrman.org/history-resources/teacher-resources/statistics-trends-american-farming.

Appleby, Arnold P. "Milestones in the Legislative History of U.S. Land-Grant Universities." October 2007. Accessed November 12, 2025. https://cropandsoil.oregonstate.edu/sites/agscid7/files/land-grant_0.pdf.

Turner, Jonathan Baldwin. *A Plan for an Industrial University for the State of Illinois, Submitted to the Farmers' Convention at Granvile, Held November 18, 1851.* Illinois Committee of Publication, 1851. **Pages:** 7–9.

Illinois History and Lincoln Collections. "Jonathan Baldwin Turner: Reformer and Visionary." September 14, 2018. Accessed November 12, 2025. https://publish.illinois.edu/ihlc-blog/2018/09/14/jonathan-baldwin-turner-reformer-and-visionary/.

Illinois History and Lincoln Collections. "Turner, Jonathan Baldwin. Papers, 1823–1924 | Illinois History and Lincoln Collections." Accessed November 12, 2025. https://archon.library.illinois.edu/ihlc/index.php?p=collections/control card&id=333.

Gates, Paul Wallace. "Free Homesteads for All Americans; the Homestead Act of 1863." Mississippi State: Mississippi State University Libraries, 1962. https://scholarsjunction.msstate.edu/cgi/viewcontent.cgi?article=1640&context=fvw-pamphlets.

Parker, William Belmont. *The Life and Public Services of Justin Smith Morrill.* Boston: Houghton Mifflin Company, 1924. **Pages:** 11–38, 50–57, 61–62, 103–32, 263–268, 280, 341.

United States Senate. "Justin S. Morrill." Accessed November 12, 2025. https://www.senate.gov/artandhistory/history/minute/Justin_S_Morrill.htm.

House of Representatives. "Speech of Hon. Justin S. Morrill, of Vermont in the House of Representatives, June 6, 1862." Accessed November 12, 2025. https://babel.hathitrust.org/cgi/pt?id=hvd.hnyplb&seq=2.

National Archives. "Morrill Act (1862)." Last modified May 10, 2022. Accessed November 12, 2025. https://www.archives.gov/milestone-documents/morrill-act.

United States Congress, "MORRILL, Justin Smith," Accessed November 12, 2025. https://bioguide.congress.gov/search/bio/m000969.

Clouatre, Douglas. "U.S. Department of Agriculture (USDA)." EBSCO. 2023. Accessed November 12, 2025. https://www.ebsco.com/research-starters/agriculture-and-agribusiness/us-department-agriculture-usda.

University of New Hampshire. "Hatch Act of 1887: Act of 1887 Establishing Agricultural Experiment Stations." Accessed November 12, 2025. https://colsa.unh.edu/new-hampshire-agricultural-experiment-station/hatch-act-1887.

Diorio, Gina L. "History of Public Education in the U.S." EBSCO. 2023. Accessed November 12, 2025. https://www.ebsco.com/research-starters/history/history-public-education-us.

University of Virginia. "February 24, 1859: Veto Message Regarding Land-Grant Colleges." Accessed November 12, 2025. https://millercenter.org/the-presidency/presidential-speeches/february-24-1859-veto-message-regarding-land-grant-colleges.

Fithian, Steve. "Daniel Coit Gilman: Transforming Higher Education in America." June 1, 2024. Accessed November 12, 2025. https://otislibrarynorwich.org/2024/06/01/daniel-coit-gilman/.

Roy, Mark J. and Anderson, Tracy. "Land Grant Status Acquired After 'Yale-Storrs Controversy.'" September 26, 2012. Accessed November 12, 2025. https://today.uconn.edu/2012/09/land-grant-status-acquired-after-yale-storrs-controversy/.

Rodriguez, Michael. "The Yale-Storrs Controversy." May 12, 2021. Accessed November 12, 2025. https://connecticuthistory.org/the-yale-storrs-controversy/.

Fernald, Merritt Caldwell. *History of the Maine State College and the University of Maine.* Orono: University of Maine, 1916. **Pages:** 20–23.

University of Massachusetts Amherst. *Factbook: University of Massachusetts Amherst.* Amherst: Office of Institutional Research, 1980. https://www.umass.edu/uair/sites/default/files/2024-07/Factbook_AY1980.pdf.

YouMass. "Morrill Land Grant Acts." Last modified September 3, 2021. Accessed November 12, 2025. http://scua.library.umass.edu/youmass/doku.php?id=m%3Amorrill_act.

Sorber, Nathan M. "Farmers, Scientists, and Officers of Industry: The Formation and Reformation of Land-Grant Colleges in the Northeastern United States, 1862–1906." n.d. **Pages:** 62–67, 87–89, 252–253. https://www.academia.edu/1474827/FARMERS_SCIENTISTS_AND_OFFICERS_OF_INDUSTRY_THE_FORMATION_AND_REFORMATION_OF_LAND_GRANT_COLLEGES_IN_THE_NORTHEASTERN_UNITED_STATES_1862_1906.

Association of Public & Land-Grant Universities. *The Land-Grant Tradition.* Washington, DC: Association of Public and Land-Grant Universities, 2012. **Pages:** 4–5. https://www.aplu.org/wp-content/uploads/the-land-grant-tradition.pdf.

CHAPTER 9: NATIONAL INSTITUTES OF HEALTH

National Institutes of Health. "Nobel Laureates." Last modified January 21, 2025. Accessed November 14, 2025. https://www.nih.gov/about-nih/nih-almanac/nobel-laureates.

Boles, Sy. "NIH Funding Delivers Exponential Economic Returns." March 11, 2025. Accessed November 14, 2025. https://news.harvard.edu/gazette/story/2025/03/nih-funding-delivers-exponential-economic-returns/.

American Presidency Project. "Address at the Dedication of the National Institute of Health, Bethesda, Maryland." Accessed November 14, 2025. https://www.presidency.ucsb.edu/documents/address-the-dedication-the-national-institute-health-bethesda-maryland.

Morens, David M. and Fauci, Anthony S. "The Forgotten Forefather: Joseph James Kinyoun and the Founding of the National Institutes of Health." June 26, 2012. Accessed November 14, 2025. https://pmc.ncbi.nlm.nih.gov/articles/PMC 3388889/.

National Library of Medicine. "The Beginnings of Organized Biomedical Research." Accessed November 14, 2025. https://www.nlm.nih.gov/exhibition/ phs_history/beginningsbio.html.

Duffy, John and Mannikko, Nancy Farm. "U.S. Public Health Service Is Established." EBSCO. 2023. Accessed November 14, 2025. https://www.ebsco.com/research-starters/public-health/us-public-health-service-established.

National Library of Medicine. *Act Establishing Narcotic Farms and a Narcotics Division in the Public Health Service*. Washington, DC: United States Government Printing Office, 1929. Accessed November 14, 2025. https://profiles.nlm.nih.gov/catalog/nlm:nlmuid-9918351284206676X308-doc.

Piotrowski, Nancy A. "National Institutes of Health (NIH)." EBSCO. 2025. Accessed November 14, 2025. https://www.ebsco.com/research-starters/health-and-medicine/national-institutes-health-nih.

Shrestha, Laura B. "Life Expectancy in the United States." Last modified August 16, 2006. Accessed November 14, 2025. https://www.congress.gov/crs_external_products/RL/PDF/RL32792/RL32792.4.pdf.

U.S. Department of Health, Education, and Welfare. "NIH: A Quarter of a Century." Accessed November 14, 2025. https://nihrecord.nih.gov/sites/record-NIH/files/pdf/1955/NIH-Record-1955-05-31.pdf.

Rusk, Howard A. "Average U.S. Adult at 40 Has Lost Half of His Teeth; Little Immediate Chance of Remedying Nation's Dental Neglect Seen at Talks." *New York Times*, November 14, 1954: **Page:** 72.

Barrett, Julia R. "An Uneven Path Forward: The History of Methylmercury Toxicity Research." August 2010. Accessed November 14, 2025. https://pmc.ncbi.nlm. nih.gov/articles/PMC2920108/.

Martinez-Finley, Ebany J. and Aschner, Michael. "Recent Advances in Mercury Research." March 28, 2014. Accessed November 14, 2025. https://pmc.ncbi. nlm.nih.gov/articles/PMC5181110/.

National Institutes of Health. "U.S. Department of Health and Human Services." Accessed November 14, 2025. https://oma.od.nih.gov/IC_Organization_Chart/ NIH%20HISTORY.pdf.

National Institutes of Health. "History of Congressional Appropriations, 1950–1959." Accessed November 15, 2025. https://officeofbudget.od.nih.gov/pdfs/

FY08/FY08%20COMPLETED/appic3806%20-%20transposed%20%2050%20
-%2059.pdf.

Kennedy, Thomas, M.D. "James A. Shannon, M.D." Accessed November 15, 2025. https://collections.nlm.nih.gov/catalog/nlm:nlmuid-101263944-vid.

National Institutes of Health. "History of Congressional Appropriations, 1960 - 1969." Accessed November 15, 2025. https://officeofbudget.od.nih.gov/pdfs/ FY08/FY08%20COMPLETED/appic3806%20-%20transposed%20%2060%20 -%2069.pdf.

National Institutes of Health. "History of Congressional Appropriations, 1970 - 1979." Accessed November 15, 2025. https://officeofbudget.od.nih.gov/pdfs/ FY08/FY08%20COMPLETED/appic3806%20-%20transposed%20%2070%20 -%2079.pdf.

Royal College of Physicians. "James Augustine Shannon." Accessed November 15, 2025. https://history.rcp.ac.uk/inspiring-physicians/james-augustine-shannon.

Patel, Sejal. "The Benevolent Tyranny of Biostatistics: Public Administration and the Promotion of Biostatistics at the National Institutes of Health, 1946–1970." *Bulletin of the History of Medicine* 87, no. 4, 2013: 622–647. https://www.jstor. org/stable/26305963.

Lyons, Michele. and Wilson, D. S. "How NIH's Main Campus Came to Be in Bethesda." *NIH Record* LXXIV, no. 18, 2022.

Living New Deal. "National Institutes of Health Campus–Bethesda MD." Accessed November 15, 2025. https://livingnewdeal.org/sites/national-institutes-of-health-campus-bethesda-md/.

Rettig, Richard A. "The Politics of Science." May 2002. Accessed November 15, 2025. https://www.healthaffairs.org/doi/10.1377/hlthaff.21.3.274.

Wallace, Langley Grace. "Catalyst for the National Cancer Act: Mary Lasker." Accessed November 15, 2025. https://laskerfoundation.org/catalyst-for-the-national-cancer-act-mary-lasker/.

National Library of Medicine. "Mary Lasker and the Growth of the National Institutes of Health." Accessed November 15, 2025. https://profiles.nlm.nih. gov/spotlight/tl/feature/nih.

Baranauckas, Carla. "Florence S. Mahoney, 103, Health Advocate." *New York Times*, December 16, 2002. **Page:** 10.

National Cancer Institute. "Grants to NCI-Designated Cancer Centers." Last modified July 30, 2025. Accessed November 15, 2025. https://www.cancer.gov/ about-nci/budget/fact-book/extramural-programs/cancer-centers.

National Cancer Institute. "Grant and Contract Awards." Last modified July 30, 2025. Accessed November 15, 2025. https://www.cancer.gov/about-nci/budget/fact-book/extramural-programs/grant-contract-awards.

National Institutes of Health. "History of Congressional Appropriations, 1938–1949." Accessed November 15, 2025. https://officeofbudget.od.nih.gov/pdfs/FY08/FY08%20COMPLETED/appic3806%20-%20transposed%2038%20-%2049.pdf.

National Institutes of Health. "History of Congressional Appropriations, 1980–1989." Accessed November 15, 2025. https://officeofbudget.od.nih.gov/pdfs/FY08/FY08%20COMPLETED/appic3806%20-%20transposed%20%2080%20-%2089.pdf.

National Institutes of Health. "History of Congressional Appropriations, 1990–1999." Accessed November 15, 2025. https://officeofbudget.od.nih.gov/pdfs/FY08/FY08%20COMPLETED/appic3806%20-%20transposed%20%2090%20-%2099.pdf.

National Institutes of Health. "History of Congressional Appropriations, Fiscal Years 2000–2009." Accessed November 15, 2025. https://officeofbudget.od.nih.gov/pdfs/FY21/Approp%20History%20by%20IC%20FY%202000%20-%20FY%202009%20(V).pdf.

National Institutes of Health. "History of Congressional Appropriations, Fiscal Years 2010–2019." Accessed November 15, 2025. https://officeofbudget.od.nih.gov/pdfs/FY21/Approp%20History%20by%20IC%20FY%202010%20-%20FY%202019%20(V).pdf.

National Institutes of Health. "Supplementary Appropriation Data Table for History of Congressional Appropriations, Fiscal Years 2020–2025." Accessed November 15, 2025. https://officeofbudget.od.nih.gov/pdfs/FY26/cy/Approp%20History%20by%20IC%20FY%202020%20-%20FY%202025.pdf.

National Institutes of Health. "Research Project Grants." Accessed November 16, 2025. https://report.nih.gov/funding/nih-budget-and-spending-data-past-fiscal-years/success-rates.

National Institutes of Health. "Budget." Last modified June 13, 2025. Accessed November 16, 2025. https://www.nih.gov/about-nih/organization/budget.

Cleary, E. Galkina, Beierlein, J. M., Khanuja, N. S., McNamee, L. M., and Ledley, F. D. "Contribution of NIH Funding to New Drug Approvals 2010–2016." *Proceedings of the National Academy of Sciences of the United States of America* 115, no. 10, 2018: 2329–2334. https://doi.org/10.1073/pnas.1715368115.

CHAPTER 10: FOUNDATIONS

Rossen, Jake. "How a 200-Year-Old Gift from Benjamin Franklin Made Boston and Philadelphia a Fortune." August 20, 2020. Accessed November 17, 2025. https://www.mentalfloss.com/article/627475/200-year-old-gift-from-benjamin-franklin-to-boston-and-philadelphia.

Smithsonian Institution Archives. "Smithsonian Institution General History." 2004. Accessed November 17, 2025. https://siarchives.si.edu/oldsite/siarchives-old/history/main_generalhistory.html.

Jones, Devry Becker. "John Quincy Adams [Founding of the Smithsonian Institution]." Last modified January 30, 2023. Accessed November 17, 2025. https://www.hmdb.org/m.asp?m=211392.

Smithsonian Institution Archives. "An Act to Establish the Smithsonian Institution, 1846." Accessed November 17, 2025. https://siarchives.si.edu/history/featured-topics/stories/act-establish-smithsonian-institution-1846.

Nasaw, David. *Andrew Carnegie*. New York: Penguin Press, 2006. **Pages:** 1, 32–33, 39–41, 113, 351, 586–587, 591, 598, 606–607, 670–671.

Fosdick, Raymond B. *The Story of The Rockefeller Foundation*. London: Odhams Press Limited, 1952. **Pages:** 15, 18–19, 24–25, 30–40, 49–51, 75–76, 84–86, 97, 125, 310.

Macdonald, Dwight. *The Ford Foundation: The Men and the Millions*. New York: Routledge, 1989. **Pages:** 4, 134–135, 166–167.

Forero, Juan. "$5 Billion Puts Gates Fund In First Place." *New York Times*, January 25, 2000. **Page:** 14.

Gates Foundation. "25th Anniversary Fact Sheet." Accessed November 22, 2025. https://www.gatesfoundation.org/ideas/media-center/25th-anniversary-facts.

Gates Foundation. "Gates Foundation Will Double Spending over Next 20 Years to Accelerate Progress on Saving and Improving Lives." Accessed November 22, 2025. https://www.gatesfoundation.org/ideas/media-center/press-releases/2025/05/25th-anniversary-announcement.

Gates Foundation. "How We Work." Accessed November 22, 2025. https://www.gatesfoundation.org/about/how-we-work.

Philanthropy. "Bill and Melinda Gates Foundation." Accessed November 22, 2025. https://philanthropy.org/bill-and-melinda-gates-foundation/.

Gates, Bill. "25 Years of Learning and Laughter." July 5, 2016. Accessed November 22, 2025. https://www.gatesnotes.com/25-years-of-learning-and-laughter.

O'Brien, Timothy L. and Saul, Stephanie. "Buffett to Give Bulk of His Fortune to Gates Charity." *New York Times*, June 26, 2006.

Stiffler, Lisa. "Warren Buffett Says 'No Money' Going to Gates Foundation After His Death." July 1, 2024. Accessed November 22, 2025. https://www.geekwire.com/2024/warren-buffett-says-no-money-going-to-gates-foundation-after-his-death/.

Lake, Sydney. "MacKenzie Scott Has Donated More Than $19 Billion—but It's Barely Made a Dent in Her Net Worth Because of the Power of Amazon Shares." November 7, 2025. Accessed November 22, 2025. https://fortune.com/2025/11/07/mackenzie-scott-19-billion-charitable-donations-amazon-shares-net-worth/.

CHAPTER 11: NATIONAL GALLERY OF ART

Love, Philip H. *Andrew W. Mellon, the Man and His Work*. Baltimore: F. H. Coggins & Company, 1929. **Pages:** 15–16, 23.

Burwood, Stephen. "Andrew Mellon." EBSCO. 2023. Accessed November 23, 2025. https://www.ebsco.com/research-starters/history/andrew-mellon.

Cannadine, David. *Mellon*. New York: Alfred A. Knopf, 2006. **Pages:** 97–98, 113, 121, 141, 177–180, 229–230, 262–263, 268–274, 278, 348–350, 355, 373, 416–425, 485, 523–525, 559–561, 606, 623.

Lee, Jim. "U.S. Government Loses Its Suit Against Alcoa." EBSCO. 2023. Accessed November 23, 2025. https://www.ebsco.com/research-starters/law/us-government-loses-its-suit-against-alcoa.

CHAPTER 12: NASA

NASA. "Didymos & Dimorphos." Accessed November 24, 2025. https://science.nasa.gov/solar-system/asteroids/didymos/.

Buckley, Michael. "NASA's Parker Solar Probe Reports Successful Closest Approach to Sun." December 27, 2024. Accessed November 24, 2025. https://science.nasa.gov/blogs/parker-solar-probe/2024/12/27/nasas-parker-solar-probe-reports-successful-closest-approach-to-sun/.

Ostovar, Michele. "The Decision to Go to the Moon: President John F. Kennedy's May 25, 1961 Speech Before a Joint Session of Congress." September 22, 1998. Accessed November 24, 2025. https://www.nasa.gov/history/the-decision-to-go-to-the-moon/.

Rice University. "We Choose to Go to the Moon." Accessed November 24, 2025. https://www.rice.edu/jfk-speech.

The Planetary Society. "How Much Did the Apollo Program Cost?" Accessed November 24, 2025. https://www.planetary.org/space-policy/cost-of-apollo.

The Brookings Institution. "The Costs of the Manhattan Project." 2002. Accessed November 24, 2025. https://www.brookings.edu/the-costs-of-the-manhattan-project/.

NASA. "A to Z List of NASA Missions." Accessed November 24, 2025. https://www.nasa.gov/a-to-z-of-nasa-missions/.

NASA. "Viking 1." Accessed November 24, 2025. https://science.nasa.gov/mission/viking-1/.

NASA. "Mars Pathfinder." Accessed November 24, 2025. https://science.nasa.gov/mission/mars-pathfinder/.

NASA. "New Horizons." Accessed November 24, 2025. https://science.nasa.gov/mission/new-horizons/.

CHAPTER 13: INTERNET

Carnegie Science. "Vannevar Bush and the Endless Frontier." February 26, 2020. Accessed November 25, 2025. https://carnegiescience.edu/news/vannevar-bush-and-endless-frontier.

Living Internet. "J. C. R. Licklider and the Universal Network." Accessed November 25, 2025. https://www.livinginternet.com/i/ii_licklider.htm.

Licklider, J. C. R. "Man-Computer Symbiosis." *IRE Transactions on Human Factors in Electronics*, HFE-1, March 1960: 4–11. https://groups.csail.mit.edu/medg/people/psz/Licklider.html.

Licklider, J. C. R. "Memorandum for: Members and Affiliates of the Intergalactic Computer Network." worrydream.com. April 23, 1963. Accessed November 25, 2025. https://worrydream.com/refs/Licklider_1963_-_Members_and_Affiliates_of_the_Intergalactic_Computer_Network.pdf.

Living Internet. "IPTO—Information Processing Techniques Office." Accessed November 25, 2025. https://www.livinginternet.com/i/ii_ipto.htm.

Computer History. Accessed November 25, 2025. https://www.computerhistory.org/internethistory/1960s/.

Norman, Jeremy M. "Paul Baran Issues 'On Distributed Communications.'" Accessed November 25, 2025. https://www.historyofinformation.com/detail.php?id=811.

Stacy, Robert N. "Leonard Kleinrock." EBSCO. 2024. Accessed November 25, 2025. https://www.ebsco.com/research-starters/computer-science/leonard-kleinrock.

Peter, Ian. "The History of Email." Accessed November 25, 2025. https://www.nethistory.info/History%20of%20the%20Internet/email.html.

Weber, Marc. "Robert W. Taylor, 2013 CHM Fellow." April 23, 2013. Accessed November 25, 2025. https://computerhistory.org/blog/robert-w-taylor-2013-chm-fellow/.

Pelkey, James L. "Chapter 4: Networking: Vision and Packet Switching 1959–1968; 4.7 Planning the ARPANET: 1967–1968." Accessed November 25, 2025. https://historyofcomputercommunications.info/section/4.7/Planning-the-ARPANET-1967-1968/.

Pelkey, James L. "Robert Taylor." Accessed November 25, 2025. https://historyofcomputercommunications.info/interviews/Robert-Taylor/.

Pelkey, James L. "Interview of Robert William 'Bob' Taylor." 2010. Accessed November 25, 2025. https://archive.computerhistory.org/resources/access/text/2017/12/102738691-05-01-acc.pdf.

Pelkey, James L. "Wesley Clark." Accessed November 25, 2025. https://historyofcomputercommunications.info/interviews/Wesley-Clark.

Internet Pioneers. "Larry Roberts." Accessed November 25, 2025. https://www.ibiblio.org/pioneers/roberts.html.

Pelkey, James L. "Chapter 4: Networking: Vision and Packet Switching 1959–1968; 4.8 The RFQ and Bidding: 1968." Accessed November 25, 2025. https://historyofcomputercommunications.info/section/4.8/the-rfq-and-bidding-1968/

Pelkey, James L. "Chapter 4: Networking: Vision and Packet Switching 1959–1968; 4.4 Paul Baran: 1959–1965." Accessed November 25, 2025. https://historyofcomputercommunications.info/section/4.4/Paul-Baran-1959-1965/.

Pelkey, James L. "Chapter 4: Networking: Vision and Packet Switching 1959–1968; 4.6 Packet Switching." Accessed November 25, 2025. https://historyofcomputercommunications.info/section/4.6/Packet-Switching/.

Pelkey, James L. "Chapter 8: Networking: Diffusion 1972–1979; 8.11 TCP to TCP/IP 1976–1979." Accessed November 25, 2025. https://historyofcomputercommunications.info/section/8.11/TCP-to-TCP-IP-1976-1979/.

Bush, Vannevar. "As We May Think." *The Atlantic*, July 1945. Accessed November 25, 2025. https://www.theatlantic.com/magazine/archive/1945/07/as-we-may-think/303881/.

CHAPTER 14: THE MARSHALL PLAN

Steil, Benn. *The Marshall Plan: Dawn of the Cold War*. Oxford: Oxford University Press, 2018. **Pages:** 20, 43–50, 87, 94–95, 98–100, 111–115, 147–165, 193–195, 198, 247–249, 304–305, 341–343, 441–444.

National Archives. "Marshall Plan (1948)." Last modified June 29, 2022. Accessed November 25, 2025. https://www.archives.gov/milestone-documents/marshall-plan.

Food and Agriculture Organization of the United Nations. "The State of Food and Agriculture 1948." September 1948. Accessed November 25, 2025. https://www.fao.org/4/ap636e/ap636e.pdf.

George C. Marshall Foundation. "The Marshall Plan Speech: 'The Whole World Hangs in the Balance . . . .'" Accessed November 26, 2025. https://www.marshallfoundation.org/the-marshall-plan/speech/.

Office of The Historian. "The Truman Doctrine, 1947." Accessed November 26, 2025. https://history.state.gov/milestones/1945-1952/truman-doctrine.

Sacquety, Troy Dr. "Gen. Lucius D. Clay, a 'Brilliant Administrator.'" January 11, 2019. Accessed November 26, 2025. https://www.army.mil/article/216006/gen_lucius_d_clay_a_brilliant_administrator.

PBS. "Lucius Clay (1897–1978) and the Organization of the Airlift." Accessed November 26, 2025. https://www.pbs.org/wgbh/americanexperience/features/airlift-lucius-clay/.

National Archives. "Truman Doctrine (1947)." Last modified February 8, 2022. Accessed November 26, 2025. https://www.archives.gov/milestone-documents/truman-doctrine.

University of Virginia. "Dean G. Acheson (1949–1953)." Accessed November 26, 2025. https://millercenter.org/president/truman/essays/acheson-1949-secretary-of-state.

Holbrooke, Richard and Clifford, Clark. "Serving the President." *The New Yorker*, April 1, 1991. Accessed November 26, 2025. https://www.newyorker.com/magazine/1991/04/01/serving-the-president-ii-the-truman-years.

United States Senate. "Arthur Vandenberg: A Featured Biography." Accessed November 27, 2025. https://www.senate.gov/senators/FeaturedBios/Featured_Bio_Vandenberg.htm.

Congressional Research Service. "The Marshall Plan: Design, Accomplishments, and Significance." Last modified January 18, 2018. Accessed November 27, 2025. https://www.congress.gov/crs_external_products/R/PDF/R45079/R45079.3.pdf#.

Kuisel, Richard F. *Seducing the French: The Dilemma of Americanization*. Berkeley: University of California Press, 1993. **Page:** 71.

The Allied Museum. "The Berlin Airlift 1948/49." Accessed December 15, 2025. https://www.alliiertenmuseum.de/en/thema/the-berlin-airlift-1948-49/ #Airlift-Statistics.

Powell, Stewart M. "The Berlin Airlift." *Air & Space Forces Magazine*, June 1, 1998. Accessed December 15, 2025. https://www.airandspaceforces.com/article/ 0698berlin/.

ACKNOWLEDGMENTS

Every book is a team effort. The key players on the team that made this book possible never met one another, but they brought their skills together in the most delightful way.

Gabriel Mairson, when a graduate student at Yale University, cheerfully gathered the source documents for each of the chapters and also evaluated the storytelling and made numerous suggestions that were presented with such grace that they were inevitably incorporated into the story.

Jack Koch took charge of the rough draft and greatly improved the text and the accuracy of the articulation of one story after another.

Maximillian Breed created the extensive citations, uncovered informational enrichments that made the storytelling more interesting and more rigorous. The extent and the richness of his enhancements of the text are balanced by the rigor of the citations he has provided readers.

Linda Lorimer, as always, provided wonderful guidance.

INDEX